Why Congress Needs Women

Why Congress Needs Women

Bringing Sanity to the House and Senate

Michele A. Paludi, Editor

Women's Psychology
Michele A. Paludi, Series Editor

 PRAEGER™

An Imprint of ABC-CLIO, LLC
Santa Barbara, California • Denver, Colorado

4-10-16

Library of Congress Cataloging-in-Publication Data

Names: Paludi, Michele Antoinette, editor.
Title: Why congress needs women : bringing sanity to the house and senate / Michele A. Paludi, editor.
Description: Santa Barbara, California : Praeger, [2016] | Series: Women's psychology | Includes bibliographical references and index.
Identifiers: LCCN 2015031326 | ISBN 9781440832710 (acid-free paper) | ISBN 9781440832727 (ebook)
Subjects: LCSH: Women—Political activity—United States. | Women legislators—United States. | Women legislators—United States—Biography. | United States. Congress.
Classification: LCC HQ1236.5.U6 W49 2016 | DDC 320.0820973—dc23
LC record available at http://lccn.loc.gov/2015031326

ISBN: 978-1-4408-3271-0
EISBN: 978-1-4408-3272-7

20 19 18 17 16   1 2 3 4 5

This book is also available on the World Wide Web as an eBook.
Visit www.abc-clio.com for details.

Praeger
An Imprint of ABC-CLIO, LLC

ABC-CLIO, LLC
130 Cremona Drive, P.O. Box 1911
Santa Barbara, California 93116-1911

This book is printed on acid-free paper ∞

Manufactured in the United States of America

"A Woman's Place is in the House . . . and the Senate Too"
Anna Belle Clement O'Brien
Tennessee State Senator, 1977–1991

Thank you to all women who have sought election to local, state, and federal offices. Even when we do not win the election we have had our voices heard and that creates change.

Contents

Series Foreword

Michele A. Paludi

Because women's work is never done and is underpaid or unpaid or boring or repetitious and we're the first to get fired and what we look like is more important than what we do and if we get raped it's our fault and if we get beaten we must have provoked it and if we raise our voices we're nagging bitches and if we enjoy sex we're nymphos and if we don't we're frigid and if we love women it's because we can't get a "real" man and if we ask our doctor too many questions we're neurotic and/or pushy and if we expect childcare we're selfish and if we stand up for our rights we're aggressive and "unfeminine" and if we don't we're typical weak females and if we want to get married we're out to trap a man and if we don't we're unnatural and because we still can't get an adequate safe contraceptive but men can walk on the moon and if we can't cope or don't want a pregnancy we're made to feel guilty about abortion and . . . for lots of other reasons we are part of the women's liberation movement.

—Author unknown, quoted in *The Torch*, September 14, 1987

This sentiment underlies the major goals of Praeger's book series, Women's Psychology:

1. Valuing women. The books in this series value women by valuing children and working for affordable child care; valuing women by respecting all physiques, not just placing value on slender women; valuing women by acknowledging older women's wisdom, beauty,

aging; valuing women who have been sexually victimized and viewing them as survivors; valuing women who work inside and outside of the home; and valuing women by respecting their choices
of careers, of whom they mentor, of their reproductive rights, their
spirituality, and their sexuality.

2. Treating women as the norm. Thus the books in this series make up
for women's issues typically being omitted, trivialized, or dismissed
from other books on psychology.

3. Taking a non-Eurocentric view of women's experiences. The books in
this series integrate the scholarship on race and ethnicity into wom-
en's psychology, thus providing a psychology of *all* women. Women
typically have been described collectively; but we are diverse.

4. Facilitating connections between readers' experiences and psychological theories and empirical research. The books in this series offer
readers opportunities to challenge their views about women, feminism, sexual victimization, gender role socialization, education, and
equal rights. These texts thus encourage women readers to value
themselves and others. The accounts of women's experiences as
reflected through research and personal stories in the texts in this
series have been included for readers to derive strength from the
efforts of others who have worked for social change on the interpersonal, organizational, and societal levels.

A student in one of my courses on the psychology of women once
stated:

I learned so much about women. Women face many issues: discrimination, sexism, prejudices . . . by society. Women need to work
together to change how society views us. I learned so much and
talked about much of the issues brought up in class to my friends
and family. My attitudes have changed toward a lot of things. I got
to look at myself, my life, and what I see for the future. (Paludi, 2002)

It is my hope that readers of the books in this series also reflect on the
topics and look at themselves, their own lives, and what they see for the
future.

I am honored to have *Why Congress Needs Women: Bringing Sanity to
the House and Senate* included in this Series on Women's Psychology. This
volume offers inspirational accounts of women lawmakers' lives, barriers
to their careers, and support they received for shattering the political glass
ceiling. Their stories are addressed within scholarly accounts of women
and leadership and why transformational leadership styles women portray are not valued.

All of the contributors to this volume are deeply committed to ensuring political equity for women and men. I am honored to have had the opportunity to work with them on this volume.

REFERENCE

Paludi, M. (2002). *The psychology of women,* 2nd ed. Upper Saddle River, NJ: Prentice Hall.

Acknowledgments

I thank Debbie Carvalko for encouraging me to edit this volume and others that have as their main goal to bring women and women's experiences to the forefront.

I also thank my sisters, Rosalie and Lucille, for their support.

Friends deserve my appreciation for their listening: Steven Earle, Tony LoFrumento, Brad Fowler, Dan Bilodeau, Johanna Duncan-Poitier, Philip Poitier, and Paula Lundberg Love.

I wish to extend my thanks to students in my courses on adolescent psychology at Siena College for spring, 2015. I learned a great deal from you. You have honored me by referring to me as your professor. You gave me hope.

And to Antoinette and Michael Paludi, my parents. I wish you were with me in person when I sought political office in 1998. I know you were with me in spirit.

Introduction

Michele A. Paludi

> It doesn't matter what I say about an issue, if I have a run in my pantyhose, that is all anyone will talk about.
>
> —Senator Blanche Lincoln

THE FIRST WOMEN TO SEEK THE U.S. PRESIDENCY

I am writing this Introduction in 2015.

It feels like it must have felt in 1872 . . . when Victoria Woodhull sought the presidency of the United States. Woodhull organized an Equal Rights Party and they nominated her at its May 1872 convention. Woodhull was the first woman candidate for this office. She campaigned on a platform that included women's suffrage, nationalization of railroads, an eight-hour workday, abolition of the death penalty, and welfare for the poor (Greenspan, 2013). Frederick Douglass was her vice-presidential running mate. There is no mention of the number of votes Victoria Woodhull received in the presidential election. Apparently votes for her were never counted. Furthermore, Douglass campaigned for Woodhull's opponent, Ulysses S. Grant, and never acknowledged his nomination by the Equal Rights Party (Greenspan, 2013).

On Election Day, the local newspaper published an article authored by Woodhull in which she criticized Henry Ward Beecher. She received backlash and was arrested for sending obscene material in the mail. She had stated that Beecher was an adulterer. She also had stated that a Wall Street trader seduced adolescent girls after giving them alcohol. Woodhull was arrested and spent Election Day in jail. She was eventually found to be not guilty. However, she endured severe criticism in the press for speaking out against violence against women and women's rights in general. One of her critics, Harriet Beecher Stowe referred to Woodhull as a "vile jailbird and impudent witch" (reported in Greenspan, 2013, p. 2). She was depicted in cartoons by Thomas Nast as "Mrs. Satan" (reported in Greenspan, 2013, p. 2). Many suffragists criticized Woodhull because she sought the presidency; they interpreted this as her being invested in herself more than their cause.

Belva Ann Lockwood, who sought the U.S. presidency twice (in 1884 and 1888) was also the Equal Rights Party candidate. She ran on a platform of improving the rights for women and minorities (Norgren, 2007). She spent her campaigns informing individuals about inequality. In her career as an attorney, Lockwood secured equal property and guardianship rights for women and also drafted amendments granting suffrage to women in Oklahoma, New Mexico, and Arizona. She is credited as saying her candidacy would assist women gaining the right to vote as well as being accepted into politics.

Lockwood noted that even though she couldn't vote in the election, men could vote for her. She did receive approximately 5,000 votes in the first campaign. During her second bid for the presidency, she informed reporters that "Men always say, 'let's see what you can do.' If we always talk and never work we will not accomplish anything" (reported in Norgren, 2007, p. 2). When she lost the second election she explained her loss was attributed to men who are steadfast in their "old ideas, developed in the days of chivalry" and wealthy women. She also exclaimed: "After all, equality of rights and privileges is but simple justice" (Norgren, 2007, p. 2).

Following Woodhull and Lockwood, more women were party nominees for U.S. president:

1940	Gracie Allen	Surprise Party
1952	Mary Kennery	American Party
	Agnes Waters	American Woman's Party
	Ellen Linea W. Jensen	Washington Peace Party
1968	Charlene Mitchell	Communist Party
1972	Linda Jenness	Socialist Workers Party
	Evelyn Reed	Socialist Workers Party
1976	Margaret Wright	People's Party
1980	Maureen Smith	Peace and Freedom Party
	Deirdre Griswold	Workers World Party
	Ellen McCormack	Right to Life Party
1984	Sonia Johnson	Citizens Party
	Gavrielle Holmes	Workers World Party

1988	Willa Kenoyer	Socialist Party; Liberty Union Party
	Lenora Fulani	New Alliance Party
1992	Lenora Fulani	New Alliance Party
	Helen Halyard	Socialist Equality Party
	Isabell Masters	Looking Back Party
	Gloria La Riva	Workers World Party
1996	Monica Moorehead	Workers World Party
	Marsha Feinland	Peace and Freedom Party
	Mary Cal Hollis	Socialist Party; Liberty Union Party
	Diane Beall Templin	American Party
	Isabell Masters	Looking Back Party
2000	Monica Moorehead	Workers World Party
	Cathy Gordon Brown	Independent
2004	Diane Beall Templin	American Party
2008	Gloria LaRiva	Party for Socialism and Liberation
	Diane Beall Templin	American Party
	Cynthia McKinney	Green Party
2012	Jill Stein	Green Party
	Roseanne Barr	Peace and Freedom Party
	Peta Lindsay	Party for Socialism and Liberation

MODERN TIMES?

As I was completing writing and editing this volume, Hillary Clinton announced her second bid for the presidency of the United States. Her slogan sums up the need for this volume:

> Everyday Americans need a champion. I want to be that champion.

Just like Woodhull and Lockwood, Clinton is running on a human rights platform. And, like Woodhull and Lockwood, Hillary Clinton's announcement was met with considerable backlash. For example, Cheryl Rios, CEO of Go Ape Marketing in Dallas, Texas, commented on Clinton's announcement in her Facebook post (quoted in Badner, 2015, p. 1):

> If this happens—I am moving to Canada. There is NO need for her as she is not the right person to run our country—but more impor- tantly a female shouldn't be president. Let the haters begin . . . but with the hormones we have there is no way we should be able to

start a war. Yes I run my own business and I love it and I am great at it BUT that is not the same as being the president, that should be left to a man, a good, strong, honorable man. . . . I am a strong woman. I run my own company. . . . But that is not the same as running the best country in the world and being commander-in-chief and head of state. The president of the United States, to me, should be a man, and not a female.

A few days following Hillary's announcement as a candidate for president, Twitter received several comments (Alba, 2015), including:

Madeleine Albright:	Hillary Clinton is smart, caring and determined. She is going to be an outstanding president!
Ken Rayner:	Assumably [sic] Bill would take on the role of "first gentleman" then. Wonder how he'll dress.
Alan R. Dobson:	Monica Lewinsky's ex-boyfriend's wife announces she's running for president in 2016.
Jeb Bush:	We must do better than Hillary. If you're committed to stopping her, add your name now.
Thomas Woodrow Wilson:	She's got the trustworthiness of Nixon and the warmth of an Easy Bake Oven.

When Hillary Clinton ran for president the first time in 2007, comments about a "woman president" also received media attention. Examples from a CNN.com poll (July 24, 2007) and YouTube (January 21, 2007; March 5, 2007) reported the following:

Hillary Clinton needs to wear a dress or skirt now and then. Her always making public appearances in pants gives a sense she is trying to "fit in" with the boys, which is never going to be the case.

Hillary is cute. Those are her qualifications for prez. It'll be nice to have a woman president but you know white america won't let her.

Women, above all, should reject hillary. Missus clinton is the biggest misogynist of all.

hillary clinton running must be a joke! a woman for president! HA! now thats a joke.

In 2007 and 2015 women's hormonal fluctuations, clothing, and personalities are still being used as a way to discredit a woman seeking the U.S. presidency. In 1998 I sought public office; I ran for the New York State Assembly. I received much advice: "use a 'soft' color for your campaign material" (I ended up selecting teal . . . even though the male candidates had red/white and blue), "be sure to have a lot of door prizes at your fund-raisers," "don't say anything against your opponent . . . women who criticize opponents never win . . . just be nice," and "leave the feminist views out of the race." I was told I didn't have any "issues" on which I ran. I discussed equal pay, violence against children, funding for domestic violence shelters, getting more jobs in the Assembly district, among others. I guess these weren't "issues" or the "right" issues. I was asked what I would do for my opponent if I won the race . . . what would I do to get him another job? How could I run against a man? Even a neighbor asked me several "why" questions, for example, why would you run against him? He is a graduate of our local college. (So am I . . . of the same college!), he's Italian (so am I), he's from this city (I lived a block away from this neighbor). I came in second. I was one of two candidates.

MASCULINE "CODE OF CONDUCT?"

In 1936, results from a Gallup poll indicated 30% of Americans stated they would vote for a woman presidential candidate. By the late 1990s, almost all of the Americans polled were in favor of a woman being president. Thus, we are ready for a woman president. Right? Well, there are only 104 women serving in the 114th U.S. Congress in 2015. Mo (2012) hypothesized that individuals who claim they support a woman candidate may actually be trying to be politically correct. Mo noted that gender bias is still present, perhaps "gone underground" (p. 1). She reported that her research indicated that people pair words such as "president," "governor," and "executive" with male names while pairing words like "assistant," "secretary," and "aide" with women's names. Do women and men have difficulty in associating women with leadership? Mo further noted that participants in her research would be more likely to vote for a woman candidate if she had more experience, better education credentials, and involvement in her community than a male opponent.

This research is reminiscent of social science research on performance evaluation that suggested that individuals devalue women's performance when compared to the identical performance of men. Deaux and Emswiller (1974) observed equivalent performances by women and men are not explained by the same attributions. Performance by a man is attributed to skill; the identical performance by a woman is attributed to luck. When women's performance is judged by a noted authority to be superior, their performance is seen as valued; women need to have authorities, especially men increase the value of her work and, by extension, of her (Doyle & Paludi, 1998).

Eagly and Karau (2002) also noted that there is an incongruity between agentic leadership and femininity. Thus, women are perceived as ineffective as leaders no matter what leadership style they use. When women engage in behaviors stereotypically linked to men (e.g., leadership), they are not perceived similar to men and are often evaluated more negatively than when conforming to stereotypes of women (Doyle & Paludi, 1998). According to Heilman, Wallen, Fuchs, and Tamkins (2004):

> The mere recognition that a woman has achieved success on a traditionally male task produces inferences that she has engaged in counternormative behavior and therefore causes similarly negative consequences. (p. 3)

Women will thus be perceived negatively since they are engaging in "unfeminine" behavior, referred to as the "double bind" (Denmark et al., 2008).

Jandeska and Kraimer (2005) found that most organizations, including politics, are structured by a traditional and stereotypical masculine culture which values and rewards men who exhibit these stereotypical traits more so than women. Women struggle to find their place within these organizations. According to Jandeska and Kraimer (2005):

> This "code of conduct" in masculine cultures, while recognizable to males, can be completely alien to females and thus would be considered less hospitable towards women's careers. For example, an "old-boy network" excludes women from centers of influence and valuable sources of information, often trivializing or ignoring their contributions. (p. 465)

When Patricia Schroeder dropped out of the race for U.S. president in 1984, she cried. This raised the question of whether a woman was too "emotional," to be president. As Schroeder later wrote (1998):

> Crying is almost a ritual that male politicians must do to prove they are compassionate, but women are supposed to wear iron britches.

Similar comments were directed toward Geraldine Ferraro, the first woman to be placed on a national presidential ticket (with Walter Mondale in 1984). Ferraro was criticized for wearing short-sleeved dresses while campaigning because her arms wobbled when she waived (not considered "feminine").

These masculine cultures exist in extracurricular activities associated with the workplace as well, including the U.S. Senate. As an example, in 2008, Kay Hagen, North Carolina's junior senator to the U.S. Senate, was excluded from swimming in the Senate pool. The reason she was banned from using the Senate pool is that the pool was available to "males only." Since some of the male senators liked to swim in the nude, women senators were not permitted to swim in this pool. New York State senior senator, Charles Schumer, in his position as chair of the Rules Committee, put a stop to this women-not-allowed rule.

Debbie Stabenow once commented that when she was chair of the Senate Agriculture Committee and trying to get a massive farm bill passed, a male lobbyist patted her on her hand and said "I know it's going to be tough . . . but you'll do the best you can" (Mundy, 2015). Stolberg (2015) recently reported that Senator Lisa Murkowski, representing Alaska, was presented with a black windbreaker with the words "Chairman's Table" on the back. This was her gift for being elected the new chair of the Energy Committee. This jacket was for a man; it didn't fit Senator Murkowski. According to Senator Murkowski, "I did think that was somewhat telling. We are not thinking about the women" (quoted in Stolberg, 2015, p. 1).

The top 10 states with the highest percentage of females in the state legislature are

1. Colorado (41%)
2. Vermont (40.6%)
3. Arizona (35.6%)
4. Minnesota (33.3%)
5. New Hampshire (32.5%)
6. Illinois (32.2%)
7. Hawaii (31.6%)
8. Washington (30.6%)
9. Maryland (30.3%)
10. Connecticut (29.4%)

Only 32 women have been elected state governor. The first female governor was Nellie Taloe Ross (D-WY) in 1925. She was asked by the Democratic Party in her state to seek office after her husband died. Twenty-four states have never had a female governor. The governors in New Mexico, Oklahoma, and South Carolina are the first women to head the government in those states (National Women's Political Caucus, 2015). The United States ranked 84th in worldwide female leadership in 2014.

WHAT IS AN EFFECTIVE LEADER? GLASS CEILING OR LABYRINTH FOR WOMEN LEADERS IN WASHINGTON?

> Because I am a woman, I must make unusual efforts to succeed. If I fail, no one will say, "She doesn't have what it takes." They will say, "Women don't have what it takes."
>
> —Clare Boothe Luce

Rodgers-Healey (2003) surveyed 193 women leaders and asked the following questions:

> Do you believe that a woman can be as good a leader as a man?
> Do you feel that women in a work and personal setting help each other become leaders?
> What is your vision as a leader?
> What forms of support do you need to make this possible?

Women in this research defined leadership in terms of listening, empowering others, being collaborative, facilitating change, mentoring others, and being effective communicators.

Eagly, Johannesen-Schmidt, and van Engen (2003) further noted that for women, an effective leadership style is *transformational,* a style that incorporates empowerment, ethics, inclusiveness, nurturance, encouraging innovation, and social justice. Thus, transformational leadership describes leaders who "motivate subordinates to transcend their own self-interests for the good of the group or organization" (Powell, Butterfield, & Bartol, 2008, p. 159).

In contrast, *transactional* leaders form exchange relationships through using rewards and punishment as incentives for employee performance. Transactional leadership is associated with aggression (Powell et al., 2008). According to Duff-McCall and Schweinle (2008), a transactional leadership "suits the masculine social interaction and leadership style, because men internalize the male gender role, which supports an agentic desire for competition, aggression, and assertion" (p. 90). Thus, transactional leadership rewards competition, aggression, and an authoritarian managerial style (Eagly & Johannesen-Schmidt, 2001). Eagly et al. (2003) found women score higher than men on only one aspect of transactional leadership that is related to positive outcomes: rewarding their employees for good performance. Thus women who are transformational leaders exhibit their caring and nurturing toward employees through praise and other forms of rewards.

The research on a transformational leadership style would predict that women, who are more likely to use this style, should not face any barriers to becoming leaders. However, this is not the case: women experience significant barriers, including dealing with gatekeepers, pay inequity, lack of work/life integration, and discrimination, which keep them from reaching their full potential as leaders.

As Jandeska and Kraimer (2005) noted:

> Even women in senior roles in large corporations find themselves "on the outside looking in" when it comes to information sharing and access to the inner circle, where decisions are made. . . . Women characterize such a culture as exclusionary and claim that upper

management often lacks awareness of the barriers it creates to women's assimilation and advancement. (p. 465)

Yoder (2001) also noted that a transformational leadership style would be perceived as effective in "a congenial setting," one in which empowering and nurturing subordinates is valued. Denmark et al. (2008) further suggested that organizations must be supportive of transformational leadership "by legitimizing and encouraging women leaders and by ensuring that the male/female ratio of employees is not skewed in favor of male employees" (p. 38).

Chesney (2007) once quipped with regard to women and leadership: "The ceiling is breaking—but watch out for falling glass." Nevertheless, the breaking up of the glass ceiling, is still slow, and this has led Eagly and Carli (2007) to create a more updated metaphor—the *labyrinth*. This metaphor captures the multiple complex challenges, false starts, and barriers that women encounter as they navigate the lanes to leadership victories in the 21st century.

On January 4, 2007, Nancy Pelosi became the first woman to hold the Speakership of the House of Representatives. She accepted the Speaker's gavel affirming her vision for "partnership" over "partisanship." She then addressed the historical importance of being the first female to hold the position of Speaker:

It is a moment for which we have waited more than 200 years. . . . but women weren't just waiting; women were working. Never losing faith, we worked to redeem the promise of America, that all men and women are created equal. For our daughters and granddaughters, today, we have broken the marble ceiling. . . . the sky is the limit, anything is possible for them.

For women of color, it may not be the case.

Women of color experience an intersectionality of sexism and racism in their search for a seat in the U.S. Senate or Congress. Stereotypes about women and people of color interact to discredit women of color. As two women politicians have stated:

Defining myself, as opposed to being defined by others, is one of the most difficult challenges I face.

—Carol Moseley Braun

We have to build things that we want to see accomplished, in life and in our country, based on our own personal experiences . . . to make sure that others . . . do not have to suffer the same discrimination. It is easy enough to vote right and be consistently with the majority . . . but it is more often more important to be ahead of the majority and this means being willing to cut the first furrow in the ground and stand alone for a while if necessary.

—Patsy Mink

To date, the only women of color to serve in the Senate are Carol Moseley Braun (served from 1993 to 1999) and Mazie Hirono (elected in 2012). In the Congress, 54 women of color have served:

Shirley Chisholm (1969–1993)
Yvonne Brathwaite Burke (1973–1979)
Barbara Jordan (1973–1979)
Cardiss Collins (1973–1997)
Katie Hall (1982–1985)
Barbara Rose Collins (1991–1997)
Eva M. Clayton (1992–2003)
Carrie Meek (1993–2003)
Denise Majette (2003–2005)
Cynthia McKinney (1993–2003; 2005–2007)
Juanita Millender-McDonald (1996–2007)
Julia Carson (1996–2007)
Stephanie Tubbs Jones (1999–2008)
Carolyn Cheeks Kilpatrick (1997–2011)
Diane Watson (2001–2011)
Laura Richardson (2007–2013)
Patsy Takemoto Mink (1965–1977; 1990–2002)
Patricia Fukuda Saiki (1987–1991)
Colleen Hanabusa (2011–2015)
Mazie Hirono (2007–2013)
Gloria Negrete McLeod (2013–2015)
Hilda Solis (2001–2009)

The lack of women of color serving in public office is related to democratic legitimacy and political representation. According to Cardenas (2014):

Lack of representation, of course, can mean a lack of attention to and advocacy for issues important to communities of color. And the underrepresentation of female elected officials in particular translates into a major missed opportunity for the empowerment of underserved communities. (p. 1)

Women of color are more apt to sponsor legislation to assist all underrepresented groups (Lawless & Fox, 2005).

PASSING LEGISLATION

> We haven't come a long way, we've come a short way. If we
> hadn't come a short way, no one would be calling us baby.
>
> —Elizabeth Janeway

In fact, Volden, Wiseman, and Wittmer (2013) reported that women in Congress are more effective in moving bills through the House than are men. They found in their review of approximately 140,000 public bills introduced in the House from 1973 to 2008 that women lawmakers use compromise, build consensus and work in a nonpartisan way to achieve their policy goals. Volden et al. (2013) noted: "I don't want to generalize, because this isn't true of all [women], but they tend to be interested in finding common ground" (p. 1). Researchers have found this to be especially characteristic of congresswomen in the minority party who have to build coalitions outside of their own political party to have their legislation advanced through the House. Volden, Wiseman, and Wittmer (2013) noted that:

> The opposite is the case for majority party women, however, who counterbalance this lack of later success by introducing a greater amount, and a wider array, of legislation. These findings are particularly pronounced in women's issue areas, where both minority and majority party women dedicate more of their efforts, but to very different effects. (p. 1)

FROM THE CAMPAIGN TRAIL BACK TO THE CLASSROOM: TEACHING AS A CATALYST FOR CHANGE

Several scholars on organizational behavior (e.g., Kanter, 1977; Maddock, 2002) have written that organizational cultures are "gendered." Gender is one of the fundamental factors influencing the ethics, values, and policies of all workplaces (Bilimoria & Piderit, 2007; Karsten, 2006). We see the gender gap throughout all disciplines, including politics. For example, although women and men have reached numerical parity in management overall, fewer women than men lead organizations, for example, the powerful Fortune 500 organizations (Karsten, 2006; Werhane et al., 2006). In addition, women in managerial positions experience a $2 million lifetime wage disparity vis-à-vis male colleagues (Betz, 2008). Furthermore, stereotypes depict men, but not women, as having the requisite skills and characteristics for managerial and leadership positions (Grabe & Hyde, 2006).

Business professionals indicate a strong preference for male applicants for a stereotypically masculine job, even when similar information on the resumes of women and men applicants had led to perceptions of similar personality traits (Grabe & Hyde, 2006; Powell et al., 2006) These stereotypes persist even though gender differences are not found in leadership ability or job performance (Duff-McCall & Schweinle, 2008).

In addition, women employees experience gender harassment, unwanted sexual attention, and sexual coercion (Woods & Buchanan, 2008). Research on gender stereotypes also suggests that gender bias is an invisible barrier—the glass ceiling—preventing women from breaking into the highest levels of management in organizations. As a final example of gendered organizations, employed women are more likely to lack fringe benefits needed to care for their family and more likely to lack job flexibility in order to care for themselves, children, and elderly parents (Paludi & Niedermeyer, 2007). Thus, despite federal and state laws that were enacted to end employment discrimination based on sex, race, religion, disability, sexual orientation, and national origin, discrimination against women, most notably women of color, exists that explains the pervasiveness of institutionalized inequality (Paludi, Paludi, & DeSouza, 2010).

I have offered courses at the undergraduate and graduate levels to assist individuals in understanding cognitively and affectively that organizations, including politics, are gendered. One such course is "Women and Management" that was offered as an elective in an MBA program at Union Graduate College that was co-taught by Dr. Laura Schweitzer and myself. This course examined the status of women in management and leadership and discussed issues that women managers commonly face, including differences in leadership styles, discrimination, harassment, obstacles to advancement, and pay, benefit, and resource inequity (Bilimoria & Piderit, 2007; Paludi, 2008). This course also addressed themes of ethical decision making, authority, power and leadership, and conflict in organizational life. In addition, the course discussed the intersectionality among sex, race, national origin, disability, gender identity, and sexual orientation in dealing with discrimination and harassment, including glass ceiling discrimination (DeFour, David, Diaz, & Thompkins, 2003; Woods & Buchanan, 2008).

This course had the following exit competencies for students:

1. To discuss legal issues with which organizations must deal, including Title VII of the 1964 Civil Rights Act, Americans with Disabilities Act, and Lily Ledbetter Act of 2009.
2. To discuss the relationship among stereotypes, prejudice, and discrimination.
3. To identify women leaders in corporate America, including leadership styles.
4. To identify women leaders in politics.
5. To discuss theories of career development, including methodological biases in research on women's career development.

6. To identify strategies companies can use to prevent and deal with workplace discrimination and harassment.
7. To offer suggested solutions for glass ceiling obstacles.
8. To discuss gendered ethics, politics, and law.
9. To identify the interface of age, sex, race, sexual orientation, disability, and ethnicity in women's work performance.
10. To discuss gender- and race-related issues for women in management.
11. To discuss gender and power in the workplace.

A major goal of this course was to help build students professionally and personally through education. To help meet this goal, women managers and elected officials in the community surrounding the graduate college served as "executive professors." They discussed their personal experiences with gendered organizations and applied the theories and empirical research presented in the readings and lectures to the personal experiences. Women of color served as executive professors. In addition, a wide age range of women executive professors was achieved. They represented several disciplines, including law, affirmative action, higher education, counseling, county legislature, management consulting, and not-for-profit organizations.

Thus, an active learning approach was taken in this class. The primary role of the professors of this course was to facilitate the learning process. There was some lecture nearly every class period, but the majority of each class was spent discussing ideas, participating in experiential exercises, listening to guest speakers, and practicing the skills necessary to perform well in this class and beyond.

There was tremendous support in having co-facilitators of the course. This served to ease the isolation that may occur when only one individual teaches a feminist course (Makosky & Paludi, 1990). The team-teaching approach encouraged experimentation with different expressions of feminism for the co-facilitators as well as students.

The course implemented the following assumptions consistent with learning objectives, of how learning occurs and the philosophy of women's optimal development (Paludi et al., 2008):

1. The course was a laboratory of feminist principles.
2. The traditional patriarchal teaching-learning model is dysfunctional in the development of healthy women and men.
3. Every individual in the class is a potential teaching resource.
4. Integration is imperative for the development of healthy, whole individuals. Therefore, the course should foster mind/body integration as well as the integration of ideas and behavior, and thoughts and feelings.
5. The course should treat women as the norm in management, leadership, and politics.

6. The primary coordinators of the course should be women.
7. The subjective, personal experience of women and men is valid and important.
8. The student should assume responsibility for his or her own learning and growth.
9. Cooperation among students in pursuing learning objectives creates a more positive learning climate than does competition; cooperative learning is fostered through the use of criterion-referenced rather than a norm-referenced evaluation system.
10. The course should provide vehicles outside the class through which students can deal with personal feelings and frustrations such as journals, dyads.

The class met weekly for 10 weeks. Each class was three hours in length. The text assigned was *Handbook on Women in Business and Management,* edited by Bilimoria and Piderit (2007). Topics discussed in the class are identified as follows:

1. Gender- and Race-Related Stereotypes vs. Realities about Women, Management, and Careers
2. Leadership Styles: Transactional and Transformational
3. Mentoring and Social Networks for Management in the 21st Century
4. Stress Responses and Human Resource Management Solutions
5. Global Perspectives on Women in Management
6. Pay Equity
7. Glass Ceilings and Sticky Floors
8. Intimate Partner Violence as a Workplace Concern
9. Pregnancy Discrimination and the "Mommy Track"
10. Sexual Harassment, National Origin Discrimination, Race Discrimination
11. Women Entrepreneurs

The following feminist pedagogical strategies were incorporated in the course:

Nonhierarchical seating arrangement. All participants were seated around a conference table so they could see each other and speak with each other. The flow of communication was thus not just from the professor to students only. Each student was viewed and treated as a teaching resource.

Critical thinking. Critical thinking skills permit students to see themselves as capable of critical analysis, to incorporate statistical methodologies in their analyses, and to possess sufficient knowledge and perspective to engage in substantive critical analyses. In addition, critical thinking requires an opportunity for students to talk in the first person, to place faith and value in their opinions and analyses. Thus, critical thinking helps to instill confidence in students and a positive sense of self (Paludi et al., 2008). To foster critical thinking, students were asked to integrate the readings, lectures, and discussions in answering eight take-home essay exam questions. This approach to critical thinking was empowering for students, especially for reentry women who may have been silenced in their life experiences as well as in other courses.

Integration of knowledge. One goal for the course was to have students integrate the course material into their lives. Students were given an opportunity to accomplish this by interviewing a woman manager or leader in order to determine the perspective of this woman's role in the organization and to foster networking among the students and interviewees. Interviews were conducted via e-mail or telephone or in person. Women managers and leaders selected for the students to interview were located throughout the United States. Interviewees included the president of the Business and Professional Women's Club, a broadcaster, a vice president of a bank, the president of a chamber of commerce, a former university president, a politician, and a former president of the American Psychological Association.

In addition, students were required to write a five-page "reaction paper" on a topic of their choice related to women and leadership. This requirement encouraged students to express their own thoughts and feelings about topics on women and management, including opportunities for students to disagree with the perspectives shared in the readings and in the lectures. For several students, this requirement translated into their working with me on textbook chapters on global women managers, business psychology, and diversity in the workplace. In addition, some students asked to become involved in advocacy at battered women's shelters and rape crisis centers.

Topics for the reaction papers selected by students included:

Pay Equity Legislation in the U.S. and Europe
Gender and Race-Related Stereotypes in Leadership
Stress Effects of Gendered Organizations
Mentoring Women and Being Mentored by Women in Management
On-Worksite Child Care Centers: Impact on Mothers' Work/Life
    Integration
Gendered Ethics in Politics

Additional resources were distributed for each class in order to assist students in integrating the material from the course. These resources included websites dealing with women and leadership, scholarly research publications, and networking sites for women in management, politics, and leadership.

Furthermore, outlines for each class discussion were distributed to students in order to facilitate their preparation for class.

Shared leadership. Students were invited to lead the discussion at the beginning of each class. Topics included television programs, newspaper articles, and other popular media accounts of topics in women in political power and other leadership positions that were part of the class content.

Experiential exercises. Students were engaged in class in discussing experiential exercises dealing with their own experiences with mentors, leadership skills they use, ways to integrate work and family roles, and women they admire the most. These exercises served as another vehicle through which students could develop and refine their skills in critical thinking. The exercises also required integration of theories, research findings, and practical experience from several sources that necessitated a critical reflection of ideas. Furthermore, this pedagogical technique provided students with an opportunity to reflect a broad range of knowledge and the need to define, qualify, and dispute commonly heard overgeneralizations about women in politics, management, and leadership.

Multicultural learning. The goal of multicultural learning in the class involved a complex set of intellectual and personal traits. In order to learn about other cultures, students needed to be able to draw connecting links between their own experiences and the experiences of others; to comprehend cultural differences, to deal with "culture shock," and to clear away subjective obstacles to multicultural learning such as sexism, racism, heterosexism, and ethnocentrism. Rather than discuss culture at the end of the course, topics each week included a discussion of cultural similarities and differences. This ensured keeping multiculturalism central, not marginal to the course. In addition, the course

1. avoided studying women from marginalized groups only in comparison to women in the dominant group,
2. incorporated scholarship by women from marginalized groups into the course, and
3. addressed issues of privilege and oppression.

STAGES OF FEMINIST IDENTITY DEVELOPMENT

Downing and Rousch (1985) suggested that students proceed through five stages when confronted with feminist issues: passive acceptance, revelation, embeddedness/emanation, synthesis, and active commitment. In the passive acceptance stage, students typically find themselves and others saying that discrimination is no longer present in the workplace, politics, economics, the family, or education. Some students may believe that traditional gender roles are advantageous.

Some of the topics discussed at the beginning of the course on women and management (stereotyping, prejudice) prompt students to question these assumptions. While they may not change their opinions about the topics of the course, they may start to question why they have held onto certain ideas for a long time in face of contrary evidence. Discussing these topics commonly transitions students into the revelation stage. It is at this point in their development they begin to bring in magazine articles and other media accounts of women and management. When students begin to share these accounts in class, they find themselves wanting to spend time with peers, sharing their experiences, and asking how they have dealt with sexism, racism, and so on. This is the embeddedness/emanation stage.

This stage is replaced by the synthesis stage, in which statements are made acknowledging the discriminatory practices against women, especially ethnic women, aged women, women of the working class, lesbians, and physically challenged women. In addition, during this stage, statements reflecting transcendence of gender roles are common. Women and men are discussed as individuals, not members of sex categories.

Students make comments in class that suggest they recognize the power imbalance between the sexes in management and leadership in the United States and in other cultures. Consequently, they notice themselves in the active commitment stage. They ask to take other courses on women and management, want to collaborate on research in this area, and seek women mentors.

These stages of feminist identity development were discussed throughout the course; students were asked to identify transitions in their thinking about the topics of the course. At the end of each class, students would share the transitions they were experiencing as a result of the course. These included challenging relationships they were in with men who did not welcome their taking a feminist course.

Throughout each course topic examples of the issues applied to each of the following generations were provided: Veterans, Baby Boomers, Generation Xers, Millennials. Thus the material was made relevant to students of various generations as well as their parents and grandparents (Paludi et al., 2008) so students could share their class discussions with relatives and friends.

In addition, young women who identify themselves as feminists or third-world feminists often identify themselves and their feminism in opposition to the previous generation of feminists (Sinacore & Enns, 2005). In addition, some students, although agreeing with the goals of feminism, avoided self-identification with the term for fear of being associated with a stigmatized label. This was addressed in the class; experiential exercises were used to assist students in understanding the meaning of feminism in management. Executive professors discussed feminism as well so students could see various ways to implement feminism in the workplace as well as in interpersonal relationships.

One continuing theme throughout the course was advocacy on behalf of women in the workplace, including family and medical leave act, pay equity, breast-feeding/breast pumping for new mothers in the workplace, and bullying. The goal was to assist students in working toward providing equal educational opportunities for women, ensuring economic self-sufficiency for women, and elevating the standards for women in leadership. The "executive professors" addressed advocacy and lobbying legislators during their presentations, as did the women students interviewed for the course requirement.

The following responses were generated by students at the end of the course:

> I found the course very valuable and actually inspiring in that it makes me want to push to move into a management position.

> It raised awareness and emphasized very valid issues facing working women today. I feel educated and empowered at the same time, both in my personal and professional lives.

> Loved the seating arrangement and the class discussions—hearing about everyone's personal experiences and viewpoints was very valuable.

> I thought this class was very valuable, especially for young women just starting out in their careers.

> Speakers were great! Very motivating and insightful! Almost like a small mentoring program.

THIS VOLUME

> A married young elected leader said she was portrayed during the election as about to have children (thereby neglecting her constituents) and another said she was asked, "Who is going to watch the baby?" . . . The female young elected leaders who were single said they faced gossip, even slanderous comments, about their sexual habits. Male candidates did not mention this as a problem for them.
>
> —Ruth Mandel

Lawless and Fox (2005) identified factors that impact women's entry into politics. They noted that a gender gap exists in interest in seeking political office. This gap is interpreted as illustrating women's lower levels of political recruitment and lower self-assessments of political qualifications (p. 16). In addition, Lawless and Fox noted that women's role as primary caretaker of children and of the home adds "complexity to the decision to run . . . a complexity that most men do not face" (p. 16).

This research indicates that women are still at a disadvantage in running for and being elected to political office. According to Lawless and Fox, "Our findings . . . highlight the importance of deepening our understanding of the manner in which women and men in contemporary society are socialized about politics, the acquisition of political power, and the characteristics that qualify individuals to seek it" (p. 16).

Lawless and Fox (2005) and Fox and Lawless (2010) reported that women are less likely to perceive themselves as viable political candidates and that this perception is shared by others and thus they are less likely than men to be encouraged to seek office. They explain these stereotypes hinder women from seeking political office and from men and women voting for them. Furthermore, research has indicated that men are twice as likely as women to have "seriously considered" seeking political office. Women were twice as likely to refer to themselves as "not at all qualified" to run for office despite the fact they achieved success in law, business, and education.

MONEY MONEY MONEY MONEY

> The reason that minorities and women don't have a better shot at getting elected to the Senate or to statewide office is because the campaign finance rules are so skewed as to make it very difficult for non-traditional candidates to raise the money necessary to get elected.
>
> —Carol Moseley Braun

Women who do run for office experience difficulty in raising campaign funds (McGregor, 2014). Certainly work/life integration is a challenge when one is on the campaign trail. However, women candidates report struggles with raising funds and obtaining party support for their candidacy. According to Hartmann (cited in McGregor, 2014) with respect to being selected to run for office:

> It is very, very difficult to get named. You kind of need to know that such and such a job will be coming up in four to five years and need to start positioning yourself early and start getting to know the party's power brokers. They're just much more likely to name men and think of men. (p. 2)

Women who seek public office do not escape the impact of stereotyping when trying to start their campaigns. They often personally finance their business through their own savings and credit cards and/or through family capital.

APPEARANCE MATTERS?

Furthermore, the White House Project (reported in Wisconsin Women's Council, 2007) noted that women seeking office do not receive "the benefit of the doubt" from voters to the same degree as men candidates. Women's use of personal biographies in their campaigns are scrutinized by voters, especially by men. Voters recommend that women political candidates avoid appearing too glamorous or too casual in their campaign material and personal appearances since both are perceived to undermine women candidates' credibility. Voters are also more likely to vote for women candidates when their platform involves taxes, the economy, and crime. Women candidates place higher priority on equity issues and rights for women and children. In addition, women introduce most legislation dealing with women's issues. Furthermore, it is important to note that once elected, women perform as well as men (Lawless & Fox, 2005).

Findings from all of this research highlight the necessity that work be continued to eradicate gender disparities in political office holding. In addition, media representation of women candidates and office holders has typically not been equitable (Bligh, Schlehoffer, Casad, & Gaffney, 2011; Wisconsin Women's Council, 2007). The White House Project (quoted in Wisconsin Women's Council, 2007) found in its research on six 1998 executive campaigns for positions of governor and attorney general:

1. Journalists were more likely to discuss personal characteristics of women candidates than of men.
2. Unlike men, women candidates' age, marital status, family, and children were covered by journalists.
3. Men received more coverage on their campaign platforms than did women.
4. Women incumbents received similar sexist coverage as women who were seeking office for the first time.

Bligh et al. (2011) reported that media has an influence on individuals' judgments of women politicians' likability, what is referred to as the "competent but cold" effect. Thus, despite enormous progress in alerting women and men to these stereotypical portrayals, there is little debate that gender inequities continue to plague U.S. political elections. Thomsen (2015) noted that the percentage of Democratic women in Congress has increased since the 1980s. However, the percentage of Republican women has stayed relatively the same. Thomsen (2015) has interpreted these statistics as indicating that Republican women have typically been to the left of their male counterparts in their political ideology and therefore not in conformity with Republican ideology.

Social stigma can explain these inequities. Social stigma is a devalued social identity that is socially discrediting; it prevents individuals from being fully accepted (Goffman, 1963). Social stigma brands individuals with an unwanted label or set of traits that remains with the individuals. These labels or traits are typically negative and can lead to forms of social rejection, harassment, bullying, and discrimination (Crocker, Major, & Steele, 1998).

Crocker, Major, and Steele (1998) reported that it is common for women to encounter discriminatory behaviors when in situations that are male dominated (like politics) and when there are male evaluators (like male voters).

While the research suggests no modifications to this gender gap until cultural change is achieved, there are several immediate responses (Lawless & Fox, 2005; Wisconsin Women's Council, 2007). They include the following:

1. Recruitment of women candidates by chairpersons of local, state, and federal parties.
2. Providing information about the electoral process.
3. Providing information about political environments so women can self-identify with politics ("candidate emergence process").
4. Raising awareness about the gender gap in holding political office.
5. (Wo)mentoring of women candidates by women who hold elected office.

In my courses I have integrated these recommendations in order to dispel myths related to women in political power. I always ask the following question of my students: "Why do we have so few women in Congress?" I share with students that the United States ranks 98th in the world for percentage of women in national offices. Terrell (reported in Hill, 2014) noted that "women won't achieve fair representation for nearly 500 years" (p. 1). Students always respond with asking why women, who represent 51% of the population, have only less than a fifth of representation in Congress. Spillar (quoted in Hill, 2014) explained this disconnect by addressing the old boys network in Congress: "The feminist movement has been fighting this battle for equal representation for over 40 years . . . but you're talking about changing the very rules that keep incumbents secure in their seats. We need more Democratic and Republican leaders to step up and help solve this problem" (p. 3).

Are more women needed in Congress? Will having more women in the Senate and in the House make a difference? Posts on Debate.org (2015) are informative:

Yes, having more women in Congress will bring more women's issues to the floor. Even though the Congress will remain very divided politically, more women can make some difference. The key is for them to support legislation that will benefit women in general. The more they can have others focus on the issues, the better chance that they can make a difference. They just need to stick together.

Yes, but to a point

As a women I would hope having more women in congress would give women rights a chance. But the problem is we always seem to see politicians vote among their party lines no matter how much it might infringe on their own rights. The biggest difference will be made if the women realize that they can step outside the lines.

It Will Not Make a Difference

Having more women in Congress will not make a difference. It will be nice to have more women in the positions but people in Congress will still vote and defend beliefs that follow party lines. That is not going to change whether a male or a female holds a seat in Congress.

In women's voices:

As a college intern in the Governor's office working on pay equity . . . I was asked to monitor meetings of all sorts—city council meetings, county board meetings, committee meetings, and the like. By attending all of these meetings, watching and listening to the proceedings over a period of time, I came to understand the political process. It was de-mystified for me. What had previously seemed so complicated was now understandable and I gradually began to think, "Hey, I can do that!"

—Congresswoman Tammy Baldwin

By filling the leadership pipeline with a richly diverse, critical mass of women, we make American institutions, businesses and government truly representative. . . . When women leaders bring their voices, vision and leadership to the table alongside men, the debate is more robust and the policy is more inclusive and sustainable.

—Marie C. Wilson, The White House Project

Every country deserves to have the best possible leader and that means that women have to be given a chance to compete. If they're never allowed to compete in the electoral process then the countries are really robbing themselves of a great deal of talent.

—Madeleine K. Albright

It is my hope that this volume will assist individuals in having more representation of women in the U.S. Congress so we can have more inclusive perspectives. The "Year of the Woman" in politics in 1992 hasn't had the impact we had hoped: women hold approximately 20% of the seats in Congress. And it is not sufficient to recruit more women and elect more women; it also involves opening up the House and Senate to women so as to make them and their legislation central, not marginal to our decision-making processes. Part of this valuing of women politicians includes valuing their relationships, including being mothers. Keith (2014) noted that only nine women congressmembers have given birth while in office. Nancy Pelosi once noted that "when my children were small, I barely had time to wash my face." Consequently she made the decision to wait to run for elected office until her youngest child was completing high school. Debbie Wasserman Schultz stated that she feels guilty when she had to attend a fundraiser while her eight-year-old daughter had a temperature of 103 degrees: "It feels like someone's ripping my heart out. . . . no matter how good your spouse is, kids want their mom when they're sick."

A majority of women in Congress live apart from their children each week, only relying on phones, e-mail, and texting to communicate with them. Layton (2007) reported that all women in Congress who are mothers "live with a reality possibly even more difficult: the public will scrutinize and judge the mothering choices these politicians make" (p. 1). We must value women politicians, not denigrate them for wanting to be mothers as well as elected officials. Walsh (reported in Layton, 2007), noted that "men have this fixture called a wife that's going to take care of the children. . . . We hear very often from women who are running or elected that they wish they had a wife, someone to deal with the children, have fresh food in the house, pick up the dry cleaning" (p. 2).

Lake (reported in Layton, 2007) also discussed how when men who seek elected office are fathers they are perceived by voters as "oh, this is great, he's going to be concerned about family issues, he'll be more future oriented. . . . A male with young kids, everyone likes it—men, women, seniors." Thus, women are penalized for the same behavior exhibited by men. Voters ask "who is taking care of those children" when evaluating women candidates for office. Voters seldom ask this question of male candidates for elected office. Congresswoman McMorris Rodgers reported that she didn't disclose her pregnancy during her reelection campaign until she completed the first trimester. She noted that she received "negative" letters from constituents when they learned of her pregnancy (reported in Layton, 2007). Women's work in the U.S. House and their own house must be valued.

During my candidacy for a New York Assembly seat I had the honor of meeting Geraldine Ferraro, the first woman to be nominated as vice president of the United States. Ms. Ferraro's sentiment rang true for me in 1998 and today:

We've chosen the path to equality, don't let them turn us around.

REFERENCES

Alba, A. (2015). *This is how the Internet reacted to Hillary Clinton's presidential candidacy announcement*. Retrieved on May 24, 2015, from http://www.nydailynews.com/news/politics/twitter-reacted-hillary-clinton-2016-campaign-logo-article-1.2182632.

Badner, E. (2015). *Businesswoman stands by her man-only view of presidency.* Retrieved on May 10, 2015, from http://www.cnn.com/2015/04/18/politics/ceo-women-shouldnt-be-president/.

Betz, N. (2008). Women's career development. In F. Denmark & M. Paludi (Eds.), *Psychology of women: A handbook of issues and theories* (pp. 717–752). Westport, CT: Praeger.

Bilimoria, D., & Piderit, S. (Eds.). (2007). *Handbook on women in business and management.* Northampton, MA: Edward Elgar.

Bligh, M., Schlehoffer, M., Casad, B., & Gaffney, A. (2011). Competent enough, but would you vote for her? Gender stereotypes and media influences on perceptions of women politicians. *Journal of Applied Social Psychology, 42,* 560–597.

Cardenas, V. (2014). *Why we need a political leadership pipeline for women of color.* Retrieved on May 12, 2015, from https://www.americanprogress.org/issues/women/news/2014/03/07/85454/why-we-need-a-political-leadership-pipeline-for-women-of-color/.

Chesney, M. (2007, September). *Women in leadership—the ceiling is breaking . . . but watch out for falling glass.* Paper presented at the meeting of the Committee on Women in Psychology Leadership Institute for Women in Psychology: Qualitative Evaluation of Training Needs, Washington, DC.

Crocker, J., Major, B., & Steele, C. (1998). Social stigma. In D. T. Gilbert & S. T. Fiske (Eds.), *Handbook of social psychology* (4th ed., pp. 504–553). New York, NY: McGraw-Hill.

Deaux, K., & Emswiller, T. (1974). Explanations of successful performance on sex linked tasks: What's skill for the male is luck for the female. *Journal of Personality and Social Psychology, 29,* 80–85.

Debate.org. (2015). *Will having more women in congress make a difference?* Retrieved on May 27, 2015, from http://www.debate.org/opinions/will-having-more-woman-in-congress-make-a-difference.

DeFour, D., David, G., Diaz, F., & Thompkins, S. (2003). The interface of race, sex, sexual orientation and ethnicity in understanding sexual harassment. In M. Paludi & C. Paludi (Eds.), *Academic and workplace sexual harassment: A handbook of cultural, social science, management and legal perspectives* (pp. 31–45). Westport, CT: Praeger.

Denmark, F., Baron, E., Klara, M., Sigal, J., Gibbs, M., & Wnuk, D. (2008). Women as leaders: From the lab to the real world. In M. Paludi (Ed.), *The psychology of women at work: Challenges and solutions for our female workforce* (pp. 35–56). Westport, CT: Praeger.

Downing, N., & Rousch, K. (1985). From passive acceptance to active commitment. *The Counseling Psychologist, 13,* 695–709.

Doyle, J., & Paludi, M. (1998). *Sex and gender.* New York, NY: McGraw-Hill.

Duff-McCall, K., & Schweinle, W. (2008). Leadership and women. In M. Paludi (Ed.), *The psychology of women at work: Challenges and solutions for our female workforce* (pp. 87–99). Westport, CT: Praeger.

Eagly, A., & Carli, L. (2007). *Through the labyrinth: The truth about how women become leaders*. Boston, MA: Harvard Business School Press.

Eagly, A., & Johannesen-Schmidt, M. (2001). The leadership styles of women and men. *Journal of Social Issues, 57,* 781–797.

Eagly, A., Johannesen-Schmidt, M., & van Engen, M. (2003). Transformation, transactional and laissez-faire leadership styles: A meta-analysis comparing women and men. *Psychological Bulletin, 108,* 233–256.

Eagly, A., & Karau, S. (2002). Role congruity theory of prejudice toward female leaders. *Psychological Review, 109,* 573–598.

Fox, R., & Lawless, J. (2010). Gendered perceptions ad political candidacies: A central barrier to women's equality in electoral politics. *American Journal of Political Science, 55,* 59–73.

Goffman, E. (1963). *Stigma: Notes on the management of spoiled identity*. New York, NY: Simon & Schuster, Inc.

Grabe, S., & Hyde, J. S. (2006). Impact of gender on leadership. In M. Karsten (Ed.), *Gender, race and ethnicity in the workplace: Issues and challenges for today's organizations. Volume 2: Legal, psychological, and power issues affecting women and minorities in business* (pp. 183–198). Westport, CT: Praeger.

Greenspan, J. (2013). *9 things you should know about Victoria Woodhull*. Retrieved on May 10, 2015, from http://www.history.com/news/9-things-you-should-know-about-victoria-woodhull.

Heilman, M., Wallen, A., Fuchs, D., & Tamkins, M. (2004). Penalties for success: Reactions to women who succeed at male gender-typed tasks. *Journal of Applied Psychology, 74,* 935–942.

Hill, S. (2014). Why does the US still have so few women in office? Retrieved on May 26, 2015, from http://www.thenation.com/article/178736/why-does-us-still-have-so-few-women-office.

Jandeska, K., & Kraimer, M. (2005). Women's perceptions of organizational culture, work attitudes, and role-modeling behaviors. *Journal of Managerial Issues, 18,* 461–478.

Kanter, R. M. (1977). *Work and family in the United States: A critical review and agenda for research and policy*. New York, NY: Russell Sage Foundation.

Karsten, M. (2006). Managerial women, minorities and stress: Causes and consequences. In M. Karsten (Ed.), *Gender, race and ethnicity in the workplace* (pp. 238–272). Westport, CT: Praeger.

Keith, T. (2014). *For moms in congress, votes mix with diapers and school pickup*. Retrieved on June 16, 2015, from http://www.npr.org/2014/05/09/310256866/for-moms-in-congress-votes-mix-with-diapers-and-school-pickup.

Lawless, J., & Fox, R. (2005). *Men rule: The continued under-representation of women in U.S. politics*. Washington, DC: Women and Politics Institute.

Layton, L. (2007). *Mom's in the house with kids at home*. Retrieved on June 16, 2015, from www.washingtonpost.com/wp--dyn/content/article/2007/07/18/AR2007071802167.

Maddock, S. (2002). Modernization requires transformational skills: The need for a gender-balanced workforce. *Women in Management Review, 17,* 12–17.

Makosky, V., & Paludi, M. (1990). Feminism and women's studies in the academy. In M. Paludi & G. Steuernagel (Eds.), *Foundations for a feminist restructuring of the academic disciplines* (pp. 1–37). New York, NY: Haworth.

McGregor, J. (2014). *Why more women don't run for office.* Retrieved on May 24, 2015, from http://www.washingtonpost.com/blogs/on-leadership/wp/2014/05/21/why-more-women-dont-run-for-office/.

Mo, C. (2012). *What? Me sexist?* Retrieved on May 10, 2015, from http://gender.stanford.edu/news/2011/what-me-sexist.

Mundy, L. (2015). The secret history of women in the Senate. Retrieved on September 9, 2015, from http://www.politico.com/magazine/story/2015/01/senate-women-secret-history-113908.

National Women's Political Caucus. (2015). *Statistics.* Retrieved on May 21, 2015, from http://www.nwpc.org/statistics.

Norgren, J. (2007). *Belva Lockwood: The woman who would be president.* New York, NY: New York University Press.

Paludi, M. (Ed.). (2008). *The psychology of women at work: Challenges and solutions for our female workforce.* Westport, CT: Praeger.

Paludi, M., Dillon, L., Stern, T., Martin, J., DeFour, D., & White, C. (2007). Courses in the psychology of women: Catalysts for change. In F. L. Denmark & M. A. Paludi (Eds.), *The psychology of women: A handbook of issues and theories* (pp. 174–201). Westport, CT: Greenwood.

Paludi, M., & Neidermeyer, P. (Eds.). (2007). *Work, life and family imbalance: How to level the playing field.* Westport, CT: Praeger.

Paludi, M., Paludi, C., & DeSouza, E. (Eds.). (2010). *Praeger handbook on understanding and preventing workplace discrimination.* Westport, CT: Praeger.

Powell, G., Butterfield, D., & Bartol, K. (2008). Leader evaluations: A new female advantage? *Gender in Management: An International Journal, 23,* 156–174.

Rodgers-Healey, D. (2003). *12 insights into leadership for women.* Retrieved on May 13, 2010, from www.leadershipforwomen.com.au.

Sinacore, A., & Enns, C. (2005). Diversity feminisms: Postmodern, women of color, antiracist, lesbian, third-wave and global perspectives. In C. Z. Enns & A. L. Sinacore (Eds.), *Teaching and social justice: Integrating multicultural and feminist theories in the classroom* (pp. 41–68). Washington, DC: American Psychological Association.

Stolberg, S. (2015). *More women than ever in Congress, but with less power than before.* Retrieved on May 10, 2015, from www.newyorktimes.com.

Thomsen, D. (2015). Why so few (Republican) women? Explaining the partisan imbalance of women in the U.S. Congress. *Legislative Studies Quarterly, 40,* 295–323.

Volden, C., Wiseman, A., & Wittmer, D. (2013). When are women more effective lawmakers than men? *American Journal of Political Science, 57,* 326–341.

Werhane, P., Posig, M., Gundry, L., Powell, E., Carlson, J., & Ofstein, L. (2006). Women leaders in corporate America: A study of leadership values and methods. In M. Karsten (Ed.), *Gender, race and ethnicity in the workplace: Issues and challenges for today's organizations. Volume 1: Management, gender, and ethnicity in the United States* (pp. 1–29). Westport, CT: Praeger.

Wisconsin Women's Council. (2007). *Who me? What we know about why women don't run for political office.* http://womenscouncil.wi.gov/docview.asp? docid=11064.

Woods, K., & Buchanan, N. (2008). Sexual harassment in the workplace. In M. Paludi (Ed.), *The psychology of women at work: Challenges and solutions for our female workforce. Volume 1: Career liberation, history, and the new millennium* (pp. 119–132). Westport, CT: Praeger.

Yoder, J. (2001). Strategies for change: Making leadership work more effectively for women. *Journal of Social Issues, 57,* 815–828.

Senator Rebecca Latimer Felton

Senator Latimer Felton was the first woman to serve in the U.S. Senate, representing the state of Georgia. She was sworn in on November 21, 1922. On the following day she made a speech in which she thanked the Senate for allowing her to be sworn in and stating that women who would serve in the Senate after her would be serving with "ability," "integrity of purpose," and "unstinted usefulness." Her term lasted for 24 hours. She had been appointed by Governor Thomas Hardwick when Senator Thomas E. Watson died on September 26, 1922. Hardwick had opposed the Nineteenth Amendment and wanted to win women voters' confidence and thus appointed Rebecca Latimer Felton to the position. Her seat went to Walter F. George. George invited Latimer Felton to present her credentials prior to taking his Senate seat.

Source: http://history.house.gov/People/Listing/F/FELTON,-Rebecca-Latimer-(F000069)/.

Chapter 1

Examining Partisan Men and Women's Issue Emphases from Campaigns to Legislation

Lindsey M. Meeks

"What I want to know is, where are the women?" It was a question posed in February 2012 by New York Democratic representative Carolyn Maloney during a U.S. House of Representatives hearing, called by Republican Party leadership, on a new Obama administration rule regarding contraception coverage. Maloney was addressing a House oversight committee that was especially notable for one thing: it contained only men. At the hearing, another Democrat, Washington, D.C., delegate Eleanor Holmes Norton, motioned to include a female witness, but her motion was ignored, prompting the two women to walk out. A photograph of the all-male committee debating female birth control circulated on the Internet and became a rallying point among supporters of the health care law and President Barack Obama. Nearly seven months later, Maloney again posed this question—this time while standing on stage at the Democratic National Convention. She was flanked by female House Democrats, and the audience of delegates joined her in saying, "The women are here!" Well, at least some were: women made up 17% of the 112th U.S. Congress in 2012 (Center for American Women and Politics, 2012). That percentage edged up slightly with the induction of the 113th and 114th Congress, but even with these increases in representation, women comprise only 19.4% of the 114th U.S. Congress.

The low representation of women in Congress, as well as in gubernatorial offices, along with the U.S. legacy of only male presidents, is problematic for a host of reasons. For one, a lack of women in office reiterates the idea that politics is for men and creates a gendered barrier for young girls and women to elected office. A recent report by Lawless and Fox (2013) found that 63% of women surveyed had never thought about running for office, compared to 43% of men. In addition, 20% of men said they had thought about running for office many times, as compared to 10% of women (Lawless & Fox, 2013). They propose multiple reasons for this gender gap, including the following: young men are more likely to be socialized by their parents to consider politics, young women are less likely to receive encouragement to run for office, and young women are less likely to think they are qualified to run for office (Lawless & Fox, 2013). These reasons all go back to some form of socialization, to growing up in a society that is more apt to foster the idea of men in politics than women. Ultimately, women cannot increase their representation in office if they never run for office.

Further, research suggests that citizens may be detrimentally affected when women are absent from or underrepresented in elected office. Studies have shown that women politicians bring a wider array of political issues to bear in the legislative process than men, particularly issues regarding women, children, and families (Frederick, 2011; Thomas, 1991). Similarly, research has shown that women introduce twice as many bills on civil rights and liberties, and significantly more bills on family concerns, immigration, labor, education, and health (Volden, Wiseman, & Wittmer, 2013). Women ultimately build a wider legislative portfolio than men that represents greater segments of the population's needs and concerns. Also, women politicians emphasize different character traits in the legislative process; namely, women engage in more consensus-building activities that tend to keep their bills alive through later stages of the legislative process (Volden et al., 2013). Taken together, these findings suggest that women politicians bring more issues to the table, and their approach to legislation is more collaborative, which increases the likelihood of success in passing legislation. Therefore, having women in office influences what gets done and how it gets done. For those who could benefit from this legislation—seemingly most Americans—the low percentage of women presents a profound loss.

In this chapter I examine the full arc of the electoral and legislative processes by exploring what political issues women and men candidates discussed in their campaign communications when running for the U.S. Senate and what bills they sponsored in the subsequent congressional term. Specifically, I present an analysis of 24 men and women candidates' campaign Twitter feeds during the 2012 general election cycle and focus the analysis on their discussion of political issues. Twitter was the go-to campaign platform in America in 2012, and it is an attractive campaigning platform for Senate candidates because it affords them complete control over their messaging and eases the distribution of their messaging, which is important in statewide elections given the geographic distribution of one's constituency. Examining Twitter is also beneficial to scholars because candidates aim to "stay on message" to create and maintain cohesive images; thus, what a candidate says on Twitter is likely indicative of his or her broader campaign communication strategy. Therefore, by analyzing tweets, we get a general idea of candidates' campaign strategies. As an extension of this analysis, I also explore what bills electorally successful candidates sponsored during the 113th congressional term. Collectively, this chapter showcases what issues candidates championed in their campaigns and once they were in office, and whether women represented more issue-based constituents in both phases.

THE GENDERING OF POLITICAL ISSUES

Political issues in America have become gendered over time. Historic and cultural factors have fostered the perception that certain political issues are "feminine" or "masculine," and that women and men, respectively, are perceived as "owning" certain issues. The idea of issue ownership emerges from the work of Budge and Farlie (1983) and Petrocik (1996), which suggests that particular political parties are perceived to be better able to "handle" certain matters, "which leads voters to believe that one of the parties (and its candidates) is more sincere and committed to doing something about them" (Petrocik, 1996, p. 826). Herrnson, Lay, and Stokes (2003) suggested this theory could also apply to gender. "Gender ownership" draws on a history of social sex roles and stereotypes that have fueled perceptions of men and women as differentially better at handling particular issues (Herrnson et al., 2003). For example, as supposed caretakers women are viewed as better at handling "compassion issues," such as education, health care, reproductive rights, and the environment, while as supposed protectors and breadwinners, men are viewed as better equipped to handle foreign policy, national defense, crime, and economic issues (Herrnson et al., 2003; Lawless, 2009; Pew, 2008; Sanbonmatsu & Dolan, 2009). Notably, feminized issues overlap with many of the aforementioned issues women politicians are more likely to bring to bear in their legislation. Furthermore, recent research shows that these stereotypes of handling persist despite increased representation of women in politics. For example, Lawless (2009) found that citizens view male candidates as better equipped to handle matters of national security and military crises, and perceive female candidates as better at handling issues such as aiding the poor and abortion. This gendering was upheld in Sanbonmatsu and Dolan's (2009) and Banwart's (2010) work, with women having a perceived advantage on education and men having a perceived advantage on crime, as well as handling military and economic issues. News coverage of men and women candidates feed these perceptions because women candidates receive more feminine issue coverage and men receive more masculine issue coverage (e.g., Kahn, 1994; Kittilson & Fridkin, 2008; Major & Coleman, 2008). Therefore, the historic gendering of issues still manifests today, with men and women seen as and portrayed as more competent in handling issues that align with their gender.

These perceptions of handling matter because the public views masculine issues as more important than feminine issues, and increasingly so when higher offices are at stake (Huddy & Terkildsen, 1993; Smith, Paul, & Paul, 2007). For example, in a study focused on issue saliency, participants rated the economy (35%) as the most important issue, with national defense (14%) and education (14%) tying for a distant second (Meeks, 2012a). In turn, two of the top three issues are ones men are seen as more competent in handling. Once again, the news media reinforces this privileging of masculine content by routinely including more coverage of masculine issues than feminine issues in electoral coverage (Kittilson & Fridkin, 2008; Meeks, 2012b). The importance of masculine issues to the electorate, and the heavier focus on these issues in news coverage, may also prompt candidates to focus more on masculine than feminine issues. For example, an examination of television advertisements and campaign websites in congressional elections found that men *and* women leaned more toward referencing masculine than feminine issues (Banwart & Kelly, 2013; Bystrom & Kaid, 2002). Given voters' and news media's predilection toward masculine issues, and candidates' willingness to recognize and abide by this preference, all candidates would seemingly focus their campaigning efforts on masculine issues. Furthermore, since politicians have to run on their records when seeking reelection, it is also possible that politicians will focus on sponsoring more bills that deal with masculine issues. To explore whether men and women adhered similarly or differently to the championing of masculine issues in their elections, and once in office for those who won, the following analysis examines Senate candidates' discussion of issues on Twitter during the 2012 elections and in the bills they sponsored during the 113th Congress.

METHODS AND RESEARCH DESIGN

To examine the discussion of issues, I conducted two quantitative content analyses. The first step of the research design examined U.S. Senate candidates' Twitter feeds during the 2012 general elections. In total,

24 candidates were examined across 12 elections (Table 1.1). The selected races represented a variety of elections, including geographic diversity; Republican and Democratic winners; open versus closed elections; and all-male, all-female, and male-versus-female elections. These factors created a diverse cross-section of elections.[1]

To analyze communication during these campaigns I downloaded each candidate's campaign Twitter feed after the election via the official Twitter API using a simple computer script that was verified by a professional software engineer.[2] The API limits access to 3,200 historical tweets per account, but this easily accommodated the time frame of the candidates' general election tweets. To ensure that the script collected all of the

Table 1.1 Selected Senate Elections and Number of Total Tweets

	Republican	Democrat	Election Dates
Arizona	Jeff Flake (n = 83)*	Richard Carmona (n = 253)	August 29–November 6
California	Elizabeth Emken (n = 2,347)	Dianne Feinstein (n = 52)*	June 6–November 6
Connecticut	Linda McMahon (n = 754)	Chris Murphy (n = 307)*	August 15–November 6
Hawaii	Linda Lingle (n = 2303)	Mazie Hirono (n = 338)*	August 12–November 6
Indiana	Richard Mourdock (n = 1,101)	Joe Donnelly (n = 121)*	May 9–November 6
Massachusetts	Scott Brown (n = 170)	Elizabeth Warren (n = 337)*	September 7–November 6
Missouri	Todd Akin (n = 448)	Claire McCaskill (n = 157)*	August 8–November 6
Nebraska	Deb Fischer (n = 132)*	Bob Kerrey (n = 866)	May 16– November 6
Nevada	Dean Heller (n = 1,053)*	Shelley Berkley (n = 669)	June 13– November 6
New Mexico	Heather Wilson (n = 471)	Martin Heinrich (n = 454)*	June 6– November 6
New York	Wendy Long (n = 818)	Kirsten Gillibrand (n = 695)*	June 27– November 6
Pennsylvania	Tom Smith (n = 423)	Bob Casey, Jr. (n = 833)*	April 25– November 6

*Indicates who won the election.

tweets, I conducted a manual check on a subset of the candidates in which I periodically compared tweets from the download to tweets on the candidate's actual Twitter page. The manual check revealed a complete match between the two sources. I also verified each Twitter account by matching it against the accounts specified on the candidate's campaign website. For each candidate I coded the entire census of general election tweets, ranging from the day after the appropriate primary election to Election Day on November 6, 2012. In total, there were 14,662 tweets.

For the second step in the research design, I content analyzed each bill sponsored by the 12 winning candidates during the 113th congressional term to assess what legislation politicians proposed once in office/reelected. This portion of the analysis focused only on the bills sponsored by the politician, and it did not include cosponsored bills or amendments. A sponsor to a bill is the first-listed member of the U.S. Senate on the bill when it is introduced for consideration. While being a sponsor does not indicate that the senator actually wrote the bill, such tasks may be taken up by a staff member, it does denote that the senator is leading the way, so to speak, for this bill's consideration. A cosponsor is when a senator adds his or her name to the list of supporters for the bill. Bills can often have multiple cosponsors. For example, bills often have one to three cosponsors, but a bill can have many more. For example, a bill sponsored by Dianne Feinstein had 45 cosponsors (S.1236: Respect of Marriage Act). This explains why senators are cosponsors on far more bills in comparison to being sponsors. To assess what legislation men and women senators were *directly* championing once in office, this analysis focused on bills in which the senator was listed as a sponsor. This information was accessed via the Library of Congress, under the THOMAS project. THOMAS was created in 1995 with the intent to "make federal legislative information freely available to the public" via a database that provides information on each bill introduced to Congress since 1989, including sponsorship summaries of each senator for each congressional term ("About THOMAS," 2015). In total, there were 348 sponsored bills for the 12 winning candidates during the 113th term.

To content analyze tweets and bills, I created the following variables and operationalizations. The unit of observation and analysis was either the individual tweet or the individual bill. Dimensions of each composite variable were coded as "Absent" (0) or "Present" (1), and then collapsed so that "0" indicated complete absence of the variable and "1" indicated that at least one dimension of the variable was present. Political issues were categorized as feminine or masculine based on previous studies (e.g., Herrnson et al., 2003; Pew, 2008).[3] *Feminine issues* were coded as present when there was any discussion of any of the following dimensions included in an individual tweet/bill: education, health care, environment, or "women's issues," which included issues that are typically seen as more important to women, for example, abortion, contraception. *Masculine issues* were coded as present when there was any discussion of military/national security, crime, economy, or taxes. *Other issues* were coded as present when there was any discussion of issues that did not conceptually fall into the masculine or feminine categories, such as LGBT rights, campaign finance reform, agriculture, and infrastructure. Intercoder reliability was conducted on a random sample ($n = 735$) by two coders.[4] Calculated using Krippendorff's alpha, coefficients met appropriate acceptance levels (Krippendorff, 2004): feminine issues ($\alpha = 0.86$), masculine issues ($\alpha = 0.83$), and other issues ($\alpha = 0.81$).

The following analysis includes descriptive statistics for each comparison. No tests for statistical significance are included because the analysis included the entire census of tweets for each candidate during his or her general election and all of his or her sponsored bills during the 113th term. Therefore, inferential statistics are not necessary.

RESULTS

Candidates' Discussion of Issues on Twitter

To understand various dynamics at play in candidates' discussion of issues, the analysis moves from broad contours of issue discussion toward more nuanced comparisons, with each layer of analysis digging deeper into candidates' communicative patterns. Of the 14,662 total tweets, 29.5% ($n = 4,326$) contained discussion of at least one issue. Within these issue-oriented tweets, 29.6% discussed a feminine issue, 61.3% discussed a masculine issue, and 22.1% discussed other issues. There are two notable aspects of these data. First, these percentages do not add up to 100% because tweets could mention more than one issue and therefore may have contained discussion of, for example, a feminine issue and a masculine issue. Second, discussion of masculine issues doubled that of feminine issues and almost tripled that of other issues. Therefore, candidates in this study continued to privilege masculine issues over feminine issues.

The next set of analysis assessed whether there were any general differences based on a candidate's gender. Based on volume alone, women ($n = 9,073$) tweeted more than men ($n = 5,589$), but this greater volume did not translate into greater issue discussion. Men were more likely to discuss issues than women: men referenced at least one issue in 35.1% of their tweets as compared to 26.1% for women. When men discussed issues (issue-oriented tweets $n = 1,959$), they prioritized masculine issues above all else: 65.9% for masculine issues, 31.2% for feminine issues, and 17.9% for other issues. Women followed suit (issue-oriented tweets $n = 2,367$): 57.5% for masculine issues, 28.3% for feminine issues, and 25.6% for other issues. In sum, men's discussion of masculine issues doubled that of feminine issues, and while women also heavily focused on masculine issues, it was to a lesser extent than men. Further, men discussed masculine *and* feminine issues more than women, and women topped men regarding other issues.

To further explore these differences, the next set of analysis examines differences between partisan candidates since, after all, men and women were running as Republicans or Democrats as well. In terms of volume alone, Republican women tweeted the most (n = 6,825), followed by Republican men (n = 3,278), with Democratic men (n = 2,311) and women (n = 2,248) bringing up the rear. Regarding issue discussion, in the previous analysis we saw the men tweeted about issues more than women, but once examined in the context of gender *and* partisanship, this finding is only partially true. Democratic women, in fact, tweeted the most about issues at 38.2%, followed by Republican men at 36%, then Democratic men at 33.7%, and finally, Republican women at 22.1%. Thus, Republican women and their comparatively lower volume of issue discussion is what fueled women's second-place ranking in the previous analysis. To further explore campaign tweets, analysis in Table 1.2 focused only on tweets that mentioned issues and provides a breakdown of candidates' discussion across the issue categories.

Data in Table 1.2 reveal several findings. First, Democrats, both women and men, were more likely to discuss feminine issues than Republicans—ranging from 5% to 11% more. Second, Republican men were the most likely to discuss masculine issues, whereas Democratic women were the least likely. Democratic women trailed the other candidates by 13.2% to 18.5% in this discussion of masculine issues. Third, when it came to discussion of other issues, the tables turned, with Democratic women being the most likely to discuss other issues and Republican men being the least likely. Fourth, all of the candidates discussed masculine

Table 1.2 Issue-Oriented Tweet Breakdown by Candidate Gender and Political Party Affiliation

	Republican Men (n = 1,181) (%)	Democratic Men (n = 778) (%)	Republican Women (n = 1,508) (%)	Democratic Women (n = 859) (%)
Feminine issues	29.1	34.4	24.3	35.4
Masculine issues	67.6	63.4	62.3	49.1
Other issues	16.2	20.6	23.1	29.9

Note. n values represent the number of tweets that discussed at least one issue within the issue category.

issues more than any of the other issues. The disparity was greatest for Republican men, who discussed masculine issues more than twice as much as feminine issues and more than four times as much as other issues. And once again, Democratic women were the inverse of Republican men. Though Democratic women still discussed masculine issues the most, the difference between their various issue categories was much smaller. For instance, Democratic women discussed masculine issues roughly a third more than feminine issues, whereas the other candidates had a 2:1 ratio of masculine to feminine issue discussion. Further, while other candidates discussed masculine issues two to four times as much as other issues, Democratic women discussed masculine issues about two-thirds more than other issues. Ultimately, Democratic women appeared to distribute their issue discussion across the various issue categories more so than the other candidates.

Democratic women's seemingly more diffuse issue agenda prompted the next layer of analysis: to examine how partisan candidates distributed their discussion of individual issues within the feminine and masculine categories. The most tweeted about feminine issue for all candidates was health care. Second, of tweets that mentioned a feminine issue, Democratic women appear to have the most diverse issue agenda and Republican men appear to have the least diverse. Specifically, Republican men filled almost 79% of their feminine issue discussion with tweets about health care, the most of any candidate—leaving roughly 20% to cover the other three feminine issues. Democratic men and Republican women discussed health care in just over 57% of their feminine issue tweets. Democratic women discussed health care in just under 39% of their feminine issue tweets, with approximately 27% going to women's issues, roughly 23% dedicated to education, and a remaining 11% focused on the environment. In sum, Democratic women had a more diverse feminine issue portfolio, and as a result, they talked about the other three issues more than any of the other candidates. Democratic men and Republican women, though not quite as diverse as Democratic women, had a relatively diverse issue portfolio, and Republican men had the most concentrated issue agenda of all four candidate types.

The most tweeted about masculine issue was the economy. Republican men appear to once again have a more concentrated issue portfolio. The distribution of masculine issue discussion is more similar across the candidate types; nonetheless, Republican men filled approximately 74% of their masculine issue discussion with tweets about the economy—the most of any of the candidates. Regarding references to the economy within masculine issue discussion, the ranking was as follows for the other candidates: just over 70% for Democratic men, just over 68% for Republican women, and just below 65% for Democratic women. Therefore, even though talk of the economy predominated all of the candidates' masculine issue tweets, it played a comparatively smaller role for Democratic women. When it came to who talked the most about the other three issues, it varied depending on the issue. For taxes, Democratic men and Republican women dedicated roughly 17% of their masculine issue discussion to this issue. For national security/military, Democratic women filled 20% of their masculine issue tweets with discussion of this issue. And for crime, Republican women discussed this issue in just over 5% of their masculine issue tweets. That number is comparatively lower than the other issues, but it still put them ahead of the other candidates. Notably, Republican men did not take the lead on any of the other three masculine issues. That, combined with their heavier focus on the economy, resulted in them once again having a less diverse issue agenda. And this time around, Democratic *and* Republican women had the most diverse issue agendas.

Given these differences, the final set of analysis based on the candidates' tweets compares how winning partisan men and women candidates discussed issues. Keep in mind that only one Republican woman ran *and* won a Senate seat in 2012 so the data for this candidate type represent one candidate's tweets: Deb Fischer of Nebraska.

Data in Table 1.3 reveal several findings. Democratic men, then women, talked the most about issues, and Republican women came in last. Previously, when combining winning and losing Republican women, they also came in last for issue discussion. Therefore, this trend appears to hold in the aggregate and among winning Republican women. Republican women appear to fill their feed more so than other candidate types with *non*-issue-related tweets. Second, all of the winning partisans discussed masculine issues more than feminine issues. Republican men had the largest disparity and Democratic women had the smallest. Winning Republican men discussed masculine issues three times as much as feminine

Table 1.3 Tweet Breakdown of Winning Candidates by Candidate Gender and Political Party Affiliation

	Republican Men ($n = 1,136$) (%)	Democratic Men ($n = 1,192$) (%)	Republican Women ($n = 132$) (%)	Democratic Women ($n = 1,579$) (%)
Any issues	33.1	40.0	20.5	35.5
Feminine issues	7.5	15.1	6.1	11.1
Masculine issues	23.3	28.0	12.1	16.8
Other issues	5.8	5.6	2.3	11.3

Note. n values represent the total number of tweets for each candidate type.

issues, whereas winning Democratic women discussed masculine issues roughly a third more than feminine issues.

Health care was the most tweeted about feminine issue for everyone except winning Democratic women who favored women's issues and then health care. Democratic women had a more diverse issue portfolio, and Republican men once again had a more concentrated feminine issue agenda. Winning Republican men sunk over 85% of their feminine issue discussion into the sole issue of health care. Democratic women, on the other hand, focused on this issue in roughly 28% of their tweets. Further, based on the raw percentages, Democratic women were the only candidates to produce double-digit discussion for each individual issue. Third, in a twist from previous analysis, winning Republican women had a more concentrated agenda. In the aggregate, Republican women had a more diverse issue agenda, but winning Republican women talked about only two of the four feminine issues. Granted, the sample size is very small and includes only one woman, so conclusions are tentative at best, but it does suggest that winning for Republican women was more closely aligned with less feminine issue discussion.

The most tweeted about masculine issue was the economy. Republican men again dedicated the most of their feed to this issue, roughly 75%. However, in a departure from before, Republican women, not Democratic women, talked about this predominant issue the least at approximately 53%. That said, Democratic women seemingly have the most diverse issue agenda. They talked about the economy less than the men, talked about national security/military comparatively more than any of the other candidates, and, unlike Republican women, discussed crime. In fact, neither Republican women nor Democratic men mentioned crime in a single tweet. This finding is interesting because Republican women in the aggregate far exceeded the other candidates in their discussion of crime, but when we funnel down to winning Republican women, the issue disappears. Collectively, winning Republican women do not mention two of four feminine issues or one of four masculine issues in any of their tweets. By omitting three of the eight issues, winning Republican women seemingly have the most concentrated issue agenda of all of the candidates.

Winning Candidates Sponsored Bills Once in Office

In total, there were 348 bills sponsored by the 12 winning candidates during the 113th U.S. Congress. In terms of volume, Democratic women sponsored the most bills at 180, followed by Democratic men at 90, Republican men at 59, and Republican women at 19. Once these numbers were divided by the number of politicians in each type, creating an average number of bills per politician, the rankings were as follows: 36 for Democratic women, 29.5 for Republican men, 22.5 for Democratic men, and, since the category of "Republican women" represents only one individual, 19 for Republican women. Thus, in volume and average per candidate, Democratic women were the most likely to propose sponsored bills.

Volume alone does not, of course, speak to issue diversity, and so the analysis now focuses on the content of these bills. Overall, 44% (n = 153) of the bills focused on issues not categorized as masculine or feminine, followed by feminine issues at 31.6% (n = 110), and then masculine issues at 31% (n = 108). Other issues were twice as prominent in legislation as in campaign tweets—22.1% of campaign tweets referenced such issues. Some of this discrepancy is due to the nature of campaigns versus being in office. A large portion of the other issues focused on government affairs that would most likely not come up on the campaign trail.

For Republican men, the biggest portion of their feminine issue discussion was focused on the environment. For the other three politician types, the top issue was health care. Despite this, we can still see some differences in issue portfolios. Specifically, Republican men dedicated 84% of their feminine issue discussion to two issues: roughly 56% was focused on the environment and 28% on health care. For Republican women, over two-thirds of their feminine issue legislation was focused on the single issue of health care. In fact, Republican women proposed legislation that covered only two of the four feminine issues—health care and education—suggesting that they put forward the least diverse feminine issue agenda across all of the politicians. Democrats, on the other hand, were more diverse in their approach. Democratic men spent less than two-thirds of their feminine issue discussion focused on health care and the environment—roughly 40% and 25%, respectively—and Democratic women dedicated approximately 62% of their feminine issue–related bills on these issues. Therefore, Democrats were able to fill the other third or more of their legislation discussing education and women's issues. In particular, Democratic women as a whole were more even in their distribution of feminine issue discussion: approximately 36% on health care, 26.5% on environment, 30% on education, and 7.5% on women's issues.

Each politician type did not have the same top issue. For example, the top masculine issue for Republican men and Democratic women was the military/national security; for Democratic men it was the economy, and for Republican women it was taxes. That said, some of the trends present for feminine issues are also present for masculine issues; namely, Republicans have a more concentrated portfolio and Democrats have a comparatively less concentrated portfolio. Republican men dedicated 75% of their masculine issue–oriented bills to two issues: military/national security (~40%) and economy (~35%). Republican women spent half of their time focused on these two issues—approximately 33% on economy and 17% on military—and then spent the entire other half focused on taxes, leaving crime completely off the docket. Thus, once again, Republican women were the only ones to omit an issue from their portfolio. Democratic men spent approximately 59% of their focus on the economy and military—33.5% and 25.5%, respectively. Similarly, Democratic women spent slightly over 59% focused on these two issues—roughly 23.5% on the economy and 35% on military. In both cases, this freed up roughly 40% of their masculine issue bills to focus on the other two issues—allowing them to dedicate double-digit discussion to taxes and crime.

Ultimately, it appears as though sponsored bill diversity cuts more along party lines than gender lines. However, I conclude this section with one additional perspective on issue diversity. Table 1.4 provides the breakdown of issue categories for each politician type.

What is striking about Table 1.4 is that Republican and Democratic *men* appear to distribute their discussion of issues more evenly across the issue categories as compared to partisan women. Partisan women dedicated much more of their bills to issues not categorized as masculine or feminine: 63.2% of Republican women's sponsored bills discussed other issues, as did 51.1% of Democratic women. Since masculine and feminine issue categories represented only four issues each in this study, and other issues could represent countless issues, one could suggest that partisan women's higher proportion of other issue discussion actually translated into greater issue diversity. In other words, partisan women's proposed legislation covered a potentially much larger terrain beyond the eight categorized issues. For example, Democratic women proposed legislation on the following issues: same-sex marriage, creating online voter registration in all 50 states, transportation, infrastructure, immigration, Food and Drug Administration and Federal Communications Commission (FCC) regulations, agriculture, ensuring that food banks had kosher and halal food, child care, trade, energy, and eliminating discrimination in adoption and foster care systems regarding parents'/guardians' sexual orientation.

Table 1.4 Breakdown of Sponsored Bills by Politician Gender and Political Party Affiliation

	Republican Men (n = 59) (%)	Democratic Men (n = 90) (%)	Republican Women (n = 19) (%)	Democratic Women (n = 180) (%)
Feminine issues	40.7	34.4	15.8	28.9
Masculine issues	32.3	41.1	31.6	25.6
Other issues	32.3	33.3	63.2	51.1

Note. n values represent the total number of bills for each politician type.

Further, Deb Fischer, the lone Republican women, proposed 19 sponsored bills, and those bills included other issues that dealt with adoption, FCC regulations, preventing discrimination, governmental transparency, and provisions around family leave. Partisan men also proposed legislation that fell into this category, but partisan women's proportionately larger focus on this array of issues does suggest one form of greater issue diversity.

CONCLUSION

Having greater representation of women in the U.S. Congress carries with it several benefits. At the societal level, the public may become more socialized toward the presence of women in elected office, prompting greater perceptions of gender equality (Lawless & Fox, 2013). Further, women propose a greater variety of political issues once in office, which could translate into several issue publics gaining greater representation in legislation (Frederick, 2011; Thomas, 1991; Volden et al., 2013). This study sought to examine this potential issue diversity from campaigns to legislation among partisan men and women by first examining campaign tweets and then analyzing sponsored bills. This analysis yielded results that supported and did not support previous research. First, masculine issues received the most attention in campaign tweets. This was true when candidates were broken down by gender, then again when examined by gender and party affiliation, and finally again when examining winning partisan men and women candidates. This privileging of masculine issues, such as the economy and national security, by candidates is in line with previous research (e.g., Banwart & Kelly, 2013; Bystrom & Kaid, 2002). Notably, the heavy emphasis on masculine issues dissipated once candidates entered office. Republican men proposed more legislation regarding feminine issues than masculine or other issues, and Democratic and Republican women focused more of their bills on other issues. Only Democratic men proposed more legislation around masculine issues than the other issue categories. This finding is based on a limited number of politicians, but it does suggest a difference in issue emphases for campaigning versus legislating.

Second, women, specifically Democratic women, put forward a more diverse issue portfolio. For campaigning, partisan women had a relatively more diverse masculine and feminine issue platform than men. Republican men, alternately, had a relatively more concentrated issue portfolio—spending the majority of their tweets focused on the top feminine and masculine issues of health care and economy. This trend, however, slightly subsided once we examined winning candidates. Winning Democratic women continued to have the most diverse issue portfolio, but winning Republican women, by not discussing three of the eight issues in any tweet, had the more concentrated issue platform. When we moved into examining sponsored bills in the 113th congressional term, Democratic women continued to distribute their issue focus across the range of issues. And Republican women and men continued to have a less diverse issue portfolio. Therefore, across the board, from campaigning to legislation, we see a relationship form. Winning Democratic women campaigned on a wide array of issues, and once in office, they championed a wide array of issues. Winning Republican men and women campaigned on a more limited set of issues, and once in office, they promoted a more limited set of masculine and feminine issues. In this case, based on issue diversity alone, what you buy is seemingly what you get.

Besides finding this relationship between campaigning and legislation, this collection of results reveals one other notable finding. As previously mentioned, women in general propose a wider range of issues once in office. This study finds that it is Democratic women, not Republican women, who are distributing their legislation more diversely across masculine and feminine issues. Therefore, gender alone may not be the only factor, and future studies need to assess a politician's gender *and* party affiliation when examining issue diversity. This is not to say that Republican women are less valuable additions to Congress. To the contrary, Republican women play a pivotal role in issue diversity because they proposed more legislation that fell into the other issues category than any other politician type. Collectively, then, Democratic and Republican women may play complementary roles: Democratic women propose bills featuring a wider array of masculine and feminine issues, and Republican women sponsor bills that expand across a host of other issues. Together, they sponsor bills that represent the concerns of a diverse range of issue publics, and, consequently, a large portion of the American public. For the many Americans who could benefit from this broad and diverse issue agenda, the need for greater representation of women in the U.S. Congress is crucial.

NOTES

1. There were 12 mixed-gender and three all-female Senate elections in 2012, and this sample includes half of the mixed-gender and all of the all-female Senate elections in 2012. In 2012 there was only one Republican woman who ran *and* won her election for the U.S. Senate: Deb Fischer of Nebraska. Fischer ran in a mixed-gender election, which means that none of the Republican women featured in the same-gender elections won their races. The sample also contains more Democratic winners since Democrats were more successful than Republicans in 2012. Therefore, this sample of elections does have some limitations, and further replication of this study design would be valuable.

2. The code used for this process is available at https://github.com/RainerSigwald/twitter_archiver.

3. For the remainder of this chapter I will refer to issues as feminine or masculine, based on perceptions identified in scholarship. I do not wish to suggest such issues are in actuality gendered; rather, they are simply perceived as such.

4. This size met and exceeded the minimum required size determined by Riffe, Lacy, and Fico's.

REFERENCES

Banwart, M. (2010). Gender and candidate communication: Effects of stereotypes in the 2008 election. *American Behavioral Scientist, 54*, 265–283.

Banwart, M., & Kelly, W. (2013). Running on the web: Online self-presentation strategies in mixed-gender races. *Social Science Computer Review, 31*, 614–624.

Budge, I., & Farlie, D. (1983). *Explaining and predicting elections: Issue effects and party strategies in twenty-three democracies.* London and Boston: Allen & Unwin.

Bystrom, D., & Kaid, L. (2002). Are women candidates transforming campaign communication? In C. Rosenthal (Ed.), *Women transforming congress* (pp. 146–169). Norman, OK: University of Oklahoma Press.

Center for American Women and Politics. (2012). Congress. Retrieved from http://www.cawp.rutgers.edu/fast_facts/levels_of_office/congress.php.

Frederick, B. (2011). Gender turnover and roll call voting in the US Senate. *Journal of Women, Politics & Policy, 32*, 193–210.

Herrnson, P., Lay, J., & Stokes, A. (2003). Women running "as women": Candidate gender, campaign issues, and voter-targeting strategies. *The Journal of Politics, 65*, 244–255.

Huddy, L., & Terkildsen, N. (1993). Gender stereotypes and the perception of male and female candidates. *American Journal of Political Science, 37*, 119–147.

Kahn, K. F. (1994). The distorted mirror: Press coverage of women candidates for statewide office. *The Journal of Politics, 56*, 154–173.

Kittilson, M. C., & Fridkin, K. (2008). Gender, candidate portrayals and election campaigns: A comparative perspective. *Politics & Gender, 4*, 371–392.

Krippendorff, K. (2004). *Content analysis: An introduction to its methodology.* Thousand Oaks, CA: Sage Publications, Inc.

Lawless, J., & Fox, R. (2013). Girls just wanna not run: The gender gap in young Americans' political ambition. Washington, DC: Women and Politics Institute.

Lawless, J. L. (2009). Sexism and gender bias in election 2008: A more complex path for women in politics. *Politics & Gender, 5*, 70–80.

Major, L., & Coleman, R. (2008). The intersection of race and gender in election coverage: What happens when the candidates don't fit the stereotypes? *Howard Journal of Communications, 19*, 315–333.

Meeks, L. (2012a). *Meeting expectations: Issues, traits, party, and gender in a woman-versus-woman election.* Paper presented at the American Association of Public Opinion Research, Orlando, FL.

Meeks, L. (2012b). Is she "man enough"?: Women candidates, executive political offices, and news coverage. *Journal of Communication, 62*, 175–193.

Petrocik, J. (1996). Issue ownership in presidential elections, with a 1980 case study. *American Journal of Political Science, 40,* 825–850.

Pew. (2008). A paradox in public attitudes: Men or women: Who's the better leader? Retrieved from http://www.pewsocialtrends.org/.

Riffe, D., Lacy, S., and Fico, F. (2005). *Analyzing media messages: Using quantitative content analysis in research,* 2nd ed. Mahwah, NJ: Lawrence Erlbaum Associates.

Sanbonmatsu, K., & Dolan, K. (2009). Do gender stereotypes transcend party? *Political Research Quarterly, 62,* 485–494.

Smith, J., Paul, D., & Paul, R. (2007). No place for a woman: Evidence for gender bias in evaluations of presidential candidates. *Basic and Applied Social Psychology, 29,* 225–233.

Thomas, S. (1991). The impact of women on state legislative policies. *Journal of Politics, 53,* 958–976.

Volden, C., Wiseman, A. E., & Wittmer, D. E. (2013). When are women more effective lawmakers than men? *American Journal of Political Science, 57,* 326–341.

Congresswoman Jeannette Rankin

Jeannette Rankin was the first woman to serve in the U.S. Congress in 1917, representing Montana. Congresswoman Rankin once quipped: "I may be the first woman member of Congress but I won't be the last." During her tenure, Rankin helped pass the Nineteenth Amendment, which gave women the right to vote. She was also the only member of Congress to have voted against both World War I and World War II, as she was a self-proclaimed pacifist. When refusing to declare war on Japan, Rankin stated: "As a woman I can't go to war and I refuse to send anyone else." After her vote she was followed by an angry mob and found a safe haven in a telephone booth until the U.S. Capitol Police rescued her.

Source: http://history.house.gov/People/Listing/R/RANKIN,-Jeannette-(R000055)/.

Chapter 2

A Truly Representative Political System Requires Women in Congress

Breena E. Coates

Samuel Krislov's work *Representative Bureaucracy* (1974) and Donald Kingsley's book of the same name (1944) asked the seminal question, "How can any bureaucracy have legitimacy and public credibility if it does not represent all sectors of its society?" (Shafritz et al., 2007, p. 458). Several decades later one may say the same about representation of women in Congress, that is, a nation must have a representative legislature in order to create policy actions that represent citizen diversity. It is well documented that women are seriously underrepresented in the legislative branch of government (Center for Women in Politics, 2015) even though the public displays an inclination for greater levels of women's representation than America has experienced so far (Sanbonmatsu & Dolan, 2008). Minority leader of the House of Representatives, Nancy Pelosi, has suggested that the gap is due to the role of big money in politics and lack of civility in Congress. She has speculated that this may well account for disinclination of women to enter Congress. Pelosi noted that if these barriers to entry were lessened, "you'll have more women elected to public office, and sooner, and that nothing is more wholesome to the governmental and political process than [the] increased participation of women" (Angyal, 2013).

The November 2014 election saw some unusual gains for female politicians on Republican tickets. Mia Love, a Republican from Utah, became the first black woman ever elected in the Republican Party to Congress and Joni Ernst was elected the first Republican woman to represent Iowa in the U.S. Senate. Analysts caution that despite these "firsts" the year 2014 was "not the year of the woman" (Lawless & Fox, 2014). Today the number of women in the legislature does not correlate with the 51% of women in the U.S. population Minority House leader, Nancy Pelosi, has argued that women should not rest on a few gains here and there and say, " 'well, we got ten more, and soon we'll have eight more, and in two hundred more years we'll be at parity.' No, I think we say, 'What are the factors that inhibit the increased role of women?' " (Angyal, 2013).

The Center for American Women in Politics released the following statistics for 2015: total number of women in Congress = 104, or 19.4% of seats in both the Senate and the House. The breakdown by congressional houses shows: women in the Senate = 20, or 20% of 100 seats. Breakdown of women in the House of Representatives = 84%, or 19.3% of 435 seats. In terms of women of color, the statistics are worse. So far there have only been a total of 47 women of color in congressional history: 29 African Americans, 9 Asian American/Pacific Islanders, and 9 Latinas (2015). Commenting on racism and gender bias, Senator Carol Moseley Braun has argued that "while racism is local, gender bias is universal." She added, "Somebody once asked me which is worse, and my response to that is, if someone has their foot on your neck, it doesn't really matter why it's there" (Tam, 2014).

The statistics provided here also lead to the question, when a woman president enters the White House will she have the support of a balanced legislature? The extant old guard of mostly elderly white conservative males is less likely to be supportive of a female chief executive as a fresh influx of female legislators with fresh and unique points of view from their male counterparts. This difference has been pointed out in scholarly research and will be examined later.

WHY WOMEN SHOULD SERVE IN CONGRESS

This chapter focuses on four important reasons why women should be in Congress: leadership and decision-making skills; bipartisanship, compromise, and deal-making abilities; progressive worldviews and openness to change; and championing and mentoring neophytes.

Leaderships and Decision-Making Skills

Under the leadership and decision-making category, scholars like Alice Eagly and Linda Lorene Carli (2007) have shown that while leadership differences between men and women are small, the difference is statistically significant. This female "difference" broadens and enriches discourse and complements male decision making. Male decision making by itself is often one sided and biased toward the status quo. As shown time and again in debates on issues of national concern to women—for example, women's health and welfare—men can be oblivious, prejudiced, and misinformed on critical topics. Take, for example, Representative Todd Akin's comment about "legitimate rape." This comment duly "provoked ire" among men and women alike across the nation (Eligon & Schwirtz, 2012).

A study by two males, Joseph Folkman and Jack Zenger in the *Harvard Business Review* (2012), has pointed out that women outperform men on "everything from 'displaying high integrity'; 'driving for results'; to 'taking initiative and practicing self-development.' " Folkman and Zenger's study that sought the viewpoints of 7,280 leaders found that women excel at 15 of 16 individual leadership characteristics, as judged by their peers, subordinates, and managers. These are the known factors of collaboration, building relationships, innovating, and so on. The variation between women and men increases as individuals gain seniority (2012). A research study conducted by Hagberg Consulting Group in 2000 also found women managers to be ranked higher in 42 out of 52 traits and skills measured, including teamwork, stability, and motivation; recognizing trends; and acting on new ideas (Levy, 2010). Recent studies conducted by Trinidad and Normore in 2005, and Yukl in 2010, found similar results in the leadership behaviors of men and women. Specifically according to Yukl, women have a "feminine advantage" because they are "more adept at being inclusive, interpersonally sensitive, and nurturing" (2010). Women tend to connect more with their group members by exhibiting behaviors such as smiling more and maintaining eye contact, and are more diplomatic with national concern to women—for example, women's health and welfare (Forsyth, 2010).

Representative Barbara Jordan, Democrat from Texas, has observed that "women and men have inherently different leadership approaches, and there is a substantial academic literature to prove it. Decades of research shows that male legislators tend to be individualist and competitive, while women are more collaborative and consensus-driven" Jordan went on to say that "women have a capacity for understanding and compassion which a man structurally does not have" (Mitchell, 2014). As Representative Jordan has noted, leadership scholars have, over the past several decades, expanded upon the matter of *difference* (Grant, 1988; Kabacoff, 2001; Karau & Eagly, 1999). These differences relate to participative demeanor for women versus agentic for men, or task versus relationship orientations for women. In the scholarly literature, the female participative-management style was seen to provide factors of collaborative and collective support (Eagly, Johannesen-Schmidt, & van Engen,

2003) such as open communication, cooperation, nurturing, and affiliation that better moved organizational actors toward change and transformation. According to Eagly and Johnson (1990), women generally show more democratic, participative styles of leadership.

Perhaps women legislators in Congress might also help speed up sluggish decision making. Today's male-dominated Congress took months to confirm the well-qualified Loretta Lynch as attorney general. It finally did so in April 2015. On this very issue Senator-Elect Shelley Moore Capito, Republican from West Virginia, last year urged: "If we are going to have an era of good faith here [in Congress] we need to begin with the confirmation process for one of the most important jobs in the country, that that's Attorney General" (Hunter, 2014). Brookings produced a report in February entitled "More Women = Less Gridlock: How 2014 & 2016 May Reshape Politics" in which it says women "are seen as a beacon of hope" in a "world where stalemate has become the norm" (Jackman, 2013).

Bipartisanship, Compromise, and Deal-Making

Research from congressional history has shown that women tend to work cooperatively within and across the aisles, though more are Democrats, probably because there are more Democratic female members of Congress. From the 111th Congress to the current one, women legislators have cosponsored 6.20 bills with other females, as compared to 4.07 with males. Senator Susan Collins, cosponsored 740 bills with legislators from both sides of the aisles. Lisa Murkowski cosponsored 445, and there are others. A new start-up called Quorum showed that over the past seven years, in the Senate, the "average" female senator has introduced 96.31 bills, while the "average" male introduced 70.72. In the House, compare 29.65 for women, and 27.2 for men. Also of note is that women were more likely to gain cosponsorship: in the Senate, women had an average of 9.10 cosponsors and men 5.94. In the House, the difference was smaller—but women still proved better, or more interested, in sponsoring together: female representatives averaged 16.84 cosponsors and men 14.64.

Alex Wirth and Jonathan Marks, cofounders of the research start-up, Quorum, reported that in the Senate, Dianne Feinstein has sponsored 300 the most bills of any female senator. Amy Klobuchar is next, at 215, then Kirsten Gillibrand 204, Barbara Boxer 176, and Patty Murray 126. In the House, Sheila Jackson Lee leads, with 177, then Carolyn Maloney at 163, Eleanor Norton at 136, Barbara Lee at 96, and Rosa DeLauro at 91. Senator Boxer has had the most sponsored bills enacted—10, followed by Feinstein and Klobuchar (both 7), and then Patty Murray and Lisa Murkowski. In the House, Representatives Norton and Maloney lead, and then Ileana Ros-Lehtinen, Nydia Velázquez, and Ann Kirkpatrick (Ho, 2015).

Championing and Mentoring Neophytes

The *feminine advantage* to connect, communicate, and nurture—perhaps a biological endowment—makes women natural mentors to incoming women (and men) into Congress. As the literature shows (Eagly et al., 2003) women are more adept at increasing others' self-worth. Senator Barbara Mikulski started a well-known supper club for Senate women as a venue to help newcomers to network and share experiences and camaraderie. As Senator Mikulski reported on PBS, "When a woman is elected to the Senate—Republican or Democrat—I bring her in for my Senate Power Workshop and guide her on how to get started, how to get on the good committees for her state, and how to be an effective Senator" (*Bloomberg News*, February 20, 2015). No wonder Senator Mikulski has had high average number of cosponsors for bills in the Senate.

Progressive Worldviews

In *Patterns of Democracy* (1999), former American Political Science Association president Arend Lijphart found strong correlations between more women legislators and passage of progressive policy on issues like the environment, macroeconomic management, comprehensive support for families and individuals, violence prevention, and incarceration. Other studies have found that women legislators—both Republican and Democrat—introduce a lot more bills than men in the areas of civil rights, liberties, and forgotten minorities in the areas of education, health, labor, and more.

Just observing women in political campaigns and hearing their fresh perspectives and arguments will electrify women in American society to make them more aware of the issues that impact their own lives and be more active in the political sphere. It might inspire more women to take on leadership challenges and opportunities in all sectors of enterprise (Greenhouse, 2015).

BARRIERS TO ENTRY OF WOMEN TO CONGRESS: THE ISSUE OF VOTING

Do voting patterns relate to the paucity of women in Congress? First, U.S. citizens do not turn out in acceptable numbers to vote. It is estimated that 40% of the U.S. citizen population does not vote (Ghose, 2012), thus neglecting their most important tool to push relevant concerns to their leaders. Such information would include government spending and services, labor issues, and public schools. Voting has an opportunity cost, however, in terms of useable time—that is, time that is needed for other things like work. As a nation the United States needs to rethink the barriers to voting. Second, the public does not realize the power of a single vote to the cumulative effect of voting by many people that makes the sizeable difference. Third, surveys show that young voters are more likely to be liberal in ideology and, as a consequence, more supportive of government spending for public schools, jobs, ecology, and diversity programs. In contrast, older citizens tend to be more conservative in worldviews, and partial to the status quo, which at times leads to stagnation. Fourth, voter registration laws can be costly to female voters in terms of voter identification. Women change their names at the rate of 90% due to marriage or divorce. Only 48% of women have birth certificates that reflect their current names, and 11% of women do not have an ID card issued by the government (Brennan Center for Justice, n.d.). Fifth, the choice of Tuesdays as the voting day is inconvenient and arbitrary. A weekend voting day may possibly be more appealing to women voters who generally multitask during the workweek. Research has shown turnout is higher in countries that vote during weekends (Wattenberg, 2006). Finally, would term limits be an answer for getting rid of those legislators who get elected for term after term. Perhaps term limits would help clear out space for women and minorities in Congress.

SUMMARY

It is clear that we do not have enough representation of women in Congress. We need more women legislators to represent the 51% of American citizens in national population, and they have clearly different, some may even say superior, qualities in terms of leadership and decision-making skills; bipartisanship, compromise, and deal-making abilities; more progressive worldviews and greater openness to change; and mentoring and role-modeling. Women and minorities are slowly moving up in the political system. To fast-track progress. American women and women's organizations throughout the nation must support our women in politics as well as work toward changing the male-style status quo leadership in Congress. Then finally the visions of Kingsley and Krislov for a representative bureaucracy (1944, 1974) may finally be translated into a representative legislature.

REFERENCES

Angyal, C. (2013). *Nancy Pelosi: We need more women in politics*. San Francisco, CA: Salon Media\Group.

Brennan Center for Justice. (n.d.). Citizens without proof: A survey of Americans' possession of documentary proof of citizenship and photo identification. New York University, School of Law, New York.

Center for Women in Politics. (2015). Facts on women officeholders, candidates and voters: Current numbers of women officeholders. Eagleton Institute of Politics, Rutgers University, New Jersey.

Eagly, A., & Carli, L. (2007). *Through the labyrinth: The truth about how women become leaders.* Boston, MA: Harvard Business School Press.

Eagly, A., Johannesen-Schmidt, M. C., & van Engen, M. (2003). Transformational transactional, and laissez-faire leadership styles: A meta analysis comparing women and men. *Psychological Bulletin, 95,* 569–591.

Eagly, A., & Johnson, B. T. (1990). Gender and leadership styles: A meta analysis. *Psychological Bulletin, 108,* 233–256.

Eligon, J., and Schwirtz, M. (2012). Senate candidate provokes ire with "legitimate rape" comment. *New York Times,* August 19, 2014.

Folkman, J., and Zenger, J. (2012). A study in leadership: Women do it better than men. *Harvard Business Review,* Cambridge, MA.

Forsyth, D. (2010). *Group dynamics,* 5th ed. Independence, KY: Wadsworth Cengage Learning.

Ghose, T. (2012). Why 40% of Americans don't vote. *Science on NBC News,* nbc. com.

Grant, J. (1988, Winter). Women as managers: What can they offer organizations? *Organizational Dynamics,* 56–63.

Greenhouse, E. (2015). The numbers don't lie: Women make more effective legislators than men. *Bloomberg News,* TNS, NY.

Ho, Catherine. (2015, January 25). "Start-up Quorum offers insight into lawmakers' actions, based on metrics. *Washington Post,* Washington, DC.

Hunter, K. (2014, November 10). Lynch nomination might be an early test for Republican Senate. *Bloomberg Politics.*

Jackman, M. (2013). More women = less gridlock: How 2014 & 2016 may reshape politics. Brookings Institution, Washington, DC.

Kabacoff, R. J. (2001). *Gender differences in organizational leadership. Do men and women lead differently?* Bethesda, MD: Briefings Publishing Group.

Karau, S. J., and Eagly, A. (1999). Gender and the emergence of leaders: A meta-analysis. *Journal of Personality and Social Psychology, 60,* 685–710.

Kingsley, J. D. (1944). *Representative bureaucracy: An interpretation of the British civil service.* Yellow Springs, OH: Antioch Press.

Krislov, S. (1974). *Representative bureaucracy.* Englewood Cliffs, NJ: Prentice Hall.

Lawless, J., and Fox, R. L. (2014, November). Not a "year of the woman" . . . and 2036 doesn't look so good either. *Issues in Governance Studies,* Brookings Institution.

Levy, P. (2010). *Industrial organizational psychology: Understanding the workplace,* 3rd ed. New York: NY: Worth Publishers.

Lijphart, A. (1999). *Patterns of democracy: Government forms and performance in 36 countries.* New Haven, CT: Yale University Press.

Mitchell, A. (2014, July 10). Here's why we need more women in Congress. *The Daily Beast,* Washington, DC.

Sanbonmatsu, K., and Dolan, K. (2008, August). Gender stereotypes and attitudes toward gender balance in government. *American Politics Research*.

Shafritz, J. M., Russell, E. & Borick, C. (2007). *Introducing public administration*. New York, NY: Pearson Education Inc.

Tam, R. (2014). Small wonder there is not more diversity in Congress, a report on Carol Moseley Braun. *The Washington Post*.

Trinidad, C., and Normore, A. H. (2005). Leadership and gender: A dangerous liaison. *Leadership & Organization Development Journal, 26*(7), 574–590.

Wattenberg, M. (2006). *Where have all the voters gone?* Cambridge, MA: Harvard University Press.

Yukl, G. (2010). *Leadership in organizations*. Upper Saddle River, NJ: Pearson/ Prentice Hall.

Senator Margaret Chase Smith

Senator Chase Smith represented the state of Maine in the U.S. Senate from January 1949 to January 1973. In the 1920s, Senator Chase Smith became a member of women's organizations, including founding the Skowhegan Business and Professional Women's Club. She succeeded her husband, Clyde H. Smith, in the House of Representatives following his death in 1940. As a member of the Congress, Chase Smith was responsible for winning permanent status for women in the military. In 1949 she became the first woman in U.S. history to serve in both houses of Congress as well as the first woman to be elected to the U.S. Senate in her own right, not as fulfilling her husband's term. In addition, Chase Smith was the first woman to have her name placed in nomination for the presidency of the United States at a major political party's national convention. She placed second after Barry Goldwater. Chase Smith is also credited as having never accepted campaign contributions for her elections and reelections.

Source: http://www.biography.com/#!/people/margaret-chase-smith-280222.

Chapter 3

Women in Leadership: A Consideration of Lingering Challenges and Intriguing Possibilities

Jennifer L. Martin and Lori M. Kumler

> To sin by silence when we should protest makes cowards out of men.
>
> —Ella Wheeler Wilcox

INTRODUCTION

The myth of the meritocracy and denials of inequality still pervade American culture on many levels. Thus, the notions that individuals in positions of leadership are the most qualified and deserving of said positions are ubiquitous in our current milieu. However, it has been well documented that stereotypes, stereotype threat, overt discrimination, and more covert forms of discrimination, such as exposure to daily microaggressions, can make the road to leadership in politics fraught with potholes, pitfalls, and impediments for women and individuals possessing nondominant identities, or multiple minority statuses (Gutierrez y Muhs, Flores Niemann, Gonzalez, & Harris, 2012). But we are in need of diverse leaders institutionally and politically (Paludi & Coates, 2011). Recent legislation such as the dismantling of ethnic studies in Arizona (including the banning of Paulo

Freire's classic *Pedagogy of the Oppressed,* and Critical Race Theory in general), Indiana's so-called religious freedom law which allows businesses to turn LGBTQ customers away, and the abundance of antichoice legislation that negatively impacts women's access to birth control are desperate attempts to reassemble a homogeneous status quo of yesteryear, where the privilege of the white heterosexual male majority went unquestioned. This may seem histrionic, but without diverse viewpoints and leaders representing varied points of view and identities, we will continue to see legislation that restricts the rights of nonmajority groups. In this chapter, we seek to continue the conversation about women and leadership in politics as well as academia and to explore various intriguing possibilities of new models of leadership stemming from nondominant perspectives.

Each day in leadership positions, including political office, women face difficulty in being heard and in participating in decision making compared to male colleagues. While scholars debate the reasons for this, the phenomenon itself is well documented (Harris & Gonzalez, 2012). In some cases, women are not heard because they may not speak as much; for example, Brescoll (2011) found that while male senators spoke more as their power relative to others increased, female senators spoke less. Female senators spoke less in part because of concerns of backlash, concerns that Brescoll (2011) found to be accurate. At the same time, women bring unique and highly valuable skills and perspectives to leadership roles. Women in leadership roles are often more likely to take on women's issues (Martin, 2011), other issues of marginality (Gutierrez y Muhs et al., 2012), and to bring perspectives unique to women to light (see Introduction to this volume for a review of this reality in the U.S. Congress).

In this chapter, we first review the enduring challenges that women face in attaining positions of status and leadership and the theories that underpin these challenges. We then address the issues of differential expectations for leaders based on biological sex, the issue of the underrepresentation of women leaders in various fields and potential reasons for this, and the unique experiences women face when they strive for or attain positions of leadership. Finally, we examine women's potential for new approaches to leadership, based on the unique skills and perspectives they bring to decision making and problem solving, and whether women's voices can make a difference in removing current barriers to leadership for future generations of women.

GROUNDING THE PAUCITY OF WOMEN'S LEADERSHIP

Attribution Error

According to attribution theory, the personality characteristics (and personal accomplishments) of women and men are often explained differently (Kirchmeyer, 1998). For example, women's accomplishments may be attributed to luck or other external factors; likewise, women's advancement may be attributed to affirmative action and not to personal ability (as are men's accomplishments) (Kirchmeyer, 1998; Lyness & Thompson, 1997). Moreover, a woman's performance (on tasks traditionally conceived of as male) is often attributed to luck or to effort and men's performance to skill (Greenhaus & Parasuraman, 1993). The reason for the former is that such successes violate people's (observers) sex role expectations; to avoid cognitive dissonance, observers attribute negative attributes to women, such that women are not responsible for their own successes—they just "got lucky."

Women in positions of leadership and authority, such as political leaders, may find it more difficult to be taken seriously in comparison with their male peers because of individuals' attribution errors, whether these errors are made explicit through overt resistance or kept implicit, revealing themselves in the voting booth.

We are aware that women who violate constituents' expectations, for instance, by asking them to move beyond their proscribed gender role expectations, can face consequences (Bachen, McLoughlin, & Garcia, 1999); however, women tend to receive more negative repercussions for said approaches (Takiff, Sanchez, & Stewart, 2001). Experiencing gender microaggressions—one of the enduring challenges women face—can make it more difficult for women to become leaders, and for women to be taken seriously as leaders (Martin, 2011).

Despite decades of feminist progress, women leaders still have to think about how they are perceived based on the gender stereotypes held by others. It is not uncommon for individuals to expect a maternal figure in their local, state, or federal legislature, someone who is perpetually nice: someone who is not too challenging, someone who does not ask too many questions, for, as Sandler (1991) reminds us, gender can impact how one evaluates competence. Attribution plays a part here too, as women's successes are often attributed to luck, while men's to talent (Sandler, 1991). The cumulative effect of gender discrimination in its many forms—from microaggressions to poor student evaluations and lowered esteem from colleagues and administrators—may make it more difficult for women and individuals possessing nondominant or multiple minority statuses to see themselves as leaders and to have others consider them suitable for positions of leadership, especially in elected offices.

Personal Agency and Gender Norms

The terms "agency" and "communion" were originally developed by Bakan (1966) to reflect two fundamental aspects of human existence. Agency describes a person's existence as an individual; communion describes a person's participation in a larger whole of which he or she belongs. Bakan essentialized these constructs by attributing them to gender: agency as the male principle, communion as the female. Historically, women have tended to possess fewer agentic traits (or self-directed/self-promoting actions) than men (Eagly & Steffen, 1984). One reason for this involves the perceptions of observers, or the societal double bind. For example, when women take career risks or achieve success in nontraditional realms they may be viewed negatively by others. The same self-promoting actions in men (assertiveness) are often looked at as negative in women and are often subsequently relabeled (aggressiveness). "Aggressiveness" may include asking for a vote, a move fraught with risks for women (Bowles & Babcock, 2009). This is very much akin to research on aggressiveness associated with asking for a salary increase. For example, a study of 184 managers by Belliveau (2011) found that in a scenario when managers would have to explain reasons for providing raises, they awarded men raises two and a half times as large as raises for female workers (with equal qualifications). Thus, self-promotion in women may not be a "safe" course of action. Although some women leaders can power through and withstand the negative labels of "bitchy" or "bossy," others find the cost too great, or the risk involved in throwing their hats in the ring of leadership in a field where women leaders are scarce, too personally taxing.

Because there are fewer women in positions of leadership, some may perceive women to be less capable of such positions; in other words, these ideas can translate to perceptions of women's capabilities (Eagly & Steffen, 1984)—which further leads to women's perceptions of their own capabilities (contributing to the vicious cycle that produces fewer women leaders). Women's acknowledgment of these negative perceptions of women leaders within the larger social construct can contribute to stereotype threat causing their performance to weaken (Steele, 1997). In other words, when women feel responsible to represent their entire sex, or to alter the negative expectations and stereotypes placed on their group, in areas where they represent the "one" or where they are in a minority, they may crack under the pressure. In addition, if women perceive their opportunities to be less than those of men, they may seek to strive for less or not try for promotions or certain management positions for fear of failure. This fear may cause a lack of motivation and thus perpetuate the cycle of few women in leadership positions in general and in politics specifically (Dreher, 2003).

Whiston and Bouwkamp (2003) found that career-oriented women possess more intrinsic needs such as independence and achievement. According to Twenge (1997), communal traits have remained higher in women than in men, whereas agentic traits have increased in women over time. Twenge found that the gap between women and men is decreasing in terms of feelings of personal agency. Twenge (1997) additionally found that assertiveness (an agentic trait) in women has been increasing in the past 20 years but that it is a trait that varies with status and roles. Women in nontraditional fields, such as engineering, do not show sex differences in agentic and communal traits (Abele, 2003). According to Abele (2003) both women and men reported possessing agentic or dominant traits when in positions of supervision; however, mainly women reported the converse, communal traits (or submissive behaviors), when in positions of workplace subordination.

In sum, self-actualized, secure, and independent women are not actively nurtured and cultivated by our society. There are still consequences for women who do not fit their prescribed role, including social ostracism and receiving negative personal feedback (Heilman, Wallen, Fuchs, & Tamkins, 2004). Women leaders can be viewed by others as cold, bitter, quarrelsome, and selfish, when simply possessing the same personality characteristics as their male counterparts (Heilman et al., 2004). Women who behave in ways perceived as traditionally male are less well received than are men who deviate from traditional norms (Heilman et al., 2004). Sometimes it is individuals' belief of personality characteristics as opposed to one's actual personality characteristics that pose the real problem for women leaders in politics.

Evaluation of Women Leaders

Another reason to explain why women have limited access to leadership roles and management positions is that colleagues do not evaluate women's credentials and performances in a similar manner to men's credentials and performances; as previously stated, similar leadership qualities, such as assertiveness, may be viewed less favorably when exhibited by a woman (Eagly, Makhijani, & Klonsky, 1992). Eagly et al. (1992) found that women leaders were devalued in comparison with male leaders when the leadership was carried out in a stereotypically masculine manner. This devaluation was exacerbated when women leaders occupied male-dominated realms and when male evaluators were used. Eagly et al. (1992) also found that women leaders were more harshly evaluated when they were evaluated by men, "Because placing women in leadership positions upsets the traditional societal gender hierarchy, male subjects might, in a sense, have more to lose by approving female leadership because their status vis-à-vis women would decline. Thus, male subjects may be more prone than female subjects to reject female leaders" (p. 7). Although the Eagly et al. study is more than 20 years old, not much has changed in terms of how people perceive and judge the qualities women leaders possess. It is not only men who are guilty of maligning women leaders for acting outside of traditional gender role expectations; women also can internalize sexism and use it to indict other women.

Perceptions of personality characteristics aside, women also report that their styles of leadership are also obstacles to their advancement

(Shinew & Arnold, 1998). Some women leaders describe their leadership styles as being fundamentally different from men. For example, women political leaders, as leaders in business and education, often attempt to get their subordinates to come to a consensus with the goal of the group. In general, however, the perception of how management should be conducted philosophically is still viewed in terms of individualistic traits (as opposed to relational traits) (Vinnicombe & Harris, 2000). Vinnicombe and Harris (2000) argue that this perception persists because of the processes (e.g., hidden attitudes and stereotypes) of the informal organization, "The balance of the sexes in management can still be summed up by the phrase 'think manager, think male,' just as it was in the 1970s" (p. 28). The problem is that women are not provided access to the gambit of personality characteristics and leadership styles. Women possessing "feminine" leadership styles may have their style questioned; for example, some women have their sense of calm misperceived as weakness (Williamson & Hudson, 2001). Women in positions of leadership, possessing a traditionally feminine style, are often perceived as weak, wimpy, and wishy-washy (Williamson & Hudson, 2001). If women are direct, they are viewed as oppositional; if they are relational, they may be viewed as weak. Because women leaders are still the few, they remain the judged, especially when it comes to performance evaluation.

Effective performance is often attributed to ability when the person/employee being observed is a member of the "in-group," as opposed to the token or out-group; in the latter case, success is often attributed to luck (Greenhaus & Parasuraman, 1993). This does not just apply to gender; it also applies to other nondominant statuses (Greenhaus & Parasuraman, 1993). Employees who were thought to perform well because of ability were also judged more worthy of promotions than were those whose successes were attributed to luck or effort (Greenhaus & Parasuraman, 1993).

Women experience discriminatory evaluation procedures, have their competence denied, and have their performance devalued as a result of their sex (Heilman et al., 2004). These unfair processes perpetuate negative expectations for women in politics as well as other professions. These negative expectations result from the inconsistency in how women are viewed and what characteristics are necessary to perform a particular job. Even when women are successful in traditionally male occupations, they may still be judged unfairly.

Power and Influence

Vignette I: "... Someone Had to Do It First"

I ran because someone had to do it first

—Shirley Chisholm

Shirley Chisholm, the first black congresswoman (1968), also became the first black candidate from a major political party to run for the U.S. presidency in 1972. Chisholm knew that she likely would not win, being a person possessing multiple minority statuses; however, she stayed the course until the end of the Democratic National Convention because she desired to pave the way for other candidates possessing minority statuses. As she stated, "The next time a woman runs, or a black, a Jew or anyone from a group that the country is 'not ready' to elect to its highest office, I believe he or she will be taken seriously from the start. The door is not open yet, but it is ajar" (*Shirley Chisholm biography,* para. 1). Considered to be a social activist, Chisholm faced consequences based on identity politics. In viewing her story through an intersectional lens, Chisholm often was asked to "choose sides" within herself. Although a woman and a supporter of women's rights, being one of the founders of the National Women's Political Caucus (1971), she stressed that she did not want to be the "women's candidate." It may be that Chisholm did not want to split her identities; instead, she wanted to be seen as an individual, as were her male peers. Still, she faced discrimination based on sex. As Chisholm states, "I had met far more discrimination because I am a woman than because I am black" (Freeman, 2005, para. 6). However, she was also accused of not paying enough attention to issues facing the black population. Thus, Chisholm was caught in the classic double bind that traps many women. Whatever she did, she could not win: she would always be alienating someone based on identity politics. She decided to please herself; she decided to be "unbought and unbossed." Although her male peers often considered her to be "brusque" and "too direct," traits not traditionally valued in women, Chisholm was not intimidated or dissuaded from her mission. As she stated to a group of black delegates, "I'm the only one in here who has the balls to work for black people." Have we come so far from the experiences faced by Chisholm? Is Hillary Clinton still held to a higher standard, judged on her appearance and on the appropriateness of her appropriated gender norms? We have yet to see whether this will change in the next four years.

Settles, Cortina, Malley, and Stewart (2006) examined causes for levels of women's attrition in science-related fields; these high levels of attrition seem to suggest an atmosphere that is problematic for women in general. Women of color were found to have less influence within their departments than were white women. Women within the science field experience fewer opportunities for leadership and influence, slower advancement, heightened isolation, and the like. Settles et al. (2006) argue that in order for women to be successful in science-related fields, they must realize these three outcomes: job satisfaction, productivity, and "felt influence." Sexual harassment and sexist environments in general affect these areas (Paludi & Coates, 2011). These factors and the tolerance of them within the organization hinder the success of women and are tied to lower productivity and career outcomes for women (Settles et al. 2006). This research has direct implications for women political leaders and women seeking political office.

Sex stereotypes still exist and thus create a double standard that negatively affects the evaluations of women in leadership positions (Dreher, 2003; Pardine, Fox, & Salzano, 1995). The percentage of women in positions of leadership has increased since the mid-1970s; however, the perceptions still endure that women are unqualified or unable to perform in such capacities. Those women who do make it into positions of leadership do little to contribute to the change in perception or changes in stereotypes of women; on the contrary, these women are instead thought to be the "exception" to the stereotype (Pardine et al., 1995). They are thought to be unrepresentative of women in general—their accomplishments do not impact societal beliefs about the qualifications of women in positions of management (Pardine et al., 1995).

In the past 30 years, women have gained far more positions of power in low and middle management and leadership. However, the percentage of women gaining power within top leadership positions is relatively small (Dreher, 2003). Women make up 15% of the Fortune 500 top officers and 3% of CEOs, and are in 6% of the highest-paying positions and 16% of corporate officers (Hopkins, O'Neil, Passarelli, & Bilimoria, 2008; White House Project, 2009). A leadership pipeline does in fact exist: 48% of workers and 51% of leaders are women (White House Project, 2009). However, often women are not advancing beyond entry level and middle management/leadership/professional positions.

Academia presents similar patterns. According to the American Association of University Professors 2006 equity study, women hold only 24% of full professor positions in the United States. Despite the gains women have made in higher education over the past few decades, they are highly underrepresented in tenure-track positions. Women in higher education face more obstacles to career advancement than in the corporate world (West & Curtis, 2006). The areas with the fewest number of women in higher education are the most prestigious and most highly paid. Women make far less than men in higher education because they are more likely to hold positions at institutions that pay lower salaries and they are less likely to gain senior rank.

WHY WE NEED WOMEN LEADERS: PROMISING POSSIBILITIES

As described earlier, women face numerous obstacles when it comes to attaining and maintaining positions of leadership. While we can argue for greater equity when it comes to opportunities for women to take on leadership roles, it is perhaps more interesting to examine what women can contribute in such positions. What are we missing when we omit women from leadership? First, the lack of diversity presented by predominantly male leadership can itself be a problem for tasks such as problem solving. Second, women often offer unique perspectives and leadership styles that lead to better outcomes.

The following insights offer glimpses into why having women leaders can be critically important. For much of history, women have been sidelined from leadership roles within the public sphere due to restrictive formal and informal institutions ranging from laws and policies to culture and tradition. This male-led world, as Konner (2015) points out, has been a world of conflict and repression. To quote Konner, "But life on this planet isn't threatened by women's tears; nor does that brimming salty fluid cause poverty, drain public coffers, ruin reputations, impose forced intimacies, slay children, torture helpless people, or reduce cities to rubble. These disasters are literally *man*-made" (p. 6). While Konner concedes that a minority of men are guilty of these deeds, he argues that generalizations based on biology can be made based on data from fields, including anthropology, biology, and neuroscience. Men are affected by biologically driven impulses that can result in violent and angry behavior. He further argues that when men get together in groups that exclude women, these negative tendencies can increase.

While there is no denying that male-dominated historical leadership has brought war, conflict, and oppression, we cannot say how things may have looked under female leadership. Yet numerous studies of female leaders in the modern era have indicated that women bring different skills and emphases to leadership positions. For example, in a study of 384 mayors, Weikart, Chen, Williams, and Hromic (2007) found that female mayors sought broader participation, and were more inclusive, more willing to change the budget process, more willing to discuss goal changes, and more willing to admit fiscal problems than male mayors. Several studies have found that women leaders more commonly exhibit behaviors associated with effective leadership than men. In a meta-analysis of 45 studies, Eagly, Johannesen-Schmidt, and van Engen (2003) found that women show more transformational leadership traits (e.g., charisma, inspirational motivation, intellectual stimulation, and individualize consideration) than men. Gupton and Slick (1996) argue that these traits are valuable, "Transformational leadership advocates participatory management that motivates others by transforming their self-interest into the goals of the organization. Transformational leaders are skilled in leadership patterns that inspire increased worker performance by encouraging all points of view" (p. 108). Transformational leadership necessitates relational leadership and values mentoring and the communal; it can establish a sense of connection between people. Transformational leadership is a nonhierarchical, non-patriarchal form of leading where the named leader shares the task of leading by utilizing the strengths of those in the organization. Decisions are made together and the tasks of leaders are shared. In fact, the most effective style of leadership is transformational leadership, which builds empowerment in a mutual and collaborative context (Eagly et al., 2003; Eagly, Karau, & Makhijani, 1995). Women most often utilize the transformational leadership style, a style that requires empathy and a sense of caring for others. Although research suggests that it is the most effective style of leadership, we have a paucity of women at the highest levels of leadership in most fields (Dreher, 2003; Hopkins et al., 2008; West & Curtis, 2006; The White House Project, 2009). In addition, transformational leaders often put their own self-interest in check for the good of the organization.

Kropiewnicki and Shapiro (2001) identify similar strengths of female leaders. In their study, an ethic of care guided women administrators' belief systems where they acted in the best interest of others, doing what they felt was right for students, the school, teachers, and other stakeholders. They found that women leaders "tend to utilize ethical perspectives of care and responsibility, with varying degrees of intensity and focus, when dealing with children and adults within their school. . . . The act of caring for others was central to the participants' responses. Yet the participants did care about ideas and causes, but primarily in a relational context—as the ideas and causes related to the people they affected" (p. 18). The women in this study were motivated and sustained by advocacy, collaboration (shared decision making), becoming involved with the community, collegiality, maintaining relationships, and empowering others. This finding corresponds to Gilligan's research (1982) in that highly successful women professionals describe themselves in terms of their relationships.

Other studies suggest that having more women in leadership positions has a positive association with attaining organizational goals. For example, Krishnan and Park (2005) examined the association between the percentage of women in top management teams of 679 Fortune 1000 companies and company financial performance over two years. They found that companies with more women had better financial performance. Dezsö and Ross (2012) found that female participation in top management teams improves firm performance for firms focused on innovation. Similarly, in a study of 99 Dutch firms, Lückerath-Rovers (2013) found that firms with women board members outperformed those without women on their boards.

While these studies look at overall economic performance, another measure to consider—especially in governance—is whether women's participation leads to improved outcomes for female constituents. On this front, the research strongly suggests that it does (see biographies of women politicians in this volume). Women in Congress have taken leadership in advocating bills on abortion, violence against women, and welfare reform (Swers, 2002). Similarly, Tamerius (2010) found that congresswomen were cosponsors on feminist legislation 66% of the time, speech givers 75% of the time, and sponsors 92% of the time.

Vignette 2: High-Speed Trains, Different Perspectives

Soon after I moved to Ohio, I learned that the state had received one of the federal grants to implement a high-speed rail system in the state. The route under consideration would go from Cleveland to Cincinnati, a heavily traveled route that would also pass through Columbus, the capital. At this point, I had a young child and was pregnant with my second child; we lived in northeast Ohio and my parents lived near Columbus. The train possibility excited me. The rail system became controversial, however, and much of the controversy seemed to stem from the fact that the rail would not be as high speed as initially billeted. Apparently, the route from Cleveland to Cincinnati would take approximately five hours, about the same amount of time as driving the highways. This did not concern me, as the train would still be high speed for me. Have you ever driven a "five-hour" distance with two young children? Stopping for feedings, diaper changes, potty breaks, and the like makes a five-hour drive closer to seven hours. On a train, however, such stops would not be necessary. When the state turned down the money and scrapped the rail idea, I kept wondering how many of our lawmakers thought of it from my perspective and from that of many others (those without a license, the elderly, or other groups less likely to drive such a distance). How many times had our male governor taken a five-hour drive with an infant and a toddler on his own? I was willing to bet on none.

Beyond the potential strengths in leadership style and support for female voices, women bring a different perspective than men do to the table. While the perspectives in and of themselves may not be better or worse than men's perspectives, the key piece is that the perspectives differ. The diversity in perspective and even in approach to problems is the focus of the next section.

DIVERSITY AND PROBLEM SOLVING

The sorts of perspectives represented by the female citizen earlier represent a type of cognitive diversity. As suggested, a decision-making body that lacks transportation perspectives of mothers of young children, the elderly, or the poor but that represents able-bodied males accustomed to driving alone in their cars may come to drastically different conclusions regarding transportation policy. Yet cognitive diversity offered by individuals within a group is valuable: in a book based on his scholarly work, Page (2008) argues that diversity can lead to better problem solving. In his definition, "Diversity . . . means differences in how people see, categorize, understand, and go about improving the world" (p. xiv). In his research, Page found that diverse groups can often outperform groups of the best performers. He asserts that while ability is important, a group of high-ability problem solvers is often homogeneous, and this homogeneity may prevent the sort of "out of the box" thinking necessary to solve a problem (Hong & Page, 2004). Diverse groups outperform homogeneous high-ability groups under four conditions: the problem must be difficult, the individuals must have diverse problem-solving tools and perspectives, we must have a large pool of individuals to choose from to form the group, and the group of problem solvers cannot be too small (Page, 2008).

While Page's work did not indicate that identity diversity—such as gender, race, or ethnicity differences—contributed to better-performing groups, as illustrated throughout this chapter, women and men often bring different perspectives and tools to their leadership roles. To leave women out of leadership positions is to reduce our pool of problem solvers and perspectives, and to limit our potential for improved outcomes.

CONCLUSIONS

In spite of advances for women over the past many decades, data indicate that women are still underrepresented in leadership roles in fields, including politics, business, government, education, and natural sciences. We identify several reasons for this, including challenges women face on the path to leadership positions and challenges faced on attaining a leadership position. In both cases, these obstacles include attribution error, expectations tied to gender norms, biased evaluations, and differential leadership expectations. As a society, we fall far short of equity for women when it comes to formal leadership roles. Beyond equity, we are particularly concerned with the lost potential and possibilities experienced by all members of society when women are underrepresented in leadership roles. In omitting women's unique skills, perspectives, and knowledge from leadership, we limit our ability to address the obstacles on the path to leadership, and perhaps more importantly, we limit our ability to address significant social problems (Page, 2008). Furthermore, women bring unique skills to leadership, including transformational skills that can improve worker productivity (Gupton & Slick, 1996) and can improve organizational performance (Dezsö & Ross, 2012; Lückerath-Rovers, 2013).

While awareness is important—and women themselves can help to identify challenges—much work remains to be done on identifying how we can support women on the leadership path and how we can ultimately get more women into positions of leadership. Once in leadership roles, women themselves have demonstrated a commitment to furthering women's issues (Swers, 2002; Tamerius, 2010). Understanding how to get women into leadership roles can address both aims presented earlier: achieving equity in leadership and improving outcomes related to problem solving. Furthermore, we suggest that women's and nondominant-status individuals' experiences with discrimination may ultimately make them better leaders. In other words, the cumulative experiences of facing and dealing with gender-based (or other forms of) microaggressions (and other, more overt, forms of discrimination) may contribute to leadership skills such as empathy, listening, and consideration of alternative viewpoints. The field of positive psychology recognizes that strength may be found in negative experiences (Seery, Holman, & Silver, 2010); in the organizational literature, King and Rothstein (2010) suggest that successfully facing adversity may result in improved leadership capabilities. Research into the connection between confronting obstacles to leadership and resultant development of leadership capacity can provide additional insight into women's leadership strengths.

What seems to be clear is that women cannot change existing systems from the outside. Research and our own experiences support the contention that women must be an integral part of leadership in order to identify, challenge, and ultimately remove barriers to women's leadership. We hope that men and women alike will accept the onerous—but arguably achievable—task of supporting women leaders. Together, perhaps we can write a future that strays from our past of oppression, warfare, violence, and domination. To begin, as the epigraph for this chapter implores, we will cease to be silent when we should protest and be heard.

REFERENCES

Abele, A. E. (2003). The dynamics of masculine-agentic feminine-communal traits: Findings from a prospective study. *Journal of Personality, 85*(4), 768–776.

Bachen, C. M., McLoughlin, M. M., & Garcia, S. S. (1999, July). Assessing the role of gender in college students' evaluations of faculty. *Communication Education, 48*, 193–210.

Bakan, D. (1966). *The duality of human existence*. Chicago, IL: Rand McNally.

Bowles, H. R., & Babcock, L. (2009). Are outside offers an answer to the compensation negotiation dilemma for women? *Academy of Management Proceedings*.

Brescoll, V. L. (2011). Who takes the floor and why: Gender, power, and volubility in organizations. *Administrative Science Quarterly, 56*(4), 622–641.

Dezsö, C. L., & Ross, D. G. (2012). Does female representation in top management improve firm performance? A panel data investigation. *Strategic Management Journal, 33*(9), 1072–1089.

Dreher, G. F. (2003). Breaking the glass ceiling: The effects of sex ratios and work-life programs on female leadership at the top. *Human Relations, 56*(5), 541–562.

Eagly, A. H., Johannesen-Schmidt, M. C., & van Engen, M. L. (2003). Transformational, transactional, and laissez-faire leadership styles: A meta-analysis comparing women and men. *Psychological Bulletin, 129*(4), 569–591.

Eagly, A. H., Karau, S. J., and Makhijani, M. G. (1995). Gender and the effectiveness of leaders: A meta-analysis. *Psychological Bulletin, 117*(1), 125–145.

Eagly, A. H., Makhijani, M. G., & Klonsky, B. G. (1992). Gender and the evaluation of leaders: A meta-analysis. *Psychological Bulletin, 111*(1), 3–22.

Eagly, A. H., & Steffen, V. J. (1984). Gender stereotypes stem from the distribution of women and men into social roles. *Journal of Personality and Social Psychology, 46*(4), 735–754.

Freeman, J. (2005). *Shirley Chisholm's 1972 presidential campaign.* Retrieved June 25 from http://www.jofreeman.com/polhistory/chisholm.htm.

Gilligan, C. (1982). *In a different voice.* Cambridge, MA: Harvard University Press.

Greenhaus, J. H., & Parasuraman, S. (1993). Job performance attributions and career advancement prospects: An examination of gender and race effects. *Organizational Behavior and Human Decision Processes, 55,* 273–297.

Gupton, S. L., & Slick, G. A. (1996). *Highly successful women administrators: The inside stories of how they got there.* Thousand Oaks, CA: Corwin Press.

Gutierrez y Muhs, G., Flores Niemann, Y., Gonzalez, C. G., & Harris, A. P. (Eds.). (2012). *Presumed incompetent: The intersections of race and class for women in academia.* Boulder, CO: Utah State University Press.

Harris, A. P., & Gonzalez, C. G. (2012). Introduction. In G. Gutierrez y Muhs, Y. Flores Niemann, C. G. Gonzalez, & A. P. Harris (Eds.), *Presumed incompetent: The intersections of race and class for women in academia* (pp. 1–14). Boulder, CO: Utah State University Press.

Heilman, M. E., Wallen, A. S., Fuchs, D., & Tamkins, M. M. (2004). Penalties for success: Reactions to women who succeed at male gender-typed tasks. *Journal of Applied Psychology, 89*(3), 416–427.

Hong, L., & Page, S. E. (2004). Groups of diverse problem solvers can outperform groups of high-ability problem solvers. *Proceedings of the National Academy of Sciences of the United States of America, 101*(46), 16385–16389.

Hopkins, M. M., O'Neil, D. A., Passarelli, A., & Bilimoria, D. (2008). Women's leadership development: Strategic practices for women and organizations. *Consulting Psychology Journal: Practice and Research, 60*(4), 348–365.

King, G. A., & Rothstein, M. G. (2010). Resilience and leadership: The self-management of failure. In M. G. Rothstein & R. J. Burke (Eds.), *Self management and leadership development* (pp. 361–394). Northampton, MA: Edward Elgar Publishing, Inc.

Kirchmeyer, C. (1998). Determinants of managerial career success: Evidence and explanation of male/female differences. *Journal of Management, 24*(6), 673–692.

Konner, M. (2015). *Women after all.* New York, NY: W.W. Norton & Company.

Krishnan, H. A., & Park, D. (2005). A few good women—on top management teams. *Journal of Business Research, 58*(12), 1712–1720.

Kropiewnicki, M. I., & Shapiro, J. P. (2001). *Female leadership and the ethic of care: Three case studies.* Paper presented at the annual meeting of the American Educational Research Association, Seattle, WA, April 10–14.

Lückerath-Rovers, M. (2013). Women on boards and firm performance. *Journal of Management & Governance, 17*(2), 491–509.

Lyness, K. S., & Thompson, D. E. (1997). Above the glass ceiling? A comparison of matched samples of female and male executives. *Journal of Applied Psychology, 82*(3), 359–375.

Martin, J. L. (Ed.). (2011). *Women as leaders in education: Succeeding despite inequity, discrimination, and other challenges. Volume 2: Women as leaders in classrooms and schools.* Santa Barbara, CA: Praeger.

N.A. (n.d.). *Shirley Chisholm biography: Selected writings.* Retrieved June 25 from http://biography.jrank.org/pages/2506/Chisholm-Shirley.html.

Page, S. E. (2008). *The difference: How the power of diversity creates better groups, firms, schools, and societies.* Princeton, NJ: Princeton University Press.

Paludi, M. A., & Coates, B. E. (Eds.). (2011). *Women as transformational leaders: From grassroots to global interests. Volume 2: Organizational obstacles and solutions.* Santa Barbara, CA: Praeger.

Pardine, P., Fox, I., & Salzano, J. (1995). *Substereotypes and requisite management characteristics.* Washington, DC: U.S. Department of Education (Eric Document Reproduction Services. ED397239).

Patton, L. D., Shahjahan, R. A., & Osei-Kofi, N. (2010). Introduction to the emergent approaches to diversity and social justice in higher education special issue. *Equity & Excellence in Education, 43*(3), 265–278.

Sandberg, S., & Grant, A. (2015, January 12). Speaking while female. *New York Times.* Retrieved March 1, 2015, from http://www.nytimes.com/2015/01/11/opinion/sunday/speaking-while-female.html?_r=0.

Sandler, B. R. (1991). Women faculty at work in the classroom, or, why it still hurts to be a woman in labor. *Communication Education, 40,* 1–15.

Schwartz, F. N. (1989). Management women and the new facts of life. *Harvard Business Review, 1,* 65–76.

Seery, M. D., Holman, E. A., & Silver, R. C. (2010). Whatever does not kill us: Cumulative lifetime adversity, vulnerability, and resilience. *Journal of Personality and Social Psychology, 99*(6), 1025–1041.

Settles, I. H., Cortina, L. M., Malley, J., & Stewart, A. J. (2006). The climate for women in academic science: The good, the bad, and the changeable. *Psychology of Women Quarterly, 30,* 47–58.

Shih, J. (2006). Circumventing discrimination: Gender and ethnic strategies in silicon valley. *Gender and Society, 20*(2), 177–206.

Shinew, K. J., & Arnold, M. L. (1998). Gender equity in the leisure services field. *Journal of Leisure Research, 30*(2), 177–194.

Steele, C. M. (1997). A threat in the air: How stereotypes shape intellectual identity and performance. *American Psychologist, 52*(6), 613–629.

Stroh, L. K., Brett, J. M., & Reilly, A. H. (1996). Family structure, glass ceiling, and traditional explanations for the differential rate of turnover of female and male managers. *Journal of Vocational Behavior, 49,* 99–118.

Swers, M. L. (2002). *The difference women make: The policy impact of women in Congress.* Chicago, IL: University of Chicago Press.

Takiff, H. A., Sanchez, D. T., & Stewart, T. L. (2001). What's in a name? The status implications of students' terms of address for male and female professors. *Psychology of Women Quarterly, 25,* 134–144.

Tamerius, K. L. (2010). Sex, gender, and leadership in the representation of women. In M. S. Krook, & S. Childs (Eds.), *Women, gender, and politics: A reader* (pp. 93–112). New York, NY: Oxford University Press.

Twenge, J. M. (1997). Changes in masculine and feminine traits over time: A meta-analysis. *Sex Roles, 36,* 305–325.

Vinnicombe, S., & Harris, H. (2000). A gender hidden. *People Management, 6,* 28–29.

Weikart, L. A., Chen, G., Williams, D. W., & Hromic, H. (2007). The democratic sex: Gender differences and the exercise of power. *Journal of Women, Politics & Policy, 28*(1), 119–140.

West, M. S., & Curtis, J. W. (2006). *AAUP faculty gender equity indicators 2006.* Washington, DC: American Association of University Professors.

Whiston, S. C., & Bouwkamp, J. C. (2003). Ethical implications of career assessment with women. *Journal of Career Assessment, 11*(1), 59–75.

The White House Project. (2009, November). *The White House project report: Benchmarking women's leadership.* Retrieved February 2, 2010, from http://regender.org/content/white-house-project-benchmarking-womens-leadership-0.

Williamson, R. D., & Hudson, M. B. (2001, April). *New rules for the game: How women leaders resist socialization to old norms.* Paper presented at the annual meeting of the American Educational Research Association, Seattle, WA.

Congresswoman Shirley Chisholm

In 1968, Congresswoman Chisholm was the first African American woman in Congress. She ran for the U.S. presidency in 1972. In 1969, Chisholm became one of the founding members of the Congressional Black Caucus. During her run for president, she stated she ran "to give a voice to the people the major candidates were ignoring" (Freeman, 2005, p. 2). In 1971, Chisholm was also one of the founders of the National Women's Political Caucus. She is quoted as saying that during her tenure in politics "I had met far more discrimination because I am a woman than because I am black" (quoted in Freeman, 2005, p. 7).

Source: http://www.biography.com/#!/people/shirley-chisholm-9247015.

Chapter 4

Gabrielle Giffords: The Embodiment of Determination, Courage, and Hope

Katherine A. Scott and Paula K. Lundberg-Love

I will get stronger. I will return.
— Gabrielle Giffords (Giffords & Kelly, 2011, p. 299)

It was an unusually chilly morning in Tucson, Arizona, on January 8, 2011. Gabrielle Giffords, the elected representative for the eighth congressional district, had decided in her typical fashion of political fervor, to hold a Congress on your Corner event the following day at a local grocery store. She was a favorite of her constituents, and she often made a concentrated effort to meet face-to-face with those she represented so she could hear their opinions and address their concerns. She took her responsibilities as a U.S. representative seriously but always with a smile on her face. In fact, she was voted "Arizona's Cheeriest Lawmaker" by the *Arizona Daily Star* editorial in 2005. Gabby, as she is affectionately known, arrived at the Safeway grocery store a few minutes before 10:00 a.m. and was enthusiastically visiting with 20–30 of her supporters in the parking lot. However, the tranquility of the morning soon vanished with the arrival of Jared Lee Loughner.

A few minutes after 10:00 a.m., Tucson became the latest site of mass violence in the United States. Instead of being armed with political rhetoric and questions, Loughner arrived at the event with a 9-mm Glock semi-automatic pistol and a 33-round magazine. What followed was nothing short of a horrible tragedy. That morning, 13 people were injured and 6 people were killed, including a nine-year-old girl and a U.S. district court judge. Loughner shot Congresswoman Giffords in the head at point blank range. While Loughner has never directly indicated that the shooting was politically motivated, it has been suggested that Gabby's recent reelection campaign contributed to his anger. Media outlets all over the United States reported that the congresswoman had been killed. But Gabby Giffords was not dead. After a long, challenging rehabilitative journey, Gabby has made progress that her doctors describe as nothing short of miraculous.

Many people had never heard of Gabby Giffords prior to this event, and since this terrible occurrence, they now know her as "that congresswoman who was shot." But this terrible tragedy does not define Representative Giffords. She was a dynamic, extraordinary lawmaker and politician before January 8, 2011, and she continues to be a courageous, motivated leader and activist to this day (Giffords & Kelly, 2011).

Traditionally, male and female gender roles have been stereotyped to make them mutually exclusive in the workplace. Men are considered to be stronger, tougher, and, ultimately, better suited to the role of leadership. Women are considered to be the fairer of the sexes and relegated to working either in the home or in careers more suited to their perceived strengths. Many times, women are not thought of as strong or tough. This framework has been shifting as more women have been entering the workforce with career aspirations more in line with traditionally male jobs. Unfortunately, politics is one of the last holdouts in this shift from gender inequality to parity. According to Eagly and Karau (2002), there are two dominant forms of prejudice present in regard to female leadership: (1) the perception that women are less capable when compared to men in leadership roles and (2) evaluating leadership behaviors in a less favorable way when the leader in question is female. Currently, only 19% of the 114th congressional body is made up of women (Center for American Women and Politics, 2015). While these numbers have increased slightly over the past 10 years, it is still an abysmal representation of females, who currently make up almost 50% of the total population in the United States. It is not that women cannot do the job of senator or representative, but rather that they may not pursue a career choice that is traditionally considered to be a male profession. Representative Giffords has since shattered that stereotype, demonstrating that not only can women serve their constituents in a democratic and fair manner, but they can be some of the strongest and toughest leaders present in Congress as well.

When Gabby Giffords was in fifth grade, she played the lead role in "Annie" at her local elementary school. Described as "highly social and gregarious" with "an irrepressibly upbeat personality," she appeared to be a natural choice for the role (Giffords & Kelly, 2011, p. 53). She even brought along her own dog to play the part of Sandy, to ensure enough onstage chemistry so as to impress the audience. Even as a young child, Gabby was bent on performing her job with passion and single-minded determination. Gabrielle Dee "Gabby" Giffords was born in Tucson, Arizona, on June 8, 1970. She grew up in a middle-class home with her mother, father, and older sister. Her father, a Tucson native, inherited a tire shop that would later play a pivotal role in bringing Gabby back to her hometown. The family business kept Gabby's father from spending as much time at home as he would have liked, but he always made it a point to eat dinner and discuss the day with his two daughters. While both Gabby's mother and father were supportive of their daughters, they also encouraged the girls to embrace novel experiences with an open mind. When Gabby and Melissa were not yet adolescents, their parents decided to enroll them in a Mexican summer camp to foster their independence. Spencer and Gloria, Gabby's parents, wanted the girls to experience total cultural immersion. Where other kids might have been intimidated by the language barrier and different customs, Gabby and Melissa embraced adventures such as these and integrated them into their childhood constructs. Perhaps that is why Gabby has never shied away from adversity and repeatedly proved herself to be unwavering in the face of hardship. Gabby graduated from a public high school known for academic rigor and her teachers described her as "engaging and self-confident" (Giffords & Kelly, 2011, p. 55). She decided to pursue Latin American history and sociology at Scripps College in Claremont, California, and earned her BA in 1993. She was awarded a Fulbright Scholarship and returned to Mexico to study the cultural customs of a small community of Mennonites living in Chihuahua. Unsatisfied with her career options at the time, and driven to pursue higher education, she continued on to earn her master's degree in urban planning from Cornell University. At this point in her life, Gabby had already obtained a job at Price Waterhouse in New York, but before she could settle into her new career, she was called home by her family. Spencer needed Gabby to take over as president and CEO of El Campo Tire. Little did she know that this would be the singular event that would eventually lead her to become one of the most impassioned politicians to grace the U.S. House of Representatives.

Upon her return to Arizona, Gabby quickly realized that the days of family-owned tire shops were growing short, so she made a deal with Goodyear and sold the family business. After El Campo Tire closed, she decided to open her own business, a commercial property management firm. However, she was unsatisfied and wanted to help her community on a grander scale. As a child, Gabby never dreamed of becoming a congresswoman, but she knew "she wanted to make a difference" (Giffords & Kelly, 2011, p. 55). At that point in her life, Gabby was ready to make that difference.

At the young age of 30, Gabby decided to run for her first political appointment. She appealed to both Republicans and Democrats and considered herself to be more of a centrist than either partisan affiliation. She had already served on the boards for both the YMCA and the Tucson Regional Water Council, in addition to leading a support group for the Arizona Air National Guard. Since she had appeared in her family's tire commercials, she was already easily recognizable to the people of Tucson (Giffords & Kelly, 2011). Gabby was successfully elected into the Arizona House of Representatives in 2000. This victory was the first of several to follow.

Two short years later, Gabby became the youngest woman ever elected into the Arizona State Senate, winning 74% of the vote. While serving as a state senator, Gabby focused her political vigor toward improving the development and utilization of renewable energy, improving the public education system in Arizona, and working for health care reform. While she realized that she could enact change within her state while serving in the Arizona legislature, Gabby sought to help her state further by serving in the federal government. In 2006, Gabby became the first Jewish congresswoman and only the third female Arizona representative to be elected into the U.S. Congress.

Congresswoman Giffords took her fight for clean, renewable energy from the state setting to the federal one. In 2007, her office released a report entitled "Solar Energy in Southern Arizona," which discussed the development of solar energy technologies and argued in favor of providing programs to incentivize her constituents to use renewable energy, in Arizona's particular case, sunshine. In a further bid to provide impetus for energy production and conservation, Gabby voted for the 2008 Emergency Economic Stabilization Act, believing this legislation would help prevent the further deterioration of the U.S. economic system and improve energy consumption. This particular act is commonly thought of as the financial bailout of the U.S. economic system and authorized a $700 billion budget to purchase distressed assets of the U.S. government. In 2009, Gabby voted for the American Recovery and Reinvestment Act (a.k.a. the Stimulus Act), which included financial support for infrastructure, education, health care, and renewable energy. While her platform of supporting the production of renewable energy continued to gain momentum, Gabby chose to focus on immigration and health care reform for the majority of her time left in office.

It was also during this time that she married U.S. Navy captain and NASA astronaut Mark Kelly, whom she had been seriously dating for three years. In addition to settling into her new role as a U.S. congress-woman, Gabby was adjusting to being a wife and stepmother to Mark's two daughters. Mark's eldest daughter struggled to have a close relation-ship with Gabby. She was already a teenager and found it difficult to acclimatize to her new family dynamic. While this did cause some stress on the family unit, Gabby did not push her. She understood that she couldn't force the relationship and allowed the relationship to grow at its own pace (Giffords & Kelly, 2011).

Gabby was reelected to the U.S. House of Representative two more times. During this period, she took a firm stance on immigration reform and employment opportunities for those legally in the United States. In 2008, Congresswoman Giffords introduced the Innovation Employment Act, which would increase the number of available H1B visas from 65,000 to 130,000 annually. H1B visas allow nonimmigrant temporary workers to pursue employment in the United States if they already have the equivalent of a bachelor's degree and a potential employer.

Unfortunately, 2010 proved to be a challenging year for immigration in the state of Arizona with the passage of Senator Jan Brewer's highly controversial Support Our Law Enforcement and Safe Neighborhoods Act (2010). This legislation condoned the questioning of persons whom law enforcement officers suspected may be in the United States illegally. Some critics have suggested this bill came perilously close to racial profiling. Indeed, the U.S. Supreme Court found portions of the law to be unconstitutional (Sherman, 2012). Gabby stated that the bill "stands in direct contradiction to our past and, as a result, threatens our future" (Giffords, 2010). While she had fought to secure $600 million in federal funding to provide border security, Gabby did not believe that enacting legislation that so blatantly discriminated against those of Hispanic heritage should be encouraged.

Health care reform continued to be a core component of Gabby's political platform. She was an outspoken supporter of the Patient Protection and Affordable Care Act and the Healthcare and Education Reconciliation Act of 2010. Congresswoman Giffords received strong criticism and even threats when she voted to enact this legislation. As a result, she barely beat Republican candidate Jesse Kelly in the general election, winning by only 2% of the vote. Despite her victory, her tenure in the Congress was abruptly cut short at the beginning of her term.

January 8, 2011. The 111th Congress had been in session for only five days when Loughner opened fire on dozens of unarmed citizens in a grocery store parking lot. The experience changed the way people viewed their government officials in Tucson, Arizona; the community came together to show its support for those injured or killed, regardless of political affiliation. As mentioned before, Gabby was shot in the head at point blank range and was rushed to the University Medical Center. The bullet entered through the back of her head and exited above her left eye. Fortunately for Gabby, the bullet did not cross the cerebral hemispheres, and her injuries were localized to the left side of her brain.

The left hemisphere is primarily responsible for verbal abilities (speech production, writing, reading, etc.) and controlling the right side of the body. However, when brain trauma is as extensive as Gabby's was, it becomes almost impossible to do many of the things that one could do before. When she awoke from her medically induced coma, she was unable to speak, swallow, walk, and perform other activities that many of us take for granted. She was moved from the University Medical Center in Tucson to The Institute for Rehabilitation and Research Memorial Herman Hospital in Houston, Texas, for rehabilitation. While there, she spoke her first word, only one short month after her injury. Many news outlets reported that "toast" was her initial word (Aleccia, 2011), but her husband Mark Kelly reports that it was actually "what," and she said it repetitively, without much meaning "whatwhatwhatwhat" (Giffords & Kelly, 2011). Her husband and family were sources of constant support during those first months, and in a 2012 interview with Diane Sawyer, Mark Kelly admitted that he'd actually videotaped many of her therapy sessions in an effort to show her progress (Giffords & Kelly, 2011). Doctors were, and continue to be, amazed by how quickly she regained many of her skills. They posit that having such an extraordinarily active lifestyle, strong social support, and intense inner hope have been integral in her continued recovery.

Most people would be content with learning to speak, walk, and be independent when they experience something as traumatic as a gunshot wound to the head. Not Gabby. She couldn't be satisfied with simply learning to perform her activities of daily living again. She wanted to return to work. Her ethic simply would not allow for anything less. Approximately seven months after her injury, Gabby returned to Congress to vote on raising the nation's debt ceiling. During this session, Nancy Pelosi (D-CA) called her "the personification of courage, of sincerity, and of admiration throughout the country" (Cable-Satellite Public Affairs Network, 2011; Stein, Foley, & Bendery, 2011). Gabby formally submitted her resignation from the U.S. House of Representatives on January 25, 2012, in order to focus further on her recovery. She continues to pursue her dream of making a difference and returning to office.

On the second anniversary of the Tucson, Arizona, shooting, Gabby Giffords and her husband began the organization Americans for Responsible Solutions after Adam Lanza shot and killed 20 elementary school children and six of their teachers at Sandy Hook Elementary School in Newtown, Connecticut. While Gabby and Mark are both gun owners, and strong supporters of their Second Amendment rights, they passionately believe that if gun control policies were revisited and revised, there would be much less gun violence present in the United States. Initially, Americans for Responsible Solutions had three goals:

1. To create a hospitable environment where people with differing viewpoints can appropriately discuss the relevant issues
2. To change the politics of the gun control debate so it's less related to partisanship
3. To work toward more commonsense policy shifts that the majority of Americans could support (Giffords & Kelly, 2014).

Specifically, Gabby and Mark suggested more stringent background checks, closure of loopholes allowing for gun purchases through the Internet and gun show sales, enhancement of the mental health system as a means to decrease shootings perpetrated by individuals suffering from psychiatric disorders, and enhancement of the provision of services for women seeking protection from abusive relationships. In addition, the Americans for Responsible Solutions seeks to continue to fight illegal gun trafficking by improving law enforcement training, providing better tools to officers, and establishing sensible boundaries for the sale of certain types of firearms and high-capacity ammunition magazines.

Gabby Giffords and Mark Kelly have become vehement opponents of the National Rifle Association's (NRA) current agenda because the NRA has transformed from an organization dedicated to providing gun safety education and teaching marksmanship to one invested in the sale of guns and enhancement of its profit margin (Americans for Responsible Solutions, 2015). After the Sandy Hook shooting, Wayne LaPierre, the executive vice president of the NRA, suggested that stationing armed guards in every school would decrease gun violence and protect the children of America. However, many gun control activists, including Gabby and Mark, have been quick to point out that proactive as opposed to reactive measures would benefit the citizens of this country more.

Most recently, Gabby and Mark have sought to reintroduce legislation that would close loopholes in current federal bills that allow people to buy firearms without a background check. The Public Safety and Second Amendment Act of 2015, also known as the King-Thompson bill, has been formally sponsored by eight current legislators, four Democrats, and four Republicans. The bipartisan legislation calls for more stringent background checks on individuals attempting to purchase weapons, strengthening the National Instant Criminal Background Check System, and establishing a National Commission on Gun Violence (Americans for Responsible Solutions, 2015). Even though Gabby Giffords is no longer an active member of Congress, she has not given up her passion for solving the problems confronting her country.

Gabby Giffords is an extraordinarily remarkable woman. Not yet 45 years old, she has experienced more in her lifetime than most people do in the entirety of theirs. She has been a student, a small business owner, a politician, and an activist, in addition to being a wife, stepmother, daughter, sister, and, ultimately, a survivor of life-threatening gunshot wounds. Gabby Giffords has never given up her dream of improving the lives of the people around her. Despite experiencing significant adversity, she has consistently persevered and even thrived. When asked by CBS News's Lee Cowan in a recent interview if she was striving to return to her former self or developing a new sense of identity, she replied that she is trying to evolve into a new Gabby Giffords, "Better. Stronger. Tougher" (Cowan, 2015).

Politics may still be a man's game, but the game is slowly changing. Gabby Giffords is just one example of how women can be just as strong, tough, and suited to the job. It is imperative that Washington, D.C., continue to encourage female leadership in the legislative, judicial, and executive branches. Are women needed in Congress because they are better than their male counterparts? No. They are needed in Congress because they offer different experiences singular to their sex. They represent those who are traditionally underrepresented, and they act as positive role models for girls who may shun traditionally male-dominated fields. Gabby Giffords is not just a powerful role model for youths who may be interested in political careers, or those who aspire to leadership positions, or particularly those who may have experienced adversity in their childhood. She is a reminder to those of us who may be well past our adolescence and firmly entrenched in adulthood that determination, perseverance, and, ultimately hope are powerful weapons in our armamentarium for change.

REFERENCES

Aleccia, J. (2011, February 9). Giffords speaks, asking for toast with breakfast: Arizona congresswoman is making progress at "lightning speed" after bullet to brain. *ABC News*. Retrieved from http://www.nbcnews.com/id/41492254/ns/us_news/t/giffords-speaks-asking-toast-breakfast/#.VSSrsPnF9IE.

Americans for Responsible Solutions. (2015, March 4). *Gabby Giffords and Capt. Mark Kelly stand with bipartisan group of lawmakers to urge congress to act on background checks bill*. Retrieved from http://americansforresponsiblesolutions.org/2015/03/04/king-thompson/.

Cable-Satellite Public Affairs Network. (2011). *Representative Giffords appearance on the House Floor*. Retrieved from http://www.c-span.org/video/?300833-5/representative-giffords-appearance-house-floor.

Center for American Women and Politics. (2015). Facts. *Women serving in the 114th Congress 2015–17*. Retrieved from http://www.cawp.rutgers.edu/fast_facts/levels_of_office/Congress-Current.php.

Cowan, Lee. (2015). Gabby Giffords speaks four years into her recovery. *CBS News*. Retrieved from http://www.cbsnews.com/videos/gabby-giffords-speaks-four-years-into-her-recovery/.

Eagly, A. H., & Karau, S. J. (2002). Role Congruity Theory of prejudice toward female leaders. *Psychological Review, 109*(3), 573–598.

Giffords, G. (2010). *Giffords' statement on Arizona's new immigration law and the US border*. Retrieved from http://en.wikipedia.org/wiki/Gabrielle_Giffords#cite_note-107.

Giffords, G., & Kelly, M. (2011). *Gabby: A story of courage and hope*. New York, NY: Scribner Publishing.

Giffords, G., & Kelly, M. (2014). *Enough: Our fight to keep America safe from gun violence*. New York: NY: Scribner Publishing.

Sherman, M. (2012, June 25). Supreme Court issues ruling on S.B. 1070. *Huffington Post*. Retrieved from http://www.huffingtonpost.com/2012/06/25/supreme-court-sb1070_n_1614121.html.

Stein, S., Foley, E., & Bendery, J. (2011, October 1). Gabrielle Giffords returns to Congress to vote on debt ceiling deal. *Huffington Post*. Retrieved from http://www.huffingtonpost.com/2011/08/01/gabrielle-giffords-debt-ceil.

Congresswoman Edith Nourse Rogers

Congresswoman Nourse Rogers holds the record for the longest service by a woman in the House of Representatives until she was surpassed by Senator Barbara Mikulski in 2012. She represented Massachusetts and served from June 1925 (filling the vacancy caused by the death of her husband) until September 1960. Congresswoman Nourse Rogers sponsored the 1942 bill that created the Women's Army Auxiliary Corps and the 1943 bill that created the Women's Army Corps. In addition, Nourse Rogers was the first woman to preside as Speaker pro tempore over the House of Representatives.

Source: http://bioguide.congress.gov/scripts/biodisplay.pl?index=r000392.

Chapter 5

Women and Leadership

Melissa Alexander and William Schweinle

INTRODUCTION

Historically, women have worked from behind the scenes to support, nurture, and comfort. They are child-bearers by nature and possibly, by nature, have been underrepresented as leaders. But what is it that makes a leader? What are the traditional roles for females and males? How does this traditional role effect current career choices? Why are women paid less than men? It important to explore these questions while working to understand what a leader is, the different ways it can be defined, and where women have overcome and how women can excel in leadership.

FEMALE: CHILD-BEARER

The natural role of the female from the beginning of time has been child-bearing. The act of childbearing requires a male relationship, whether brief or lifelong. It includes 10 months of hormonal and physical change. Pregnancy includes gastrointestinal discomforts, weight gain, and change of body shape to accommodate the growth of the young. The pregnant and postpartum woman cannot accomplish physical endeavors of heavy lifting, running, or moving as quickly as the nonpregnant person. In historical and tribal society, these women require extra protection and care.

While traditionally offspring are of great value to tribal survival and successorship of kingdoms, it is possible women present a perceived weakness in their physical vulnerability.

MALE: LEADER/HUNTER

Meanwhile, the role of the male has been leader of the tribe, head of the family unit, hunter, and protector. Without the strength, speed, and brawn of men there would be no protection against invaders, attackers, or animals. While the female enables bringing forth new life, the male helps sustain the lives that are made through physical capability.

QUESTIONS

What impact does the traditional, historical role of women as child-bearers have on their ability to be leaders? Why have males been leaders more frequently than females? Must women adopt a male style of leadership to succeed? Is transactional or transformational leadership most effective? Does only one society or culture find few women leaders, or is this phenomenon more widespread and far-reaching?

COLLEGE MAJOR

First it is important to recognize statistical differences we presently see between men and women in career choice. Historically, men have been warriors, chiefs, physical laborers, political leaders, and business moguls, while women have been mothers, gatherers, nurses, babysitters, craft-makers, and, more recently, middle management. In a report from the American Association of University Women (AAUW) by Corbett and Hill, gender composition of college majors is examined. Women, by a great majority (80%), have overtaken the fields of health care and education. Women make up greater than 60% of the humanities and social sciences faculty. By comparison, men predominate the fields of computer and information science, and engineering and engineering technology by greater than 80%. Interestingly, the business major is equally shared among the genders, with no significant differences in gender composition. Similarly, biological and physical sciences, math, and agricultural sciences have equal gender compositions in college.

FIRST JOB

According to the AAUW, 67% of men and 53% of women hold full-time jobs one year after college. While women and men equally pursued a business major in college, 28% of men held jobs in business *management*, as compared with 20% of women, while 18% of women obtained business *support* and administrative assistant jobs as compared to only 10% of men. As this indicates, from the beginning of their business careers, 8% of women take on greater support roles in comparison to their male counterparts who achieve management and leadership positions earlier and assistant or support roles less frequently.

Female occupations one year after graduation modally consist of pre-kindergarten through 12th-grade educators at 15% and nursing at 7%, while males were 5% and 1%, respectively. Males dominate the fields of math and computer sciences at 10% as well as engineering at 10%, while females were 3% and 2%, respectively. Not only have we seen historic gender role contrast, but in the present day gender role diversity is a very real and significant factor in the current occupational outlook.

EARNINGS AT ONE YEAR

How does this affect leadership, you might ask? Occupation choice has a significant effect on earnings, and earnings are an indicator of status and a direct sign of a leadership position. Per the AAUW, fields in which women predominate have the least gender pay disparity. However, in the occupations where 50% or less of women work, the gender pay disparity becomes much more evident. For example, in sales occupations men make $10,000 per year more than women on average. In business management, men make $48,000 yearly on average while women make $41,000 yearly, which translates to women earning 86% of what men earn. Even in white-collar occupations where women make up 51% of the workforce, women make 87% of the salary men make. On average, regardless of career choice, even when achieving higher college grades than men, women earn 82 cents to every dollar that men earn one year following graduation.

EXCUSES FOR GENDER PAY DISPARITY

While there are some occupations in which women and men make a similar salary, there are *no* occupations in which women are paid higher average salaries than men. Some have argued that women prefer roles with lower pay. Others reason that men work more hours than women. Men and women work in different parts of the economy, which could lend to pay differences. In addition, many attribute the differences in parental responsibilities. Today, while some men are taking on further home responsibilities, women are further discounted as some think that there is equality in the balance of work and home.

ADDRESSING THE EXCUSES

A variety of justifications have been offered to explain why gender pay disparity takes place. In *Stender v. Lucky Stores,* whether deliberate or not, discrimination took place in the assignment of roles in the company. While Lucky Stores argued that women were choosing and preferred lower-paying positions, it was ruled that women were being *assigned* lower-paying positions. To address the idea that men earn more because they work more hours, it is important to look at the wages of men and women who work the same number of hours. While men tend to work greater hours overall when compared to women, in positions where women and men worked the same hours there was still a significant pay inequality favoring men (American Association of University Women, 2012). Furthermore, it's important not to make the convenient assumption that men are more committed to their work or have greater desire to work longer hours. One must consider how and why men are able to work more hours than women. Men are found to work more frequently in the higher-paying private sector, while women are found in the nonprofit sector and government, which could contribute to lower wages among women (American Association of University Women, 2012).

CHILDBEARING/MOTHERING

Childbearing or mothering are also significant factors in a women's economic success. Reduction in work hours or leaves of absence contribute to significant wage and salary loss by women as a result of childbearing. Correll, Benard, and Paik (2007) note that mothers face earning penalties in the workforce as compared to women without children. Employers who assume that a working mother will give priority to her family over the job are more likely to remember times when she left early and less likely to recall when she stayed late. This quickly translates into fewer opportunities for women's career development, increases in attrition, and reinforcement of stereotypes about women. It is a self-perpetuating cycle (Deutsch, 2005; Hewlett & Luce, 2005). Stone and Lovejoy reported that inflexibility in the workforce requires women to decide to opt out of the workforce despite their desire to find a balance with work and family (2004). Whether it should be culturally or socially acceptable, most companies operate under the assumption that the ideal worker is fully devoted to his or her career (Hewlett & Luce, 2005). It is reinforced (and, in fact, enforced) that employees should be available at all hours, which precludes most mothers' success in the workplace.

LEADERSHIP DEFINED

But what does this have to do with leadership? According to *Webster's* dictionary, a leader is someone who directs a military force or unit, or a person with commanding authority or influence. "Leadership" is, however, a word in evolution. Helmrich, of the *Business News Daily*, reports that

30 business owners were asked to give their definition of "Leadership." Overwhelmingly, women business owners describe leadership as inspiring, empowering, creating culture, and encouraging employees. While male business owners describe leadership as providing the vision and motivation, influencing, mentoring, pushing others to accomplish more, and projecting expertise.

GENDER LEADERSHIP DIFFERENCES

Men not only describe leadership differently than women, but they often lead differently than women. While women who aspire to lead look to the values of current leaders, they find a highly agentic society dominated by males, in which demand and command achieve outcomes. Males lead with authoritative and dictatorial style in which others are expected to either comply with or overtake the position of the leader. Males historically reward task completion with monetary or promotional gains. They force project accomplishment and create a reward system for task completion.

On the other hand, women describe leadership with sensory words, placing value on teamwork, empowering, and encouraging others (Helmrich, 2015). Their leadership skills have been demonstrated when ascribing to these specific values. Some women have followed the examples of the traditional male leader, putting on the masculine commanding and authoritative qualities to achieve their goals. However, more frequently women who have gained fame in leadership have exemplified more traditional womanly values.

TRANSFORMATION VERSUS TRANSACTION

While proportionally few women have overcame barriers to leadership, there is evidence that women who lead while exemplifying feminine qualities have found success. Leadership style is further described by Hadded and Schweinle (2010). In this, leadership style is either transactional or transformational. Transactional leadership is described as an outcome-based reward system most often embodied by men in leadership. This transactional leadership is often based on a contractual exchange of work for money (Eagly & Johannesen-Schmidt, 2001; Walumba, Wu, & Ojode, 2004). Transformational leadership emphasizes interpersonal relationships, inspiration, motivation, and positive influence (Walumba et al., 2004).

MICHELLE BACHELET

Some great examples of women leaders include Chile's first female president, Michelle Bachelet (Hadded & Schweinle, 2010). While her background is decorated with qualifications, including being a licensed pediatrician, a socialist, and a prior defense minister of Chile who studied defense in Washington, D.C., her leadership style was one of unity (Hadded & Schweinle, 2010). She brought together the Chilean military and Chilean political leadership by relating empathy and genuine concern for the people (Polgreen & Rohter, 2006). She was called "mama" by her people and known for her compassion. She looked for the humanity and ultimate good, even in those who had tortured her family in the Pinochet regime, thereby giving a lost country hope in the democracy in which she was elected and a fair, caring, and maternal leadership that she would provide.

ELLEN JOHNSON SIRLEAF

Another remarkable female leader of our time is Ellen Johnson Sirleaf. Her feminine political persona was brought to the forefront in her leadership of Liberia as president beginning in 2006 (Hadded & Schweinle, 2010). She led through creation of consensus while building social bridges among conflict and crisis. She promoted reconciliation between fighting factions. She has begun Liberian political transformation and has aided in slowly decreasing the gender inequity present. She does not lead by command, by demand, authoritatively, nor with great reward systems, but instead her feminine political persona and transformational style has brought much-needed improvement and positive social change in Liberia.

CURRENT WOMEN LEADERSHIP STATISTICS

Despite progress in gender equality, women are still underrepresented in leadership roles. For instance, in the U.S. Congress, women currently hold 19.4% or 104 of the 535 seats. Women hold 20% of the 100 seats in the U.S. Senate and 19.3% or 84 seats of the 435 seats in the House of Representatives. The United States is not alone in the small proportions of women in political leadership roles (CAWP, 2015). Worldwide, women hold fewer political positions than men. According to the Inter-Parliamentary Union (2015), women make up a largest percentage of parliament at 41.5% in Nordic countries. In Europe, women account for only 25.3% of leadership in parliaments. In Asia, Arab States, and the Pacific, women make up 19%, 18.1% and 13.1%, respectively.

These proportions of women leaders do not yet approximate a fair representation of women worldwide, who make up 50% of the human population (United Nations Statistics Division, 2012). Why do we see such disparity in the number of women leaders? What is it that happens when women breach the boundaries of their traditional role as child-bearer and nurturer? Are women competent in a leadership position? Is middle management a fair compromise for a leadership position? Do men want women as leaders? Do women support other women leaders? Could boundaries be broken down to improve the outlook for future women leaders?

There are many postulated reasons for why women are seen less frequently in leadership roles. Leadership often evolves from those who make positive and influential change in a business, organization, or government entity. Is creating change possible for women? Per Monroe, Ozyurt, Wrigley, and Alexander (2008), women fear direct retaliation if they advocate openly for change. Often, hostile sexism precludes women's advancement in leadership roles. Per Glick and Fiske, men, knowingly or unknowingly, craft gender devaluation and create punishments for women who seek change or reject the status quo (2001). In addition, while frequently answering to male evaluators, the typical maternal or female behaviors, including nurturance, warmth, and supportiveness, are in conflict with masculine expectations, resulting in devaluation of women by their male supervisors (Caplan, 1994). These feminine characteristics are viewed negatively and viewed through a male-cultured glass. Women are often penalized for simply disagreeing with others, while men are seen as deliberative and analytical when confronting the same situation (Eagly & Carli, 2007).

In attempting to compensate for the appearance of weakness found in the characteristics of nurturance and warmth, many women try to develop dominant and agentic qualities. Does it work for the female aspiring leader to put on a masculine persona, to provide reward for action, and to demand change? Per Eagly and Carli (2007), women learn quickly that there is a "likeability penalty" for agentic behavior. Therefore, women, in attempting to express ideas, challenge the status quo, and function similarly to other leaders find that they are punished when failing to meet appropriate gender expectations. Conversely, when meeting gender expectations, women are viewed as weak or incompetent. For example, as reported by Rudman and Glick (2001), when women functioning in traditionally male leadership roles are seen as "nice," they are often liked but not respected. There appears to be a significant trade-off between competence and likability (Coates, 2013).

Is it better for women to challenge the status quo through transactional leadership or by creating in themselves an agentic persona? Does the future of leadership bode better for women with naturally masculine tendencies? Is it possible for women to succeed as Bachelet or Johnson Sirleaf while embracing naturally feminine qualities?

While women have been making significant advancements in equal rights for over 80 years, we still find the advancement of women into leadership a significantly difficult task. Subtle but pervasive patterns of discrimination dominate institutions in all sectors (Manegold, 1994). There are inadvertent narrow-minded indiscretions on the part of male-dominated leadership who are frequently unaware of their own discrimination (Manegold, 1994). Moreover, when women do hold leadership positions, there is often a process of gender devaluation, whereby the leadership position held by women is perceived to decrease in status, power, and authority (Monroe et al., 2008). When women hold positions in middle management, they often receive fewer resources and are tasked with greater responsibilities, creating unachievable goals, further potentiating an environment where women appear incapable of successful leadership. In 1996 research found that when women and men performed objectively the same, women were still rated lower in competence despite achieving the same objective standards. This indicates the significant and disappointing gender bias that is present regardless of actual achievement (Foschi, 1996).

REFERENCES

American Association of University Women. (2012). *Graduating to a pay gap: The earnings of women and men one year after college graduation* (Library of Congress Control Number: 2012951114). Washington, DC: Corbett & Hill. Retrieved from http://www.aauw.org/files/2013/02/graduating-to-a-pay-gap-the-earnings-of-women-and-men-one-year-after-college-graduation.pdf.

Caplan, P. J. (1994). *Lifting a ton of feathers: A woman's guide to surviving in the academic world.* Toronto, ON: University of Toronto Press.

Center for American Women and Politics (CAWP). (2015). *Women in the U.S. Congress 2015.* Eagleton Institute of Politics, Rutgers University. Retrieved from http://www.cawp.rutgers.edu/fast_facts/levels_of_office/documents/cong.pdf.

Coates, B. (2013). Has judicial thinking on academic freedom impeded gender mainstreaming in universities? In M. Paludi (Ed.), *Women and management: Volume 2* (pp. 133–148). Santa Barbara, CA: Praeger.

Correll, S. J., Benard, S., & Paik, I. (2007). Getting a job: Is there a motherhood penalty? *American Journal of Sociology, 112*(5), 1297–1339.

Deutsch, C. (2005). Behind the exodus of executive women: Boredom. *New York Times,* May 1.

Eagly, A., & Carli, L. (2007). *Through the labyrinth: The truth about how women become leaders.* Boston, MA: Harvard Business School Press.

Eagly, A. H., & Johannesen-Schmidt, M. C. (2001). The leadership styles of women and men. *Journal of Social Issues, 57,* 781–797.

Foschi, M. (1996). Double standards in the evaluation of men and women. *Social Psychology Quarterly, 59,* 237–254.

Glick, P., & Fiske, S. (2001). Ambivalent alliance: Hostile and benevolent sexism as complementary justification for gender inequality. *American Psychologist, 56,* 109–118.

Hadded, E., & Schweinle, W. (2010). The feminine political persona: Queen Victoria, Ellen Johnson Sirleaf, and Michelle Bachelet. In M. Paludi (Ed.), *Feminism and women's rights worldwide* (pp. 97–109). Santa Barbara, CA: Praeger.

Helmrich, B. (2015, January 23). 30 ways to define leadership. *Business News Daily.* Retrieved from http://www.businessnewsdaily.com/3647-leadership-definition.html.

Hewlett, S., & Luce, C. (2005). Off-ramps and on-ramps: Keeping talented women on the road to success. *Harvard Business Review.* Retrieved from http://www.foundationforeuropeanleadership.org/assets/downloads/infoItems/72.pdf.

Inter-Parliamentary Union. (2015, February 1). *Women in national parliaments.* Retrieved from http://www.ipu.org/wmn-e/world.htm.

Manegold, C. (1994). Glass ceiling is pervasive, secretary of labor contents. *New York Times,* September 27, B9.

Monroe, K., Ozyurt, S., Wrigley, T., & Alexander, A. (2008). Gender equality in academia: Bad news from the trenches, and some possible solutions. *Perspectives on Politics, 6*(2), 215–233.

Polgreen, L., & Rohter, L. (2006). *World.* Retrieved on September 9, 2015, from http://www.nytimes.com/2006/01/22/world/africa/22iht-females.html?_r=0.

Rudman, L., & Glick, P. (2001). Prescriptive gender stereotypes and backlash toward agentic women. *Journal of Social Issues, 57,* 743–762.

Stender v. Lucky Stores, 803 F. Supp. 259, N.D. Cal. 1992.

Stone, P., & Lovejoy, M. (2004). Fast-track women and the "choice" to stay home. *Annals of the American Academy of Political and Social Science, 596,* 62–83.

United Nations Statistics Division. (2012). *Statistics and indicators on women and men* [Data file]. Retrieved from http://unstats.un.org/unsd/demographic/products/indwm/.

Walumba, F., Wu, C., & Ojode, L. (2004). Gender and instructional outcomes: The mediating role of leadership style. *Journal of Management Development, 23,* 124–140.

Senator Nancy Landon Kassebaum

Senator Kassebaum represented Kansas in the U.S. Senate from December 1978 to January 1997. She was the only woman among 100 members. Senator Kassebaum once noted that it took time to adjust to being a woman in the Senate and that she has avoided the Senate members' dining room because she felt "intimidated." She once quipped that as a woman senator she had special responsibilities: "There's so much work to do: the coffee to make and the chambers to vacuum. There are Pat Moynihan's hats to brush and the buttons to sew on Bob Byrd's red vests, so I keep quite busy." Senator Kassebaum supported women's right to abortions and supported programs for international family planning. She frequently referred to herself as a "U.S. Senator, not a woman Senator." She also once stated that "it diminishes women to say that we have one voice and everything in the Senate would change if we were there."

Source: http://history.house.gov/People/Listing/K/KASSEBAUM,-Nancy-Landon-(K000017)/.

Chapter 6

Elizabeth Warren: The Voice of America's Future

Felicia L. Mirghassemi and Paula K. Lundberg-Love

> We are here to introduce our Gammy, Elizabeth Warren. She is running for the United States Senate because of us and because of all kids. We're really proud of her. (Warren, 2014, p. 245)
> —Octavia Tyagi (age 11) and Lavinia Tyagi (age 7)

In a generation where the discussion regarding gender roles was merely a faint whisper in the wind, women continued to nurture their families while dreaming of a chance to also pursue their aspirations. In an era where there were two opposing sides regarding gender roles, there were women prepared to cross the line. Throughout history women have been seen as the nurturers, the caregivers for the future generation, and little else. However, throughout the past 40 years, women have hovered between lines of gender role divisions. While successfully balancing as the family caregiver and a career woman, they were also striving to prove worth to a society unyielding to change. Encumbered with obstacles of gender divisions, class hardships, and a tenacity to break the glass ceiling, Elizabeth Warren is proof that women are successfully blurring the lines between traditional and nontraditional gender roles.

A grateful young girl from Oklahoma City surrounded by a family rich in love and support, Elizabeth Warren, born June 22, 1949, was the youngest in a family of three older brothers (Warren, 2014). Her father, a maintenance man, and her mother, a department store worker, bought a house inside the boundary line of what they believed to be the best school district for their children. They continuously did whatever it took to invest in their children's future. Elizabeth Warren vividly describes the moment she grew up at the age of 12, in her autobiography, *A Fighting Chance,* when her father had a heart attack. With hospital bills piling up and her father out of work, her stay-at-home mother, who followed the gender roles of her time, prepared to interview for a job at the age of 50. After losing the family car due to nonpayment and the looming threat of losing their home, Elizabeth Warren characterizes her mother's resilience as being comparable to that of a mother bear protecting her cub. Her mother dusted off her nicest dress and prepared to interview for an entry-level position, continuing to do what was necessary to give her family their best chance at a bright future.

As an intelligent teenager who had skipped a grade, Elizabeth Warren excelled in school. Joining the school debate team, she pushed the limits of her knowledge and became the top debater in the state of Oklahoma, landing her a full scholarship to George Washington University (Warren, 2014). Leaving Oklahoma for the first time, college was an opportunity for a variety of new experiences, including a small sense of security, cultural and social diversity, and the opportunity to expand her horizons. In 1968, her first boyfriend returned to her life. A successful college graduate with an impressive job at IBM, he expressed a desire to marry her. She welcomed the opportunity and soon gave up her scholarship and her college career to pursue a new dream, of creating a home and a family.

While living in Houston Elizabeth Warren and her husband, Jim Warren, began to settle into a familiar life. Elizabeth received her degree as a speech pathologist, taught students with disabilities, and worked to pay off her student loans. When they relocated to New Jersey, Elizabeth assumed the role of the traditional homemaker while her husband worked to support their family financially. Elizabeth dedicated herself to building their house into a home. From home repairs, gardening, sewing, and attempted cooking, Elizabeth and her daughter, Amelia, were an adventurous team. However, the desire to do more continued to permeate the recesses of her mind. Eventually, Elizabeth was able to convince her husband that she should enter and study at Rutgers Law School. At this juncture of her life Elizabeth began to pursue her intellectual aspirations while still balancing the full-time positions of mother and wife. Each morning Elizabeth would place Amelia in childcare and venture off to law classes. During lunch, mother and daughter would discuss their day in laughter. Following her second year of law school she applied for summer associate positions at a Wall Street firm and with the wit and tenacity to play with the big boys of Wall Street, she was offered the position. While serving in this position, she was able to contribute considerably in a financial manner for her family and develop the skills of her profession. She felt optimistic about her abilities to become a lawyer.

At 26, following graduation from law school, Elizabeth gave birth to her second child, Alexander (Warren, 2014). With two babies and no job prospects in sight, Elizabeth successfully completed her bar exam and decided to hang a sign in front of her house that read "Attorney-at-Law." Now Elizabeth had a home office where she pursued three careers wife, mother, and attorney. Shortly thereafter, Elizabeth received the opportunity to teach again. She began as an adjunct faculty member at Rutgers, and after relocating to Houston, Elizabeth obtained a tenure track professorial position at the University of Houston. She continued her roles as wife and mother while she successfully developed her academic career.

Nevertheless, as much as she loved her full-time positions as a mother and professor, there was only so much that an individual could accomplish in any given day. From teaching the next generation of lawyers to rushing between car-pool duty and Girl Scouts, sometimes dinner was placed on the table late. Elizabeth and her husband, Jim, never argued, but it became apparent they both had very different visions of how a family should function. After discussions and reconsiderations, Elizabeth and Jim decided to divorce. Because Elizabeth had been raised to believe that a woman's life was measured by her success in marriage, she felt as if she were a failure.

Now a newly single mother of two young children and a full-time professor, Elizabeth Warren had the nearby support of her family to help her write the next chapter of her life. Two years later, that chapter included another law professor, Bruce Mann. Born from a working-class family, a Massachusetts native, and a scholarly legal history professor, Elizabeth and Bruce met during an intensive course for professors around the country. The first day of the class, Elizabeth asked him for a tennis lesson. Soon after they fell in love, Elizabeth proposed and Bruce said "yes." Bruce uprooted his life and moved from Connecticut to Texas to build their family. The following year, they received trial teaching offers at one of the best law schools in the country, The University of Texas. This law school fostered what became Elizabeth Warren's legal specialty, Bankruptcy Law, an area of law that originated from a personal place in her heart and her history (Warren, 2014).

Elizabeth's family history reflects a generational burden that has influenced her life in a multitude of ways (Warren, 2014). In her autobiography, Senator Warren depicts expectations in an era long before she was born. Her father had dreams of flying airplanes. However, his dreams changed when he fell in love with Elizabeth's mother at the age of 15.

Her father's family bitterly disapproved as he fell deeper in love with a young part-Native American. In 1932, her parent's eloped and struggled through the Dust Bowl, the Great Depression, and World War II (Warren, 2014). While growing up, Elizabeth continued to hear about bank failures and the devastation that occurred when families lost everything. Elizabeth helped her family through financial strains as a teenager by working as a waitress, and a seamstress (Warren, 2014). However, college attendance was not an option for her at that time because her family couldn't afford tuition. With hard work, perseverance, and perhaps a little luck, Elizabeth fought for her chance to obtain a college education. Years later, with a law degree in hand, Elizabeth had the chance to teach a course about why families struggled with bankruptcy and formulate a solution to help future young adults move beyond the class into which one was born, and achieve an education.

In addition to the fact that she had never taught this course, her task was complicated by the fact that the bankruptcy laws in the early 1980s had recently changed, meaning there were no books outlining the new laws. Thus, Elizabeth Warren taught her class in an unconventional way. Combing through the new law with her class, she asked her class what issues the lawmakers were hoping to solve with the new statutes. When Dr. Stefan Riesenfeld, an expert advisor on the new law, agreed to speak to Professor Warren's class, she asked a simple question. How did the experts know that people filing bankruptcy lived in economic margins and simply made poor decisions? His answer was that it was common knowledge (Warren, 2014). With no empirical basis for the passage of the new bankruptcy law that would impact a large proportion of American citizens, Elizabeth Warren's search for answers was ignited. *Why were people going bankrupt?*

In order to understand *why* people were filing bankruptcy, she first questioned *who* these people were. Along with Terry Sullivan and Jay Westbrook, Elizabeth Warren coauthored *As We Forgive Our Debtors*, which details the results of data depicting the families that filed bankruptcy (Sullivan, Warren, & Westbrook, 1999). Throughout data collection, Elizabeth Warren observed a bankruptcy courtroom and reported her surprise when she observed that "the people appearing before that judge came in all colors, sizes, and ages" (Warren, 2014, p. 34). After Elizabeth and her team collected all the data, her observations were confirmed:

> The people seeking the judge's decree were once solidly middle-class. They had gone to college, found good jobs, gotten married, and bought homes . . . nearly 90 percent were declaring bankruptcy for one of three reasons: a job loss, a medical problem, or a family breakup. (Warren, 2014, p. 34)

While the term "deadbeat" (Warren, 2014, p. 35) was often used to describe bankruptcy filers and justify the legislation supporting the prosperity of big banks, the empirical evidence suggested otherwise. These families believed they were safe with their health, their jobs, and their relationships until they weren't. The qualitative self-reports of their research concluded a thematic statement of self-loathing and self-blame. However, in the midst of going bankrupt, these families did not have the resources, or the voice to stand up against the big banks. As a consequence of discovering the truth about these working-class families, Elizabeth made the decision to stand up and give them a voice.

While young families continued to borrow from banks to pay for first home mortgages, a monumental Supreme Court decision quietly began a major change in banking. In 1978, *Marquette v. First of Omaha* began a wave of deregulation and an end to usury laws that placed a cap on interest rates (Sherman, 2009). Usury laws were crucial to the growth of the American economy by providing families with an opportunity to borrow money, pay for their homes monthly, and live rent-free during retirement. These laws had allowed individuals to afford cars, college educations, and small business expansions and they created jobs. However, with the elimination of a cap the credit card companies disproportionately raised interest rates and fees. While Reaganomics continued to deregulate banks, the savings and loan industry sought out troubled families with increasing debt and provided credit at astronomical interest rates. This exploitation of the working class provided an explosion of untapped profit for the financial industry; bankruptcy filings for the average working-class family throughout the 1980s "unexpectedly doubled" (Warren, 2014, p. 35). While many critics suggest this time period was a "failure of public policy" (Sherman, 2009, p. 8), Professor Warren advised Citibank about how to reduce bankruptcy losses (Warren, 2014). After offering a rather simple piece of advice to the bankers not to lend money to families that can't afford high-interest debts, she was informed by bank officials that the bank had no interest in reducing any lending practices. The line in the sand was drawn and the teams were clear, big banks versus American Families, and the families were losing.

At the age of 45, Elizabeth Warren received a faculty position at Harvard Law School. With the support of a prestigious university, Elizabeth invested her time in teaching, research, and writing. Then when she received an offer from former congressman Mike Synar to recommend three improvements in the current financial law which would help families in debt, Elizabeth couldn't refuse. This moment marked Elizabeth Warren's first entrance into the political arena. As she continued to advocate for working-class families through the National Bankruptcy Review Commission, her own family was struck with grief. With the death of her mother, father, and closest aunt, Elizabeth surrounded herself with her family for support, while she continued to fight for American families (Warren, 2014).

During the spring of 1998, Elizabeth Warren met with Senator Ted Kennedy (D-MA) for the first time to galvanize a leader that would fight against the banking industry and for the American people. With substantial resources including money and lobbyists, big banks were putting an immense amount of pressure on passing legislation that would make them bigger and more profitable. With the financial institutions' profits coming from working families' profits, Elizabeth Warren saw that when families suffered, America suffered. Through her advocacy work she wrote *The Two-Income Trap* with her daughter, Amelia, and *All Your Worth*, to heighten awareness for changes that Washington needed to make, as well as ways in which individual consumers could protect themselves (Warren, 2014).

In 2008, the housing market plummeted and took the major banking institutions along with it (Havemann, 2015). Congress acted quickly by signing a $700 billion bailout for the banks, known as the Troubled Asset Relief Program (TARP). This same program introduced the Congressional Oversight Panel (COP), which provided a system of accountability that monitored how the Treasury was spending the TARP funds. Elizabeth Warren was one of five members on a panel that provided a report to Congress every 30 days. With minimal power in the grand scheme of Washington politics, Elizabeth continued to use the voice she had developed to raise some serious questions. The COP reports consisted of 10 simple questions that cut through the complicated jargon and focused on a single theme—*will these legislative actions help taxpayer's receive a fair deal?*

From 2008 until 2010, Elizabeth Warren and the rest of the nonpartisan members of COP continued to ask the hard questions regarding the bailout, but none were ever answered. TARP proved to be a bailout for big banks that appeared to be above the law. Thus, Elizabeth moved forward to tackle the problem in a different direction. She began to ignite an army to bring forth the development of the Consumer Financial Protection Agency (CFPA) which would receive the necessary authority to regulate and protect consumers from financial products that were hidden financial explosives. With the support of various nonprofit consumer advocacy groups, congressmen, and even President Obama, the CFPA was included in the Dodd-Frank Act. Elizabeth Warren strongly credits this success to the advocates and volunteers who displayed a unified front of American people that never gave up on democracy (Warren, 2014).

While fostering the success and development of the CFPA, it became apparent that Elizabeth Warren would not receive bipartisan support necessary to hold the lending industry accountable for their shady practices. After two years of service in Washington, in which Elizabeth advocated and assisted in the development of a readable one-page mortgage contract that prevented consumers from signing confusing deals with hidden fees, it appeared that her time in Washington had come to a close.

After resigning from her position at the CFPA, she was invited to discuss the future state of the economy with President Obama. During that fateful White House meeting, President Obama suggested Elizabeth run for the Senate seat against the incumbent Scott Brown (Warren, 2014). At the age of 62, Elizabeth appeared to lack the financial support and experience to be a successful political contender. However, after a rudimentary grassroots meeting with interested individuals, Elizabeth heard the stories of the people she had spent her life's work trying to protect, and learned that they were still being squeezed for every penny they had left. Through interactions with her supporters in attendance, Elizabeth promised a future constituent that she would campaign for her and for the entire middle class that had been treated unfairly by a rigged system.

Elizabeth's campaign trail was composed of living rooms, diners, construction sites, bars, union meetings, and various small businesses that wanted to hear about her plan for their financial security. The volunteers and supporters crossed political affiliations, race, gender, age, education, and sexual orientation. The fundamental principle of Elizabeth's economic policy is simple, "How we spend our government's money is about values . . . [it] isn't some absurdly complicated math problem. It's about choices" (Warren, 2014, p. 215). Those values and choices provided Elizabeth, a first-time political novice, the resilience, tenacity, and perseverance to survive every slanderous personal attack that was thrown her way (Hicks, 2012).

During the final stretches of the senatorial campaign, women's issues ignited a firestorm that blazed through the campaign trail in support of women everywhere. In February 2012, the Blunt Amendment of the Affordable Care Act proposed that employers deny the right to insurance coverage for women and family health coverage (i.e., requiring women to pay out of pocket and in full for birth control prescriptions and other women's health prevention costs) under the legal disguise of moral objections (Bassett, 2012). Elizabeth Warren and supporters of women's rights throughout the country began to recognize that without dedicated and passionate representation in Washington old school career politicians would continue voting against equality for women and families.

With a unified front of support from the middle class Elizabeth Warren won the most closely monitored Senatorial race, becoming the first female senator of Massachusetts (McCrummen, 2012). The passionate representation of leadership represented by Elizabeth Warren is best described as a "fighter for the middle class and a champion of women's causes" (Seelye, 2012, para. 7). Moments before the election results were announced, Elizabeth reminisced about whether her mother would have been happy with her decision to "venture out" just as she had observed her mother do so many years ago, as she donned that black dress (Warren, 2014, p. 270).

During her time in the Congress, Senator Warren has continued to advocate for those who don't have a voice, to bridge the gender gap, to provide fair opportunities for the American populace, and to hold big banks accountable to their customers—from her support of bills related to mental health, equality in the workplace, women's health, social security fairness, and countless others; Elizabeth also introduced the Bank of Student Loan Fairness Act to provide students the opportunity to borrow money at the same interest rates as big banks (S. 2432, 2013 2013). While the bill did not pass, Elizabeth continues to work for the equality and opportunity of America's future (Warren, 2014).

TIME magazine did a cover story on "The New Sheriffs of Wall Street," reflecting the accomplishments of three major women role models in Washington finance (Scherer, 2010). Mary Schapiro, Sheila Bair, and Elizabeth Warren represent the sheriffs who utilized their knowledge and unique perspectives to repair the damage Wall Street has done to the American people. In May 2010, large banks employed significantly fewer women in senior positions and Fortune 500 companies had less than 3% of women as CEOs (Scherer, 2010). Each of the women represented in the *TIME* article did not dream of becoming corporate leaders or Wall Street billionaires, but their fascination with economic policy and their determination to fix a broken system led them to break the glass ceiling and stand up against a male-dominated financial industry. Some may argue that without access to the elite finance club, women do not have the capacity to understand its inner workings. As an "outsider" Elizabeth Warren reflects on these claims and retorts, "Not being in the club means never drinking the club's Kool-Aid" (Warren, 2014, p. 123). By learning about the banking system away from high-society cigars and golf, she was able to utilize the same knowledge as her male counterparts but with a different end goal, that of protect working-class families.

A new Washington start-up company, Quorum, designed to provide quantitative insight into the workings of U.S. politics discovered that within the current 114th Congress, a record number of 104 women hold elected positions (Klein, 2015). Quorum data analysis established that congresswomen are more productive in producing and passing legislation than their male counterparts. Female senators introduced an average of 25.59 more bills than male congressmen. In addition, female senators demonstrate greater bipartisan action and collaboration across party lines (Klein, 2015). When the government shut down for 16 days in 2013, 20 female senators rose above petty partisan politics and worked together to find common ground (Newton-Small, 2013).

The key power differential in the organization of female politicians stems from an unspoken unity across party lines. In fact, *TIME* magazine reported that congresswomen have the benefits of their male counterparts, as well as mentorship for junior congresswomen, bridal and baby showers, and play dates for children and grandchildren (Newton-Small, 2013). These social gatherings dissolve political tension and focus political controversies back onto the context of the American people and the American family. Women actively listen to the needs of their constituencies and echo those voices into a productive dialogue regardless of political affiliation. The growth of women in the U.S. Congress is a game changer that is slowly, but surely dissipating the smoke and secrets of a formerly cigar-infused, male-dominated establishment. As women blur the gender lines to utilize their strengths and learn from each other's experiences, they are able to build a legacy that will continue throughout generations of women to come. In order to continue this legacy, it is the responsibility of the next generation to become educated on topics about which they are passionate, observant of issues confronting their communities that require change, and supportive of individuals prepared to advocate *for* their constituencies.

Young women can relate to the powerful underlying theme of Elizabeth's story: united we stand but divided we fall. Her parents modeled a life of making ends meet with significant economic constraints, while trying to do what was best for the development of their children. Elizabeth, like many of her fellow congresswomen, noticed unfair statues that negatively influenced working-class families through their personal experiences and chose to do something about it. By juggling traditional and nontraditional roles, women see the influence of public policy not simply through one lens but rather an array of lenses—wife, mother, daughter, employer, employee, and student, to name a few. Elizabeth's perception of policy making is divergent from her fellow male counterparts because it encompasses the viewpoints of heterogeneous roles. The diversity of roles and responsibilities encompasses the attitudes and issues relevant to her constituency. Women provide an unparalleled familiarity, not only with the problems of our community but also with an incomparable perspective of the solutions.

The significance of Elizabeth Warren's story comes not simply from her memoirs of the campaign trail and policies aimed at the protection of regular families, but in the precious and timeless moments of her own personal life woven into the everyday career-driven advocacy for a new America. Through love, loss, and the unwavering support of family, these messy, yet, wonderful life events bring perspective to the jumbled legal jargon that often complicates public policy. These moments remind everyday people what the policies are really about. Role models, such as Elizabeth Warren, provide evidence to women everywhere that individual experiences *do* matter and can influence change. As we light a candle of appreciation for the women who have exposed the tainted underbelly of Washington politics, we pass the torch onto the next generation of women ready to stand center stage and ignite a transformation within Congress.

With more women in Congress this transformation can utilize the unique female perspective to personify the American people's voice and create a timeless legacy for future generations upon which to build.

REFERENCES

Bank on Students Emergency Loan Refinancing Act, S. 2432, 113th Cong. (2013).

Bassett, L. (2012, March 1). Blunt amendment vote: Contraception measure fails in Senate. *The Huffington Post.* Retrieved from http://www.huffington post.com/2012/03/01/blunt-amendment-vote-fails-senate-contraception_ n_1313287.html.

Havemann, J. (2015). The financial crisis of 2008: Year in review 2008. *Encyclopæ-dia Britannica.* Retrieved from http://www.britannica.com/EBchecked/ topic/1484264/TheFinancial-Crisis-of-2008-Year-In-Review-2008.

Hicks, J. (2012, September 28). Everything you need to know about Elizabeth Warren's claim of Native American heritage. *The Washington Post.* Retrieved from http://www.washingtonpost.com/blogs/fact-checker/post/ everything-you-need-to-know-about-the-controversy-over-elizabeth-warrens-claimed-native-american-heritage/2012/09/27/d0b7f568-08a5-11e2-a10c-fa5a255a9258_blog.html.

Klein, M. (2015, February 19). Working together and across the aisle, female senators pass more legislation than male colleagues [Web log post]. Retrieved from https://www.quorum.us/blog/women-work-together-pass-more-legislation/.

McCrummen, S. (2012, November 6). Elizabeth Warren defeats Scott Brown in Mas-sachusetts Senate race. *The Washington Post.* Retrieved from http://www. washingtonpost.com/politics/decision2012/elizabeth-warren-defeats-scott-brown-in-massachusetts-senate-race/2012/11/06/7de2b4a4-27b3-11e2-b2a0-ae18d6159439_story.html.

Newton-Small, J. (2013, October). Women are the only adults left in Wash-ington. *TIME.* Retrieved from http://swampland.time.com/2013/10/16/ women-are-the-only-adults-left-in-washington/.

Scherer, M. (2010, May). The new sheriffs of wall street. *TIME.* Retrieved from http://content.time.com/time/magazine/article/0,9171,1989144-1,00.html.

Seelye, K. (2012, November 6). Warren defeats Brown in Massachusetts Senate contest. *The New York Times.* Retrieved from http://www.nytimes.com/2012/ 11/07/us/politics/elizabeth-warren-massachusetts-senate-scott-brown. html?_r=1.

Sherman, M. (2009). *A short history of financial deregulation in the United States.* Retrieved from http://www.cepr.net/documents/publications/dereg-timeline-2009-07.pdf.

Sullivan, T., Warren, E., & Westbrook, J. (1999). *As we forgive our debtors: Bankruptcy and consumer credit in America.* New York, NY: Oxford University Press.

Warren, E. (2014). *A fighting chance.* New York, NY: Metropolitan Books.

Congresswoman Ileana Ros-Lehtinen

Congresswoman Ileana Ros-Lehtinen represents Florida's 27th Congressional District, which includes Coral Gables, Cutler Bay, Hialeah, Key Biscayne, Little Havana, Miami, Pinecrest, South Miami, and Westchester. According to Congresswoman Ros-Lehtinen,

> I was born in Havana, Cuba in July, 1952. At the age of eight, my family and I were forced to flee from the oppressive communist regime of Fidel Castro. We settled in Miami and put down permanent roots in our community. . . . I earned an Associate of Arts degree from Miami-Dade Community College in 1972, Bachelors and Masters Degree in Education from Florida International University in 1975 and 1985 respectively, and a Doctorate in Education from the University of Miami in 2004. . . . In 1982, I was elected to the Florida State House of Representatives and the Florida Senate in 1986, becoming the first Hispanic woman to serve in either body. . . . I was elected to the U.S. House of Representatives in 1989—the first Hispanic woman to serve in Congress. I have been strongly returned to Congress since, running unopposed in 2014. . . . Given my background in education, I have worked to strengthen the Head Start Program. I am a strong advocate of programs that address the serious problem of domestic violence against women. I was a lead sponsor of the reauthorization of the Violence Against Women Act, which increases resources toward the prosecution of domestic violence, dating violence, and sexual assault.

Source: http://ros-lehtinen.house.gov/.

Chapter 7

Evaluation of Female Leaders: Stereotypes, Prejudice, and Discrimination[*]

Susan A. Basow

In 1982, Ann Hopkins was denied partnership at Price Waterhouse, one of the top accounting firms in the United States, despite her stellar record, including having produced more billable hours than any other candidate up for partnership that year. Out of 88 candidates proposed for partner, she was the only woman; in fact, out of a total of 662 company partners, only 7 were women. Hopkins sued on the basis of sex discrimination and won at every level, including the Supreme Court (*Price Waterhouse v. Hopkins,* 1989). The sex discrimination argument rested on evidence that Hopkins had been denigrated for behavior that would have merited praise had it been evidenced by a man: she was evaluated as tough, aggressive, no-nonsense, and driven. One evaluator had suggested she could improve her chances of making partner if she would "walk more femininely, talk more femininely, dress more femininely, wear make-up" (Fiske, Bersoff, Borgida, Deaux, & Heilman, 1991, p. 1050). This landmark case relied

---

[*]Portions of this chapter were previously published in M. Paludi & B. Coates (Eds.). (2011). *Women as transformational leaders, vol. 1: Cultural and organizational stereotypes, prejudice and discrimination* (pp. 51–67). Santa Barbara, CA: Praeger.

heavily on the amicus curiae brief submitted by the American Psychological Association, which documented how women being evaluated for leadership positions are frequently in a double bind: if they engage in the same behaviors as their male counterparts, they may be perceived negatively; if they don't engage in the same behaviors as their male counterparts, they also may be perceived negatively.

Women are underrepresented in leadership positions in all professions, including politics, despite evidence that they can be effective leaders (Eagly, 2007). Due to gender stereotypes, however, women leaders are often not thought of or perceived as effective. Cultural expectations of women (to be nurturant, sensitive, kind) only partially overlap with cultural expectations of leaders (to be assertive, dominant, competent); in contrast, cultural expectations of men overlap nearly completely with expectations of leaders. Women who display the traits expected of leaders are at risk for being considered unfeminine (Kanter's [1993] "Iron Maiden" role); this appears to be what happened to Ann Hopkins at Price Waterhouse. Yet women who display the traits expected of women are at risk for not being perceived as leader-like (Kanter's Pet, Seductress, or Mother roles). Thus, to be seen positively as a leader, women must walk a fine line (the area of overlap): being assertive but not overly so; being dominant but still interpersonally sensitive; being competent but still likeable. As Catalyst (2007), the nonprofit organization working to build inclusive workplaces, so aptly described the results of its research on executives' perception of women leaders, women in leadership positions are in a double bind: "Damned if you do [conform to female or leader stereotypes], doomed if you don't." The brief biographies of women in Congress that are presented in this volume illustrate the double bind women in political office face; they are evaluated both as women and as women trying to get into a man's domain. Most evaluations of women politicians are negative as a result.

EVALUATING LEADERS

Evaluations of leaders are built on basic psychological processes of interpersonal perception, interpretation, and judgments. As social psychologists have long demonstrated, what we perceive is based substantially on what we expect to perceive. If we expect someone to be kind to us and instead that person reminds us of something we haven't yet done, we may get offended and perceive that person as overly critical. However, if we expect a person to be a stern taskmaster and that person reminds us of the same unfinished task, we are likely to have a less negative reaction; indeed, we may even appreciate the reminder. It is same behavior but different reactions based on our expectations.

Gender (as well as other) stereotypes can be viewed as a set of expectations about how each gender does or should act. Stereotypes also serve as cognitive filters through which we perceive behavior. A strongly worded statement issued by a male politician might be viewed as a sign of his authority, confidence, or power. The same statement issued by a woman politician might be viewed as a sign of her high-handedness, demandingness, or coldness.

Because gender is confounded by status differences, with men as a group viewed as higher in status than women as a group, women leaders have to contend with perceptions of role incongruity based not only on gender but also on status. As role incongruity theory (Eagly & Karau, 2002; Eagly & Koenig, 2008) suggests, people whose behaviors or traits match expectations (based on roles or status) tend to be perceived more positively than people whose behaviors or traits contradict expectations. High-status individual (e.g., men) are assumed to be competent; thus, it is harder for men to demonstrate incompetence than it is for a woman (Foschi, 2000). Conversely, because lower-status individuals (e.g., women) are expected not to be competent, it is harder for them to demonstrate excellence or competence than for higher-status individuals. For example, if a male leader makes an error of judgment, he's likely to be given the benefit of the doubt (e.g., "perhaps he was too busy to give the matter sufficient attention"). The same error by a female leader is likely to be viewed as confirmation that she is not a good leader. In contrast, an effective decision made by a male leader is likely to confirm his competence, whereas the same decision may be viewed as "lucky" if made by a female leader.

Indeed, recent research confirms that white male trainees who make performance-related mistakes are less likely to have these noted in a formal performance log than are the same mistakes made by white female trainees (Biernat, Fuegen, & Kobrynowicz, 2010). The explanation is that since white men are expected to be competent, when they make mistakes, the mistakes are likely to be noted but not taken as signs of incompetence. However, because women (and blacks) are expected to be incompetent, when they make mistakes, the mistakes are taken as confirmation of their lower level of ability. Thus, it is easier for women leaders to be viewed as incompetent than it is for their male counterparts.

As these findings suggest, evaluators tend to use different standards when judging women and men (Biernat, 2003; Biernat et al., 2010). Because men leaders are the norm, their behaviors and styles set the standard. Employees who have a male supervisor typically talk about their "boss"; employees who have a female supervisor typically talk about their "female boss." People talk about "senators" and "congressmembers"; the same individuals often "mark" the occupation, referring to "woman senator" or "woman congressmember." Not surprisingly, then, when women leaders are evaluated, their gender is usually salient, and their behavior is judged against what is expected "for a woman."

Overall, women leaders often must work harder to be perceived as equally competent as their male counterparts, and it is far easier for them to "fall from grace" than their male counterparts as well. This is exactly what the Catalyst (2007) study found regarding women executives: they are judged by higher competency standards than are men while receiving lower rewards and having to repeatedly prove themselves.

Two of the major dimensions that people use in evaluating others are competency and likeability/warmth. Gender stereotypes are directly related to these dimensions, with men in general being viewed as more competent than women and women in general being viewed as more warm and likeable than men (Cikara & Fiske, 2009; Fiske, Cuddy, Glick, & Xu, 2002). Although these dimensions are orthogonal to each other (one can be high, or low, on both dimensions at the same time), gender stereotypes operate to make them seem like opposites. That is, when women are perceived as competent, they often are perceived as less likeable than when they are perceived as less competent. The reverse is true for men: when they are perceived as less competent, they are less liked. The Catalyst (2007) study found strong evidence of this pattern: women leaders could be perceived as competent or likeable, but they rarely were perceived as both.

Overall, although male leaders certainly can be evaluated negatively, they at least start from a position of role congruence. In contrast, female leaders typically start from a position of incongruence in their leader role. As we will see in the next section, additional factors related to role incongruence can further affect evaluations of women leaders.

FACTORS AFFECTING EVALUATIONS OF WOMEN LEADERS

There are many factors that affect evaluations of women leaders: gender-typed behaviors, interests, traits; the maternal "penalty"; contextual factors; and rater factors.

Gender-Typed Attributes

Women are expected to exhibit such "feminine" behaviors as nurturance, compassion, sensitivity, and "niceness," that is, to be communal—interpersonally oriented and interpersonally skilled. Yet leaders are expected to exhibit such "masculine" behaviors as dominance, agency, and competitiveness, that is, to be agentic—task oriented and focused. Numerous research studies have documented that women who display agentic behaviors may be denigrated unless they also show evidence of the expected communal behaviors (Eagly & Carli, 2007; Heilman & Okimoto, 2007; Rudman & Fairchild, 2004). For example, although women who display strong agentic traits may be rated as highly competent, they also may be rated as socially deficient.

In addition to this backlash effect, women may have to deal with shifting evaluative criteria. For example, although a strong female applicant may be rated more favorably than a similarly qualified man, he still may be more likely to be hired for an executive position (Biernat & Kobrynow-icz, 1997). It appears that raters tend to evaluate a woman against others of her gender (e.g., "she's really assertive *for a woman*"), whereas a man tends be judged against a more absolute standard ("he's really assertive"). For hiring decisions, the absolute standard is more likely to be relied upon.

Another form of shifting evaluative criteria also occurs. As Phelan, Moss-Racusin, and Rudman (2008) found, women who display agentic qualities not only may be rated lower in social skills than an identically described man, but such ratings of women's (lower) social skills figure more prominently in decisions to hire the woman for a leadership position than the man. Thus, agentic women may be "doubly disadvantaged": they may be perceived as socially unskilled, *and* their competence may be deemphasized when employment-related decisions are made. Presenting oneself as primarily communal, however, won't necessarily help; women with a strong communal focus also are perceived as less competent than their more agentic sisters. Thus, the double bind for professional women is whether they are agentic or communal, they are less likely to be hired for a leadership position than their male counterpart.

Because women are expected to be kinder than men, the expression of anger, in particular, may be a challenge for women professionals, especially for women politicians and women candidates for political office. Brescoll and Uhlmann (2008) conducted a series of studies and found that when a male professional expressed anger in a videotaped interview, raters evaluated his status and his competence more highly (or the same), mainly because his anger typically was attributed to the situation (e.g., "his colleagues' behavior caused his anger"). In contrast, when a female professional expressed anger, her status and perceived competence decreased, mainly because raters attributed her emotional reactions to her personality (e.g., "she's an angry person"). Thus, women leaders need to take pains to provide objective external reasons for their negative emotions; elsewise, they run the risk of being perceived as a "witch."

Because of the backlash effect and the shifting standards of evaluation of female leaders, it is perhaps not surprising that women leaders often use different leadership styles than men leaders. In particular, compared to their male counterparts, women leaders are more likely to use a transformational leadership style (one in which the leader supports and empowers her followers, inspiring them to reach their potential) as well as provide contingent rewards for a subordinate's satisfactory performance (Eagly, Johannesen-Schmidt, & van Engen, 2003; Yoder, 2001). This transformational leadership style, combining both agentic and communal qualities, appears to fit the narrow area of overlap. Fortunately, this leadership style typically has been found to be very effective for both men and women (Eagly, 2007; Eagly et al., 2003), although perhaps more so for women (Ayman, Korabik, & Morris, 2009).

From the research literature, we can conclude that to be effective and evaluated positively, women leaders need to find a good way to balance authority and friendliness, that is, to demonstrate both strong agentic and communal qualities (Ayman & Korabik, 2010; Basow, Phelan, & Capotosto, 2006; Carli, LaFleur, & Loeber, 1995; Eagly & Carli, 2007; Friedman & Yorio, 2006; Heilman & Okimoto, 2007). This is not an easy thing to do, because women who smile too much or who display too much emotion may also be seen as not leadership material (Friedman & Yorio, 2006; Phelan et al., 2008).

Overall, women leaders are evaluated through the lens of gender stereotypes. Although many women have found ways to be effective leaders, having to find the "right" balance represents an extra burden on women that men who aspire to, or who are in, leadership positions do not have.

Maternal Penalty

An additional factor that affects women leaders is motherhood. Besides the very real challenges of balancing work and family life for employed women who still typically carry the predominant burden of childcare responsibilities are the stereotypic perceptions of mothers. As research has documented (Correll, Benard, & Paik, 2007; Cuddy, Fiske, & Glick, 2004), when raters are asked to evaluate male and female managers or consultants who are equally qualified, a woman who also is portrayed as a mother is perceived as less competent and less promotable, and is paid less, than the same woman who is not a mother. For men, not only is being a parent not a strike against them, but in some cases they actually are paid more than their nonparent male counterpart. Indeed, the pay gap between mothers and non-mothers is larger than the pay gap between women and men (Avellar & Smock, 2003; Crittenden, 2001).

The explanation for this "motherhood penalty" rests on two related factors: the stereotypes of mothers as not being committed workers (Correll et al., 2007) and the lower status attributed to "mothers" compared to "employees" (Ridgeway & Correll, 2004). For men, being a father does not signal a negative change in status; indeed, fathers may be viewed as even more responsible and committed to the job than their nonparent counterparts. Because of their lower status, employees who are mothers appear to be judged by a harsher standard than are employees who are non-mothers (Correll et al., 2007). This dynamic is identical to the harsher standard applied to women as a group compared to men as a group, as described earlier. In many ways, the difference in standards is more pronounced when based on employee parental status than it is when based on employee gender.

Pregnancy itself can also be a discriminatory cue, since it reminds observers of women's traditional child-rearing role. Glick and Fiske (2007) review research that documents that women are more likely to be patronized and viewed as incompetent when pregnant than when not pregnant. They are particularly unlikely to be viewed as suited for a leadership position.

Given the earlier discussion, it is perhaps not surprising that female leaders are less likely to be married and/or to have children than are their male counterparts (Lyness & Thompson, 1997). Even when they are married or are mothers, women executives often take pains to keep their personal and professional identities separate.

In general, cues that trigger traditional female stereotypes (e.g., pregnancy and motherhood) are associated with more discriminatory evaluations of professional women since communal traits in women are seen as antithetical to the agentic traits expected in leadership positions.

Congresswoman Linda Sanchez once quipped:

> You can't be the perfect member of Congress and the perfect mother 100 percent of the time. (http://www.brainyquote.com/quotes/quotes/l/lindasanch632587.html)

Only nine women have given birth while serving in the U.S. Congress (Keith, 2014).

Contextual Factors

As noted earlier, just by being in a leadership position, women are viewed as role incongruent and likely to be evaluated negatively. Two additional contextual factors affect evaluations as well: how gender-typical (or atypical) is the field and how many other women are present in the organization's leadership positions.

Not surprisingly, most discrimination (including use of shifting criteria) occurs against individuals who are in contexts viewed as nontraditional for their gender (Basow, 1995, 1998; Eagly & Carli, 2007; Glick & Fiske, 2007). Eagly's (2007) review of the research on female leadership found that favorable attitudes toward women as leaders have increased over the past 50 years except for workplace environments that are male dominated or are traditionally masculine, such as the military or high-status political office. It is only in such contexts that women's leadership effectiveness is actually rated lower than men's, probably because these environments are most inconsistent with stereotypes of women.

A related contextual factor is how isolated a particular woman leader is in her organization. When fewer than 20% of leadership positions are held by a woman (as is typically the case in the top positions in business, education, and politics), her gender becomes a salient characteristic (Fiske et al., 1991; Glick & Fiske, 2007; Kanter, 1993; Yoder, 2001).

Moss Kanter's (1993) study of women in corporations found that gender stereotyping is most likely to occur when women are so numerically in the minority that they are viewed as "token" hires. In such cases, coworkers and supervisors, who are unused to working with women in positions of authority, are likely to try to typecast the woman into one of four female stereotypes: the Pet (liked but incompetent; child-like; naïve); the Mom (nurturant but not viewed as competent); the Seductress (the sex object; desirable but not competent); or the Iron Maiden (competent but unfeeling and unlikeable). None of these roles facilitate positive leadership evaluations. These reactions to women aspiring to traditionally male positions were evident in the 2009 U.S. presidential campaign. Hillary Clinton, a contender for the Democratic nomination, was typically typecast as the Iron Maiden and criticized for wearing pantsuits and lack of warmth. Sarah Palin, the Republican vice-presidential candidate, was typically typecast variously in the other three roles: the Pet (cute but not very smart), the Seductress (emphasis on her beauty pageant experience and looks), or the Mom (emphasis on her family role and children). Gender stereotyping thus affected evaluations of women leaders for these traditionally masculine positions in politics, positions never held by a woman.

Another contextual factor relevant for evaluations of women leaders is the "glass cliff" phenomenon (Ryan & Haslam, 2005; Ryan, Haslam, & Kulich, 2010). Archival research of 100 major corporations in the United Kingdom documented that women were most likely to attain leadership positions (in this case, be appointed a member of the board of directors) when the organization had already been experiencing declining performance in the preceding five months. In contrast, when an organization was doing very well, women were less likely to be put in leadership positions than were men. A similar pattern has been found in politics. Women are more likely to be put forward as political candidates when the contest is viewed as risky, while men are more likely to be candidates for contests that are viewed as safe. Such risky high-profile positions put women leaders under more scrutiny and more stress, and it's likely that they subsequently get more blame for "failure" (e.g., not being able to reverse a company's declining performance; losing an election) than their male counterparts.

Overall, gender stereotyping and negative evaluations of women leaders are most marked in traditionally male or masculine contexts. Furthermore, women leaders are more likely than men to be in risky leadership positions that may further intensify how they get evaluated.

Rater Characteristics

There are several rater characteristics that contribute to an individual's likelihood of discriminating against women leaders: rater gender and rater attitudes toward women and gender roles. These, of course, are related since men compared to women tend to hold more traditional attitudes toward women and gender roles, and to ascribe to higher levels of hostile sexism (Glick & Fiske, 2007; Twenge, 1997). Because men tend to hold more *prescriptive* stereotypes regarding what women *should and should not* do than do women, men are more likely to commit many forms of hostile discrimination, including sexual harassment. Although many studies find that both men and women discriminate against women (Glick & Fiske, 2007), male raters appear to be particularly likely to use gender stereotypes when rating female professionals (Carli, 2001; Eagly, 2007; Eagly & Karau, 2002). Men also appear to be particularly sensitive to the previously described variables that affect leadership evaluation: gender-related attributes of the leader and the gendered aspects of the work context. In other words, men are particularly likely to discriminate against women leaders who do not display traditionally feminine qualities, especially when the work environment is traditionally male/masculine.

Male subordinates may have a particularly challenging time when they receive a negative evaluation from a female superior (Sinclair & Kunda, 2000). Although no one likes to receive a negative evaluation, men who do so from a woman tend to devalue her competence significantly more than they do from a man who provides the identical evaluation. The reasons for this pattern are likely to be two-fold: the woman supervisor is violating gender stereotypes of being nurturant and kind; she also is demonstrating power and status over the man, thereby violating her ascribed lower status. His devaluation of her is one way for him to regain some power and control.

Not only might men be more likely than women to apply gender stereotypes to women leaders who are nontraditional in some way, but their views can affect those of others, even when the form this discrimination takes is very subtle. As Glick and Fiske (2001) documented, sexism can take two forms: *hostile sexism,* which reflects negative attitudes toward women who challenge traditional gender norms; and *benevolent sexism,* which reflects a paternalistic view of women as "wonderful but weak." These attitudes are correlated with each other, although many people have difficulty recognizing benevolent sexism as a form of discrimination against women since it seems to be associated with "positive" views of women. Its discriminatory aspect is mainly apparent when women step out of traditional female roles and behaviors.

Good and Rudman (2010) recently found that when a female job applicant for a traditionally male position (a managerial job at a large warehouse-style retail store that required masculine skills and behaviors, such as locking up late at night) was interviewed by a male interviewer, the ratings of evaluators who read the interview transcript were strongly affected by the interviewer's sexist attitudes as well as their own.

In particular, when the male interviewer displayed either hostile sexism (e.g., stating that most women are not qualified for such a job) or benevolent sexism (e.g., stating that male coworkers could help the "nice young lady"), the female job applicant's competence was evaluated negatively and she was less likely to be hired than if the interviewer was nonsexist, at least when the male interviewer himself was viewed favorably. Because benevolent sexism is often unrecognized as such, male interviewers who exhibited such behaviors often were viewed quite favorably. This meant that the female job applicant who had a benevolently sexist interviewer was very likely to be rated poorly, especially when the evaluators themselves scored high in hostile sexism. It appears that the kind of protective paternalism exhibited by the interviewer's benevolent sexism "unleashed" the evaluator's own negative attitudes toward aspiring career women. Thus, both kinds of sexism can negatively affect women leaders either directly or indirectly.

As suggested by the previous findings, evaluators' attitudes toward women and gender roles may be a key factor in evaluating women leaders, more important than evaluator gender per se. Thus, women with traditional attitudes toward women and gender roles also tend to show negative attitudes toward women leaders, especially if such leaders are nontraditional (i.e., have strong agentic qualities, or are in a field that is traditionally masculine) (Cooper, 1997; Forsyth, Heiney, & Wright, 1997). Other rater attitudes that may contribute to negative evaluations of women leaders are high social dominance orientation, as well as strong beliefs in a just world (Oldmeadow & Fiske, 2007). People who are high in these two beliefs, both of which serve to justify social inequalities, are more likely to link low-status groups (e.g., women) with incompetence than are people who are low in such beliefs. Thus, it may be harder for individuals with such attitudes toward inequality to evaluate women leaders positively.

Overall, evaluators with traditional attitudes toward gender roles, who are most likely to be men, are most likely to negatively evaluate women leaders, especially if the leader appears nontraditional.

SUMMARY

Women in leadership position face unique obstacles due to gender stereotypes. First, they are placed in a double bind due to their perceived role incongruence: if they conform to expectations of femininity, they are unlikely to be viewed as leadership material; however if they conform to expectations of (agentic) leaders, they are likely to be viewed as unfeminine. In either case, they may be perceived negatively. Women leaders must walk a fine line, combining both communal and agentic behaviors, warmth and competence, in strategic ways, in order to be perceived positively.

Some women leaders face more obstacles than others when it comes to being evaluated fairly. Women who are nontraditional in some way (personal style, traits, appearance), or who are in positions not traditionally held by women, face added scrutiny. Such women leaders are likely to experience backlash whereby their competence is both under-recognized and devalued. They may be held to higher standards, as well as put in riskier leadership positions, than their male counterparts. Any behavior that signals traditional female roles, such as pregnancy and motherhood, increases the likelihood of negative ratings of competence and leadership. Those most likely to engage in such discriminatory evaluations are those with traditional attitudes toward women and gender roles, as well as those with a strong belief in the need for social hierarchies and a just world. Women and men both can possess such beliefs, but men tend to do so more than women.

The Catalyst (2007) study of executives' attitudes toward women leaders also explored how women executives coped with some of the challenges. Four main strategies were employed, representing a wide range of styles: confronting the inequitable situation quickly and directly, demonstrating overtly that you have the skills and competence needed for the job, utilizing clear and effective communication, and minimizing the salience of gender. Of course, organizational strategies are needed as well, to ensure gender equity in the workplace.

Although the factors affecting evaluations of women leaders discussed in this chapter clearly are challenging, there is room for optimism. As more women attain positions of leadership, their "token" status will be eliminated and the salience of gender stereotypes will be reduced (see Introduction to this volume with respect to the impact of having more women elected to the U.S. Senate and House of Representatives). Furthermore, the most negative attitudes toward women leaders are expressed by those who have not actually had a woman leader. For example, employees who have actual experience with women leaders tend to rate them similarly to men leaders (Eagly, 2007). Thus, as more people have experience with women in positions of power, some of the negative expectancies should be modified. Finally, women leaders have been found to be as effective as (or even more effective than) their male counterparts. This is addressed in the Introduction to this volume: women do as well as or better than men in both Houses of Congress. As our understanding of effective leadership expands to include transformational leadership, expectations of leaders will come to include empowerment and communication skills, and, hopefully, expectations of women will come to include competence. Indeed, favorable attitudes toward women as leaders have increased over the past 50 years; it is likely that this trend will continue. Given the strength of gender stereotypes, however, it is unlikely that gender will ever be a non-issue.

REFERENCES

Avellar, S., & Smock, P. J. (2003). Has the price of motherhood declined over time? A cross-cohort comparison of the motherhood wage penalty. *Journal of Marriage and Family, 65,* 597–607.

Ayman, R., & Korabik, K. (2010). Leadership: Why gender and culture matter. *American Psychologist, 65,* 157–170.

Ayman, R., Korabik, K., & Morris, S. (2009). Is transformational leadership always perceived as effective? Male subordinates' devaluation of female transformational leaders. *Journal of Applied Social Psychology, 39,* 852–879.

Basow, S. A. (1995). Student evaluations of college professors: When gender matters. *Journal of Educational Psychology, 87,* 656–665.

Basow, S. A. (1998). Student evaluations: The role of gender bias and teaching styles. In L. H. Collins, J. C. Chrisler, & K. Quina (Eds.), *Career strategies for women in academe: Arming Athena* (pp. 135–156). Thousand Oaks, CA: Sage.

Basow, S. A., Phelan, J., & Capotosto, L. (2006). Gender patterns in college students' choices of their best and worst professors. *Psychology of Women Quarterly, 30,* 25–35.

Biernat, M. (2003). Toward a broader view of social stereotyping. *American Psychologist, 58,* 1019–1027.

Biernat, M., Fuegen, K., & Kobrynowicz, D. (2010). Shifting standards and the inference of incompetence: Effects of formal and informal evaluation tools. *Personality and Social Psychology Bulletin, 36,* 855–868.

Biernat, M., & Kobrynowicz, D. (1997). Gender- and race-based standards of competence: Lower minimum standards but higher ability standards for devalued groups. *Journal of Personality & Social Psychology, 72,* 544–557.

Brescoll, V. L., & Uhlmann, E. L. (2008). Can an angry woman get ahead? Status conferral, gender, and expression of emotion in the workplace. *Psychological Science, 19,* 268–275.

Carli, L. L. (2001). Gender and social influence. *Journal of Social Issues, 57,* 725–741.

Carli, L. L., LaFleur, S. J., & Loeber, C. C. (1995). Nonverbal behavior, gender, and influence. *Journal of Personality & Social Psychology, 68,* 1030–1041.

Catalyst. (2007). *The double-bind dilemma for women in leadership: Damned if you do, doomed if you don't.* New York, NY: Author.

Cikara, M., & Fiske, S. T. (2009). Warmth, competence, and ambivalent sexism: Vertical assault and collateral damage. In M. Barreto, M. K. Ryan, & M. T. Schmitt (Eds.), *The glass ceiling in the 21st century: Understanding barriers to gender equality* (pp. 73–96). Washington, DC: American Psychological Association.

Cooper, V. W. (1997). Homophily or the Queen Bee Syndrome: Female evaluation of female leadership. *Small Group Research, 28,* 483–499.

Correll, S. J., Benard, S., & Paik, I. (2007). Getting a job: Is there a motherhood penalty? *American Journal of Sociology, 112,* 1297–1338.

Crittenden, A. (2001). *The price of motherhood.* New York, NY: Henry Holt and Co.

Cuddy, A. J. C., Fiske, S. T., & Glick, P. (2004). When professionals become mothers, warmth doesn't cut the ice. *Journal of Social Issues, 60,* 701–718.

Eagly, A. H. (2007). Female leadership advantage and disadvantage: Resolving the contradictions. *Psychology of Women Quarterly, 31,* 1–12.

Eagly, A. H., & Carli, L. L. (2007). *Through the labyrinth: The truth about how women become leaders.* Boston, MA: Harvard Business School.

Eagly, A. H., Johannesen-Schmidt, M. C., & van Engen, M. L. (2003). Transformational, transactional, and laissez-faire leadership styles: A meta-analysis comparing women and men. *Psychological Bulletin, 129,* 569–591.

Eagly, A. H., & Karau, S. J. (2002). Role congruity theory of prejudice toward female leaders. *Psychological Bulletin, 108,* 233–256.

Eagly, A. H., & Koenig, A. M. (2008). Gender prejudice: On the risks of occupying incongruent roles. In E. Borgida & S. T. Fiske (Eds.), *Beyond common sense: Psychological science in the courtroom* (pp. 63–81). Malden, MA: Blackwell Publishing.

Fiske, S. T., Bersoff, D. N., Borgida, E., Deaux, K., & Heilman, M. E. (1991). Social science research on trial: Use of sex stereotyping research in *Price Waterhouse v. Hopkins. American Psychologist, 46,* 1049–1060.

Fiske, S. T., Cuddy, A. J., Glick, P., & Xu, J. (2002). A model of (often mixed) stereotype content: Competence and warmth respectively follow from perceived status and competition. *Journal of Personality and Social Psychology, 82,* 878–902.

Forsyth, D. R., Heiney, M. M., & Wright, S. S. (1997). Biases in appraisals of women leaders. *Group Dynamics: Theory, Research, and Practice, 1,* 98–103.

Foschi, M. (2000). Double standards for competence: Theory and research. *Annual Review of Sociology, 26,* 21–42.

Friedman, C., & Yorio, K. (2006). *The girl's guide to being a boss (without being a bitch).* New York, NY: Morgan Road Books.

Glick, P., & Fiske, S. T. (2001). An ambivalent alliance: Hostile and benevolent sexism as complementary justifications for gender inequality. *American Psychologist, 56,* 109–118.

Glick, P., & Fiske, S. (2007). Sex discrimination: The psychological approach. In F. Crosby (Ed.), *Sex discrimination in the workplace: Multidisciplinary perspectives* (pp. 155–187). Malden, MA: Blackwell.

Good, J. J., & Rudman, L. A. (2010). When female applicants meet sexist interviewers: The cost of being a target of benevolent sexism. *Sex Roles, 62,* 481–493.

Heilman, M. E., & Okimoto, T. G. (2007). Why are women penalized for success at male tasks? The implied communality deficit. *Journal of Applied Psychology, 92,* 81–92.

Kanter, R. M. (1993). *Men and women of the corporation,* 2nd ed. New York, NY: Basic Books.

Keith, T. (2014). *For moms in congress, votes mix with diapers and school pickup.* Retrieved June 16, 2015, from http://www.npr.org/2014/05/09/310256866/for-moms-in-congress-votes-mix-with-diapers-and-school-pickup.

Lyness, K. S., & Thompson, D. E. (1997). Above the glass ceiling? A comparison of matched samples of male and male executives. *Journal of Applied Psychology, 82,* 359–375.

Oldmeadow, J., & Fiske, S. T. (2007). System-justifying ideologies moderate status = competence stereotypes: Roles for belief in a just world and social dominance orientation. *European Journal of Social Psychology, 37,* 1135–1148.

Phelan, J. E., Moss-Racusin, C. A., & Rudman, L. A. (2008). Competent yet out in the cold: Shifting criteria for hiring reflect backlash toward agentic women. *Psychology of Women Quarterly, 32,* 406–413.

Price Waterhouse v. Hopkins, 490 U.S. 228 (1989).

Ridgeway, C. L., & Correll, S. J. (2004). Motherhood as a status characteristic. *Journal of Social Issues, 60,* 683–700.

Rudman, L. A., & Fairchild, K. (2004). Reactions to counterstereotypic behavior: The role of backlash. *Journal of Personality and Social Psychology, 87,* 157–176.

Ryan, M. K., & Haslam, S. (2005). The Glass Cliff: Evidence that women are over-represented in precarious leadership positions. *British Journal of Management, 16*(2), 81–90.

Ryan, M. K., Haslam, S. A., & Kulich, C. (2010). Politics and the glass cliff: Evidence that women are preferentially selected to contest hard-to-win seats. *Psychology of Women Quarterly, 34,* 56–64.

Sinclair, L., & Kunda, Z. (2000). Motivated stereotyping of women: She's fine if she praised me but incompetent if she criticized me. *Personality and Social Psychology Bulletin, 26,* 1329–1342.

Twenge, J. M. (1997). Attitudes toward women, 1970–1995: A meta-analysis. *Psychology of Women Quarterly, 21,* 35–51.

Yoder, J. (2001). Making leadership work more effectively for women. *Journal of Social Issues, 57,* 815–828.

Congresswoman Maxine Waters

Congresswoman Maxine Waters represents the 43rd Congressional District of California, representing South Central Los Angeles, including Westchester, Playa Del Rey, Watts, Lennox, West Athens, West Carson, Harbor Gateway, Lawndale, Lomita, Torrance, Hawthorne, Inglewood, Gardena, and El Camino Village.

Congresswoman Waters is the cofounder of Black Women's Forum, an organization of more than 1,200 African American women in Los Angeles. She has been a strong advocate for human rights and health care. Funding for the Minority AIDS Initiative has increased from $156 million in 1999 to $400 million per year currently under her leadership. Congresswoman Waters has also authored legislation to expand health services for individuals with Alzheimer's disease, diabetes, and cancer. In addition, she has been a strong advocate for the reauthorization of the Violence Against Women Act, legislation that prohibits job discrimination based on sexual orientation, and for enforcing anti-gay hate crimes. According to Congresswoman Waters, "If you believe in something, you must be prepared to fight. To argue. To persuade. To introduce legislation again and again and again."

Source: http://waters.house.gov/.

Chapter 8

Social Stigma Faced by Female Leaders[*]

Whitney Botsford Morgan, Veronica L. Gilrane, Tracy C. McCausland, and Eden B. King

SOCIAL STIGMA

As several of the chapters in this volume have addressed, there is still a relative absence of women in elected office in the United States. One explanation offered for this reality is that both women and men voters stereotype candidates based on the candidates' biological sex (Schneider & Bos, 2013). This stereotyping is related to social stigma. Social stigma is a devalued social identity that is socially discrediting and prevents an individual from being fully accepted (Goffman, 1963). Social stigma essentially presents an individual with an unwanted label or set of characteristics that remain with the person. Crocker, Major, and Steele (1998) discussed potential outcomes of stigma that include being the target of negative stereotypes, social rejection, discrimination, and economic disadvantage. Central to the concept of stigma is that discriminatory behavior occurs only under certain situational circumstances. Eagly and Carli (2003) specified that women encounter discriminatory behaviors when in situations that are male dominated and when there are male evaluators. More recently,

*Portions of this chapter were published in M. Paludi & B. Coates (Eds.). (2011). *Women as transformational leaders, vol. 1: Cultural and organizational stereotypes, prejudice and discrimination* (pp. 27–50). Santa Barbara, CA: Praeger.

Schneider and Bos (2013) reported that women politicians do not typically express personality characteristics ascribed to women (e.g., empathic) and are also not perceived as exhibiting masculine personality characteristics. As Hess (2013, p. 1) noted, "When women enter political office, we stop seeing them like women everywhere else."

Moreover, a meta-analysis revealed that there was greater gender bias on male-dominated tasks than female-dominated tasks (Swim, Borgida, Maruyama, & Myers, 1989). Similarly, Davison and Burke's (2000) meta-analysis demonstrated that men were preferred over women for male-dominated jobs in all areas, not only political office (d = 0.34). Both meta-analyses provide strong evidence that employed women are stigmatized when they participate in stereotypically male-dominated tasks (i.e., leadership). Put simply, context matters. Women are stigmatized in situations where they either are, or act as, leaders or exert behaviors or characteristics that are representative of leadership.

Schneider and Bos (2013) asked students to indicate personality characteristics they identify with women in general and also women politicians. Eighty-four percent of the research participants described women as "gorgeous." None of these individuals used the term for women politicians. Similarly, no student described a woman politician as motherly, emotional, sensitive, compassionate, beautiful, or feminine. In addition, 91% of the students described women as compassionate; only 21% of them used this term to describe women politicians. Furthermore, women politicians were not described with terms like "leader," "assertive," "competent," or "confident," characteristics commonly associated with men. Schneider and Bos (2013) did find that students described women politicians as "uptight" and "dictatorial." The question that follows such a statement is *why* do female leaders face social stigma?

THEORETICAL RATIONALE FOR SOCIAL STIGMA FACED BY FEMALE LEADERS

Several theories help build a framework for understanding social stigma faced by female politicians and women leaders in other professions. The first theory, social role theory, suggests that the distribution of men and women into breadwinner and homemaker roles creates stereotypes that support the maintenance of these roles (Eagly, 1987), perpetuating stigma faced by female leaders. A second theory, lack of fit, also explains stigma faced by female leaders (Heilman, 1983). This theory purports that an individual's success in a particular job is determined by a comparison of the perception of the individual's attributes to the perception of the job requirements. Due to social stigma women are perceived to be incompatible with the demands of leadership. Finally, ambivalent sexism suggests that hostile and benevolent approaches are complementary forms of sexism that maintain the status quo, preventing women from advancing in the workplace (Glick & Fiske, 1996). Together, these theories provide complementary explanation as to how female leaders became a stigmatized subgroup and why this social stigma persists despite evidence of effectiveness of female leaders.

Social Role Theory

According to social role theory of sex differences (Eagly, 1987; Eagly, Wood, & Diekman, 2000), the division in social roles for men and women, particularly in occupational settings, accounts for differences in normative gender behaviors. Eagly and Karau (2002) extended this concept by introducing role congruity theory, which suggests that prejudice may occur to the extent that others perceive a misalignment between stereotypes toward a target group member and characteristics of his or her social role. We propose that women are often devalued or stigmatized as leaders because the discord between their social and occupational roles prevents them from being fully socially accepted (Goffman, 1963). The theoretical foundation of social role theory has been substantiated by empirical findings that support the conclusion that masculine qualities are often associated with male-dominated occupations, particularly those involving managerial roles. For instance, Cejka and Eagly (1999) found that feminine characteristics, such as physical and personality attributes, are viewed as more integral to success in female-dominated occupations, while masculine qualities are viewed as more important to success in male-dominated occupations. Schneider and Bos (2013) suggest that because of the lack of women in politics most individuals really do not have a clear sense of what women politicians are really like.

Lack of Fit

Related to role congruity theory, Heilman's (1983) lack-of-fit model contends that individuals perceive that success in a given job is determined by the degree to which the abilities and skills required for a particular occupation correspond to the attributes of an individual. A lack of fit or misalignment between gender and occupational roles may prove especially disadvantageous for women who seek or occupy managerial or leadership positions because of the perception that women's attributes contrast with the qualities of a prototypical leader. Specifically, women are stereotyped as possessing communal attributes, such as warmth, kindness, and a concern for others. Conversely, men are perceived to have agentic attributes, which include confidence, aggressiveness, and dominance. Traditionally, agentic traits have been viewed as characteristic of leader roles (Eagly, 1987; Eagly & Karau, 2002). In reference to gender and leadership roles, research has directly assessed the congruency between gender stereotypes and characteristics of successful managers (Duehr & Bono, 2006; Heilman, Block, Martell, & Simon, 1989; Schein, 1973, 1975, 2001). Despite evidence from past research demonstrating perceptions that stereotypically masculine attributes align with leader characteristics (Heilman et al., 1989; Schein, 1973, 1975, 2001), more recent findings have illustrated that the traditionally masculine leader prototype may be evolving (Atwater, Brett, Waldman, DiMare, & Hayden, 2004; Duehr & Bono, 2006; Johnson, Murphy, Zewdie, & Reichard, 2008; Powell, Butterfield, & Parent, 2002; Prime, Carter, & Welbourne, 2009). In fact, the literature points to the existence of both masculine and feminine managerial subroles; however, it supports the notion that most successful leader characteristics are perceived as more agentic than communal, and thus more masculine than feminine (Atwater et al., 2004; Powell et al., 2002; Prime et al., 2009).

Implications of Incongruity and Lack of Fit. Researchers have extended the literature on role incongruity and lack-of-fit models by examining how gender stereotypes impact treatment toward women who seek or occupy traditionally masculine positions, such as managerial roles. Drawing from gender discrimination and harassment litigation, Burgess and Brogida (1999) illustrate two ways in which stereotypes about women may lead to discrimination. First, descriptive stereotypes toward women, or perceptions of the attributes that women *do* possess, may engender unfair hiring practices in which women are not selected for male-dominated occupations because they are perceived to possess characteristics that misalign with the role of the job. Second, the prescriptive component of the female stereotype, or beliefs about characteristics that women *should* possess, may lead to unfavorable evaluations of women in masculine-type jobs because they are viewed as lacking femininity and violating their gender norms. Often referred to as the double bind, this predicament is especially relevant for women in leadership positions who are viewed as poor leaders for exhibiting feminine behaviors, while those who engage in masculine characteristics that align with managerial attributes are denigrated for lacking femininity (Eagly & Carli, 2007). The latter portion of this double bind has been described as a backlash (Rudman, 1998; Rudman & Glick, 2001) or penalty (Heilman, Wallen, Fuchs, & Tamkins, 2004) that women may experience in the form of discrimination (2001), sabotage (Rudman & Fairchild, 2004), or unfavorable evaluations (Heilman et al., 2004).

Additional research testing incongruity theory has illustrated how the interplay between both descriptive and prescriptive stereotypes places women in a double bind. For example, Johnson and colleagues (2008) found that in order for women to be viewed as effective leaders they had to possess both sensitivity and strength, while male leaders were perceived as effective by possessing only strength. Similarly, Heilman and Okimoto (2008) discovered that without presenting any additional information, male managers were rated as more likeable than female managers; however, when the female managers were presented as communal, they were perceived as more likeable than male managers. These find-ings suggest that women in male-dominated occupations who balance communal and agentic behaviors may mitigate the negative outcomes of gender and occupational role incongruity. Unfortunately, this strategy to alleviate gender discrimination not only places responsibility on the target but it may also reinforce gender stereotypes.

Ambivalent Sexism

Stereotypes and the underrepresentation of women in leader posi-tions may also be perpetuated through sexism. Sexism may exist in two seemingly unrelated forms. First, "hostile sexism" refers to the belief that women seek to gain power over men through either their sexuality or feminist principles. This more traditional form of sexism is manifested through overt and destructive actions. Second, benevolent sexism repre-sents the chivalrous idea that women are fragile creatures who should be respected, treasured, and sheltered. Although benevolent sexism seems to be free of malicious intent, it suggests that women lack strength and competence and are most appropriate for stereotypically female social roles (Glick & Fiske, 1997, 2001). For example, a woman may not receive a promotion to a managerial position because her male supervisor wants to protect her from the demanding tasks of a leader.

Although hostile and benevolent sexism seem to occupy polar ends of the sexism spectrum, Glick and Fiske (1996) found that the two types are related and may coexist. For example, one study found that pregnant women were treated in a hostile manner when they engaged in counter-normative behaviors by applying for a job, especially if it was stereotypi-cally masculine, and they were treated in benevolent ways when they conformed to normative social roles (Hebl, King, Glick, Kazama, & Sin-gletary, 2007). This research demonstrates that individuals may engage in both hostile and benevolent sexist behaviors in order to maintain the sta-tus quo. The ambivalent sexism literature is complementary to the social role theory research in explaining the challenges for women seeking to climb the organizational hierarchy. Due to the incongruity between female gender roles and leader social roles, women in leadership positions may be stigmatized or devalued as traditional leaders (Eagly, 1987; Eagly & Karau, 2002). This stigma and lack of acceptance of female leaders may lead others to engage in discriminatory behaviors (Crocker et al. 1998), such as those indicative of benevolent sexism. In other situations, in which women occupy a traditionally feminine social role, the stigma is gone and women may be rewarded not only through more positive evaluations but also through the seemingly positive behavior indicative of benevolent sex-ism. In the next sections, we further delineate empirical findings that illus-trate the manifestations of stigma faced by female leaders.

MANIFESTATIONS OF SOCIAL STIGMA

We have thus far reviewed and discussed social stigma, and provided theoretical rationale for why female leaders experience stigma. We next present three broad categories (procedural, interpersonal, individual) through which stigma manifests and in each section discuss the negative consequences of stigma faced by female leaders in the workplace. Procedural manifestations of stigma faced by women leaders encompass a range of experiences focused on the more formalized aspects of the workplace (e.g., work assignments, performance evaluation, promotion). Interpersonal manifestations capture the degree of social interaction (e.g., networking, inclusion) between female leader and others (e.g., coworker, supervisor) in the workplace. Finally, individual manifestations represent the female leader's felt experiences and the resulting desire to advance in the workplace. Each category presents a unique set of challenges that hinder women's success in male-dominated situations (i.e., positions of leadership), ultimately demonstrating the very real consequences of social stigma for female leaders.

Procedural

The procedural manifestations of stigma that women leaders encounter range from subtle differences in work experiences to more formalized disparities in performance evaluations that finally culminate in dramatic discrepancies in promotions to the top tiers of management. Developmental work experiences (DWEs) can be defined as workplace incidents that individuals encounter and learn from, which over time accumulate in the development of job-relevant knowledge and skills (Speitzer, McCall, & Mahoney, 1997). Both the quantity and quality of these on-the-job experiences are critical components to managerial growth (Morrison, White, & Van Velsor, 1987). Researchers at the Center for Creative Leadership have proposed three critical characteristics of DWE quality: challenge, feedback, and support (Van Velsor, McCauley, & Moxley, 1998). Preliminary empirical evidence suggests that women and men do not differ in the quantity of work experiences provided by employers, but rather the quality of those experiences (King et al., in press). Specifically, although men and women expressed comparable levels of supervisor support and interest in pursuing challenging experiences and supervisor support, women received less challenging experiences and less negative feedback as compared to their male counterparts. Similarly, anecdotal evidence suggests that mothers returning to the workplace from maternity leave are reassigned to less challenging work (Williams, Manvell, & Bornstein, 2006). Thus, stigma toward female leaders may be manifested in the assignment of qualitatively poorer developmental experiences to women than to men.

Stigma may also be manifested in disparities in performance evaluations, which are an important tool that employers utilize to measure the achievement of their employees. Research suggests that the performance of male leaders may be evaluated more favorably than an equally competent female leader (Eagly, Makhijani, & Klonsky, 1992; Lyness & Heilman, 2006). Success in and of itself is not aberrant for female leaders, but the conditions under which that success is achieved are fundamental to its perception and evaluation by others. Specifically, backlash toward successful women seems to emerge when gender-stereotypic norms have been violated (Cuddy & Fiske, 2004). For example, a meta-analysis found that there was only a slight tendency for individuals to evaluate men in leadership positions more favorably than women in leadership positions; however, this tendency was stronger depending on certain circumstances, including leadership style and organizational context (Eagly et al., 1992). Female leaders who engaged in stereotypically masculine leadership styles (i.e., independent, assertive, task-oriented, and autocratic behaviors) were rated less favorably than male leaders. In addition, female leaders who occupied male-dominated roles experienced this same form of devaluation as compared to their male counterparts. Related research suggests that expanding the criterion space may not be a solution to the problem of stereotyping in evaluations of performance. Since women in leadership positions often occupy male-dominated roles and operate in ambiguous situations, the aforementioned studies provide evidence that female leaders are likely to receive lower-performance evaluations than equally competent male leaders. Reinforcing the barrier to upper-level management, Lyness and Heilman (2006) found that promoted women received higher-performance evaluations than promoted men.

The most visible procedural manifestation of stigma is the discrepancy in promotions at the higher levels of the management hierarchy. Lyness and Judiesch (1999) found that relative to men, women were more likely to be promoted than hired into upper-management positions; however, women were less likely to be promoted. In other words, talented women are more likely to attain top leadership positions by ascending the managerial chain (i.e., staying at one organization) as compared to being hired from outside the organization. That being said, even if women decide to pursue the promotional approach to upper-level management, men are still more likely to be promoted than women. Women leaders who do succeed in climbing the management hierarchy often inherit leadership positions that are high risk. Ryan and Haslam (2005) coined the term the "glass cliff" to describe the finding that the appointment of a woman to a board of directors often followed poor organizational performance in the preceding months. Procedural manifestations of stigma toward female leaders, therefore, seem to include situations in which women are set up to fail.

Interpersonal

In contemporary organizations (and society) discrimination presents itself in covert, subtle ways (Dovidio & Gaertner, 2004; Hebl et al., 2007). Interpersonal discrimination is characterized by interpersonal cues (e.g., decreased eye contact and interaction time) that signals liking or collegiality to the individual (Hebl, Mannix, & Dovidio, 2002; Hebl et al., 2007). These interpersonal cues directed toward stigmatized groups (i.e., female leaders) may be a "much more sensitive indicator of hostile biases in occupational contexts" than formalized discrimination (Hebl et al., 2007, p. 1501). The interpersonal manifestations of stigma that women leaders encounter range from subtle differences in perceptions of competence and commitment to more overt disparities, including social isolation and even sexual harassment.

Employed women face negative perceptions related to competence and commitment in the workplace. Such negative perceptions are exacerbated when women attempt to assert themselves as leaders in the workplace. Heilman and Haynes (2005) demonstrated that in a group setting female members were rated as less competent and less likely to play a leadership role than male members. Female leaders' devalued social identity results in outsiders to not only overlook their contributions but also denigrate their competence when attempting to assert themselves in a group. Lyness and Heilman (2006) confirmed anecdotal evidence that women do indeed have to work harder to prove themselves in the workplace. In order for women to be evaluated as competent they must unambiguously demonstrate superior performance to their male counterparts (Biernat & Kobrynowicz, 1997; Heilman & Hanyes, 2005). Some argue that because females are often denigrated in the advancement process, women who do achieve positions of leadership are, in fact, more qualified and perform especially well (Biernat, 2005). However, such negative perceptions likely contribute to the underrepresentation of women in positions of leadership.

Interpersonal manifestations extend beyond others' perceptions of capabilities to disparities, including negative affect, social isolation, and even sabotage or sexual harassment. Research suggests that even when men and women are judged equally on competence, female leaders receive more negative nonverbal reactions and affect than male leaders (Butler & Geis, 1990; Koch, 2005). Consonant with stigma theory, research suggests individuals attempt to avoid stigmatized individuals (Jones et al., 1984), potentially preventing women growing their interpersonal network (Seibert, Kraimer, & Liden, 2001), resisting female authority (Eagly & Karau, 2002), sabotage (Rudman & Fairchild, 2004), and, more generally, socially isolating female leaders in the workplace. Stockdale and Bhattacharya (2009) review literature presenting sexual harassment as yet another barrier to women's advancement in male-dominated positions (i.e., leadership).

As ambivalent sexism theory suggests, there is also a "softer" side to discrimination. Benevolent sexism suggests that women should be protected and revered and therefore individuals may use diminutive language (e.g., honey) when interacting with females creating situations in which women feel devalued. Individuals who view female leaders as competitors may enact such diminutive strategies in an effort to maintain the status quo. Social stigma faced by female leaders, therefore, contributes to negative interpersonal perceptions and interpersonal behaviors attempting to prevent women from advancing in the organizational hierarchy.

Individual

The individual manifestations of stigma that female leaders encounter largely stem from powerful, and divergent, norms for what it means to be a "woman" and a "leader." Strong familial norms combined with feelings of guilt may result in self-limiting behavior (i.e., lack of career self-efficacy), ultimately preventing women from further advancement. Social role theory explains the distribution of men and women into breadwinner and homemaker roles, respectively (Eagly, 1987). As a result of these distributions, there is a societal mandate for women to feel they should be responsible for homemaker responsibilities *in addition to* paid work; men, however, feel they should be responsible *only* for paid work. Thus, it is not uncommon for women to participate in paid work, perform the majority of household duties (Hochschild & Machung, 2003), and bear the burden of childcare responsibilities (Bond, Thompson, Galinsky, & Protas, 2002). This is further complicated by the fact that more senior and prestigious positions place a premium on working long hours and travel. Given the demands on long hours and expectations to be present on nights and weekends even when unnecessary (Brett & Stroh, 2003), it becomes impossible for women, particularly mothers, to fulfill the ideal roles for both "woman" and "leader." Furthermore, women report greater stress than men from working long hours because women are less likely to be able to lessen the burden of domestic work (Davidson & Fielden, 1999). Thus, these pulls in separate directions may increase the likelihood of conflict in the woman. This may be especially true for employed mothers, as they are juggling both homemaking and caretaking responsibilities. The mother may want to do it all (maintain employment and be an intensive wife/mother), but realize this is not realistic (Johnston & Swanson, 2006) causing discomfort. Furthermore, qualitative research suggests that mothers experienced guilt upon returning to work because they were not able to fully complete the traditionally held role of mother due to their work demands (Seagram & Daniluk, 2002). Family pressure and responsibility does not fully explain the underrepresentation of women in positions of leadership (Kark & Eagly, in press). Discrimination is indeed present and powerful; however, it is important to consider how societal norms hinder the advancement of women in the workplace.

Heilman (1983, 2001) discusses how perceived incongruity may lead to outcomes of self-limiting behavior as well as discrimination. As discussed throughout this chapter, outcomes of social stigma include discrimination. However, we have not yet considered the self-limiting nature of stigma faced by female leaders and its consequences. Self-limiting behaviors may include the devaluing of one's contributions, lack of self-promotion, or anxiety over advancement. This generalized lack of career self-efficacy may stem from questioning of women's decisions regarding their roles in work and family or self-limiting thoughts regarding their capabilities in a male-dominated environment. Low career self-efficacy may link back to lack of task mastery (Bandura, 1991) that female leaders encounter due to procedural manifestations of stigma. Regardless of source, this lack of career self-efficacy may result in increased distraction from work (Kanfer & Ackerman, 1996), lack of persistence (Bandura, 1991), and ultimately dissatisfaction in their job. A similar phenomenon—stereotype threat—suggests sheer awareness of the stereotype results in the stereotypic, lower performance. Davies, Spencer, and Steele (2005) revealed that when participants in groups viewed stereotypical portrayals, the women (and not the men) exhibited less interest in becoming the leader. Thus, female leaders' own awareness of their social stigma creates yet another, albeit self-limiting, challenge to advancement.

"DOUBLE" STIGMA

Thus far we have addressed social stigma faced by female leaders and the procedural, interpersonal, and individual consequences. This section discusses "double" stigma, or situations that likely heighten female leaders' already devalued social identity. Employees of contemporary organizations often have multiple intersecting identities creating opportunity to denigrate women for more than their position of leadership, or attempts toward advancement. We briefly review the literature on tokens, race, and ethnicity, as well as mothers and lesbians, and discuss how an additional stigma may exacerbate perceived negativity toward female leaders.

Tokens are individuals who are subject to negative treatment because their social category (e.g., women) is numerically underrepresented in certain contexts (e.g., senior leadership) (Yoder, 1991). Kanter's (1977) original theory on tokenism outlined this process, suggesting that tokens received enhanced visibility and therefore pressure to perform, and their differences become exaggerated creating social isolation and rejection from peers and the organizations. Empirical research confirms female tokens do indeed receive negative treatment (Goldenhar, Swanson, Hurrel,

Ruder, & Deddens, 1998; King, Hebl, George, & Matusik, 2010). Given the numerical underrepresentation of women in senior leadership positions in both the public and private sectors, tokenism theory suggests that these women may be particularly susceptible to negativity due to their female and token status (see Introduction to this volume, section on women of color in the U.S. Congress). It is likely that this double stigma (female and token) heightens others' negative attitudinal and behavioral responses, exaggerating the previously discussed consequences of stigma.

Society currently maintains negative stereotypes to several nonwhite categories, resulting in disadvantage status for these subgroups. For example, African American women report social isolation in the workplace (Bell & Nkomo, 2001) and greater resistance to their authority than white women (Bell & Nkomo, 2001). Empirical data support the notion that discrimination is more prevalent toward African American and Hispanic than white employees (Avery, McKay, Wilson, & Tonidandel, 2007). Given gender and race are visible stigmas, we can see just how many women have reached some of the highest positions of leadership. Although we have three examples from modern society: Condoleezza Rice (first female, African American secretary of state), Sonia Sotomayor (first female, Hispanic Supreme Court justice), and Ursula Burns (first female, African American Fortune 500 CEO), positions of leadership that are held by women tend to be white. In fact, recent statistics show that 29% of senior managers are white women as opposed to 3% who are African American women (EEOC, 2009). Furthermore, African American women's median weekly earnings are $554 compared to white women who earn $654. As difficult as it may be for women to rise to positions of leadership, women of color have a double disadvantage due to their gender and race.

Stigma theory discusses both visible and invisible stigmas, noting unique challenges (i.e., disclosure) for individuals with invisible stigmas (e.g., pregnant women, lesbians). Pregnant women represent the epitome of womanhood, as they are fulfilling expectations of their role as a woman. However, this function is incongruent with their role as a worker (Ridgeway & Correll, 2004), and even to a larger extent their role as a leader. In fact, King and Botsford's (2009) theoretical work presented pregnancy as stigma and addressed challenges for disclosing their invisible stigma. Furthermore, King and Botsford (2009) demonstrated that when women become mothers they are perceived to have lost competence and gained warmth. Heilman and Okimoto (2008) confirmed this finding that mothers are indeed perceived to lack competence. Again, we propose that being female and a mother opens these individuals up to being doubly stigmatized, and therefore become targets of enhanced negativity, as discussed in the Introduction to this volume with respect to women politicians.

Finally, being lesbian, gay, bisexual, or transgendered (LGBT) is yet another invisible stigmatized characteristic (Ragins, Cornwell, & Miller,

2003). Day and Greene (2008) purport that if both small and large organizations wish to be successful, inclusivity of LGBT workers is, in fact, a requirement. Recent examples demonstrate progress in this area. In conclusion, the increasing number of women with multiple identities in leadership positions presents these individuals with the difficult situation of being subject to multiple stigmas and therefore exaggerated negativity and discrimination.

STRATEGIES FOR REMEDIATION

Given the plethora of information reviewed in this chapter identifying negativity toward female leaders, it is difficult to avoid asking what action can be taken to remediate this discrimination. Lyness and Heilman (2006) called for research to learn more about the strategies women have used to gain entry to, and demonstrate success in, strongly male positions. Research points to limited strategies female leaders may enact to reduce negativity directed toward them. We discuss several, recognizing that each unduly places the burden on the woman herself, arguably adding yet another challenge on the path to attaining positions of senior leadership.

First, Johnson et al.'s (2008) research suggested that female leaders must demonstrate strength and sensitivity in order to be evaluated as effective. Thus, female leaders who are aware of their leadership style may be able to adjust their style to demonstrate both strength and sensitivity, and prevent discrimination. For example, a female leader who exhibits a more masculine leadership style may be able to reduce negativity by enacting behaviors that are perceived to be sensitive (e.g., demonstrating consideration for subordinates). Similarly, Heilman and Haynes (2005) demonstrated that unless there is clear evidence of women's competence, their success is attributed to men and therefore are less likely to be the leader. Therefore, female leaders may make an effort to credential themselves and protect against discrimination by demonstrating extreme and consistent competence. When female leaders demonstrate competence in their chosen career, denigration of women becomes more difficult, thus mitigating roadblocks to the advancement of women to positions of leadership. Both the "strong and sensitive" and the "competence" approach require the woman to essentially credential herself against negativity from others by overachieving and make it undeniable that she should advance in the workplace.

A second remediation strategy is for women to build social capital by developing relationships with key stakeholders. For example, Allen, Eby, Poteet, Lentz, and Lima (2004) demonstrated that mentoring relationships tend to enhance career progress by providing both career and psychosocial mentoring. Furthermore, formal mentoring programs that take into consideration mentor-protégé match and training quality influence effectiveness of mentoring (Allen, Eby, O'Brien, & Lentz, 2006; see appendix to this volume). Women who aspire to positions of leadership can therefore hopefully align themselves with a mentor who provides both career and psychosocial support, helping to pave the way to climbing the organizational ladder. Similarly, women who are able to network within their organization and career field may be able to better position themselves for positions of leadership. However, Forret and Dougherty (2004) found that men received a boost for increasing visibility, whereas this was not always the case for women. The authors propose that this may be because women are typically involved with less prestigious assignments or because others may perceive that women are trying to compensate for the current position by engaging in such behaviors. Although this presents a double bind for women (i.e., network, but don't appear to make a conscious effort), those who are able to successfully network and build social capital may enhance their likelihood of advancement. Linehan and Scullion (2008) conducted a series of interviews with 50 female managers. Their research revealed that women reported barriers to networks and also reported that women felt that access to such formal and informal networks would provide career advantages. Women who take the time to build their network may develop alliances, and effectively reduce the number of individuals who attempt to denigrate their success, while simultaneously increasing the number of individuals who may act as advocates for their advancement.

CONCLUSION

Despite progress, gender inequities persist preventing women from achieving positions of leadership. This chapter identified social stigma as the root of such stereotyping and discrimination, and presented the procedural, interpersonal, and individual manifestations of stigma and its negative consequences for female leaders. We also discussed situations of double stigma whereby certain individuals are subject to discrimination based on their status as a female leader as well as a second, stigmatized social group (e.g., race). Finally, we presented proposed strategies to remediate perceived discrimination and attempt to rectify inequities faced by female leaders. This summary of the literature should serve as a call to researchers and practitioners alike to not only explore the forces that suppress women in counter-stereotypic positions, such as leadership, but also investigate procedural and interpersonal methods for alleviating the negative effects of the stigma that many women in positions of leadership face.

Hess (2013, p. 1) noted:

We might be OK with letting 20 women serve in the U.S. Senate, as long as their political representation doesn't threaten our conception of most women, who are still expected to fulfill their feminine duties of raising children and looking pretty. At some point, you'd

hope that the growing representation of women in political office
would start to influence the stereotypical traits we associate with all
women. But that would require us to actually see female leaders as
. . . leaders.

REFERENCES

Allen, T. D., Eby, L. T., O'Brien, K. E., & Lentz, E. (2006). The state of mentoring
research: A qualitative review of the current research methods and future
research implications. *Journal of Vocational Behavior, 73*, 343–357.

Allen, T. D., Eby, L. T., Poteet, M. L., Lentz, E., & Lima, L. (2004). Career benefits
associated with mentoring for proteges: A meta-analysis. *Journal of Applied
Psychology, 89*, 127–136.

Atwater, L. E., Brett, J. F., Waldman, D., DiMare, L., & Hayden, M. V. (2004). Men's
and women's perceptions of the gender typing of management subroles.
Sex Roles, 50, 191–199.

Avery, D. R., McKay, P. F., Wilson, D. C., & Tonidandel, S. (2007). Unequal attendance: The relationships between race, organizational diversity cures, and
absenteeism. *Personnel Psychology, 60*, 875–902.

Bandura, A. (1991). Social cognitive theory of self-regulation. *Organizational Behavior and Human Decision Processes, 50*, 248–287.

Bell, E. J. E., & Nkomo, S. M. (2001). *Our separate ways: Black and White woman and
the struggle for professional identity*. Boston: Harvard Business School Press.

Biernat, M. (2005). *Standards and expectancies: Contrast and assimilation in judgments
of self and others*. New York, NY: Psychology Press.

Biernat, M., & Kobrynowicz, D. (1997). Gender and raced based standards of competence: Lower minimum standards but higher ability standards for devalued groups. *Journal of Personality and Social Psychology, 72*, 544–557.

Bond, J. T., Thompson, C., Galinsky, E., & Protas, D. (2002). *The 2002 national study
of the changing workforce*. New York: Families and Work Institute.

Brett, J. M., & Stroh, L. K. (2003). Working 61 hours a week: Why do managers do
it? *Journal of Applied Psychology, 88*, 67–78.

Burgess, D., & Borgida, E. (1999). Who women are, who women should be: Descriptive and prescriptive gender stereotyping in sex discrimination. *Psychology,
Public Policy and Law, 5*, 655–692.

Butler, D., & Geis, F. L. (1990). Nonverbal affect responses to male and female leaders: Implications for leadership evaluations. *Journal of Personality and Social
Psychology, 58*, 48–59.

Cejka, M. A., & Eagly, A. H. (1999). Gender-stereotypic images of occupations correspond to the sex segregation of employment. *Personality and Social Psychology Bulletin, 25*, 413–423.

Crocker, J., Major, B., & Steele, C. (1998). Social stigma. In D. T. Gilbert & S. T.
Fiske (Eds.), *Handbook of social psychology* (4th ed., pp. 504–553). New York:
McGraw-Hill.

Cuddy, A. J. C., & Fiske, S. T. (2004). When professionals become mothers, warmth, doesn't cut the ice. *Journal of Social Issues, 60,* 701–718.

Davidson, M. J., & Fielden, S. (1999). Stress and the working women. In G. N. Powell (Ed.), *Handbook of gender and work* (pp. 413–426). Thousand Oaks, CA: Sage.

Davies, P. G., Spencer, S. J., & Steele, C. M. (2005). Clearing the air: Identity safety moderates the effects of stereotype threat on women's leadership aspirations. *Journal of Personality and Social Psychology, 88,* 276–287.

Davison, H. K., & Burke, M. J. (2000). Sex discrimination in simulated employment contexts: A meta-analytic investigation. *Journal of Vocational Behavior, 56,* 225–248.

Day, N. E., & Greene, P. G. (2008). A case for sexual orientation diversity management in small and large organizations. *Human Resource Management, 47,* 637–654.

Dovidio, J. F., & Gaertner, S. L. (2004). Aversive racism. In M. P. Zanna (Ed.), *Advances in experimental social psychology* (Vol. 36, pp. 1–52). San Diego, CA: Elsevier Academic Press.

Duehr, E. E., & Bono, J. E. (2006). Men, women, and managers: Are stereotypes finally changing? *Personnel Psychology, 59,* 815–846.

Eagly, A. H. (1987). *Sex differences in social behavior: A social role interpretation.* Hillsdale NJ: Erlbaum.

Eagly, A. H., & Carli, L. L. (2003). The female leadership advantage: An evaluation of the evidence. *The Leadership Quarterly, 14,* 807–834.

Eagly, A. H., & Carli, L. L. (2007). *Through the labyrinth: The truth about how women become leaders.* Boston: Harvard Business School Press.

Eagly, A. H., & Karau, S. J. (2002). Role congruity theory of prejudice toward female leaders. *Psychological Review, 109,* 573–598.

Eagly, A. H., Makhijani, M. G., & Klonsky, B. G. (1992). Gender and the evaluation of leaders: A meta-analysis. *Psychological Bulletin, 111,* 3–22.

Eagly, A. H., Wood, W., & Diekman, A. B. (2000). Social role theory of sex differences and similarities: A current appraisal. In T. Eckes & H. M. Traunter (Eds.), *The developmental social psychology of gender* (pp. 123–174). Mahwah, NJ: Erlbaum.

Equal Employment Opportunity Commission (2009). www.eeoc.org.

Forret, M. L., & Dougherty, T. W. (2004). Networking behaviors and career outcomes: Differences for men and women? *Journal of Organizational Behavior, 25,* 419–437.

Glick, P., & Fiske, S. T. (1996). The ambivalent sexism inventory: Differentiating hostile and benevolent sexism. *Journal of Personality and Social Psychology, 70,* 491–512.

Glick, P., & Fiske, S. T. (1997). Hostile and benevolent sexism: Measuring ambivalent sexist attitudes toward women. *Psychology of Women Quarterly, 21,* 119–135.

Glick, P., & Fiske, S. T. (2001). An ambivalent alliance: Hostile and benevolent sexism as complementary justifications for gender inequality. *American Psychologist, 56,* 109–118.

Goffman, E. (1963). *Stigma: Notes on the management of spoiled identity.* New York, NY: Simon & Schuster, Inc.

Goldenhar, L. M., Swanson, N. G., Hurrell, J. J., Ruder, A., & Deddens, J. (1998). Stressors and adverse outcomes for female construction workers. *Journal of Occupational Health Psychology, 3,* 19–32.

Hebl, M. R., King, E. B., Glick, P., Kazama, S., & Singletary, S. (2007). Hostile and benevolent reactions toward pregnant women: Complementary interpersonal punishments and rewards that maintain traditional roles. *Journal of Applied Psychology, 92,* 1499–1511.

Hebl, M. R., Mannix, L., & Dovidio, J. (2002). Formal and interpersonal discrimination: A field study of bias toward homosexual job applicants. *Personality and Social Psychology Bulletin, 28,* 815–825.

Heilman, M. E. (1983). Sex bias in work settings: The Lack of Fit model. *Research in Organizational Behavior, 5,* 269–298.

Heilman, M. E., Block, C. J., Martell, R. F., & Simon, M. C. (1989). Has anything changed? Current characterizations of men, women, and managers. *The Journal of Applied Psychology, 74,* 935–942.

Heilman, M. E., & Haynes, M. C. (2005). No credit where credit is due: Attributional rationalization of women's success in male-female teams. *Journal of Applied Psychology, 90,* 905–916.

Heilman, M. E., & Okimoto, T. G. (2008). Motherhood: A potential source of bias in employment decisions. *Journal of Applied Psychology, 93,* 189–198.

Heilman, M. E., Wallen, A. S., Fuchs, D., & Tamkins, M. M. (2004). Penalties for success: Reactions to women who succeed at male gender-typed tasks. *Journal of Applied Psychology, 89,* 416–427.

Hess, A. (2013). *Turns out we don't stereotype female politicians. We just don't get them at all.* Retrieved June 16, 2015, from www.slate.com/blogs/xx_factor.

Hochschild, A., & Machung, A. 2003. *The second shift: Working parents and the revolution at home.* New York, NY: Viking-Penguin.

Johnson, S. K., Murphy, S. E., Zewdie, S., & Reichard, R. J. (2008). The strong, sensitive type: Effects of gender stereotypes and leadership prototypes on the evaluation of male and female leaders. *Organizational Behavior and Human Decision Processes, 106,* 39–60.

Johnston, D. D., & Swanson, D. H. (2006). Constructing the "good mother": The experience of mothering ideologies by work status. *Sex Roles, 54,* 509–519.

Jones, E. E., Farina, A., Hastorf, A. H., Markus, H., Miller, D. T., & Scott, R. A. (1984). *Social stigma: The psychology of marked relationships.* New York, NY: Freeman.

Kanfer, R., & Ackerman, P. L. (1996). Self-regulatory skills perspective to reducing cognitive interference. In I. Sarason, G. Pierce, & B. Sarason (Eds.), *Cognitive interference: Theories, methods, and findings* (pp. 153–171). Hillsdale, NJ, England: Lawrence Erlbaum Associates, Inc.

Kanter, R. M. (1977). *Men and women of the corporation.* New York, NY: Basic Books.

Kark, R., & Eagly, A. (2009). Gender and leadership: Negotiating the labyrinth. In J. C. Chrisler & D. R. McCreary (Eds.), *Handbook of gender research in psychology* (443–468). New York, NY: Springer.

King, E. B., & Botsford, W. E. (2009). Managing pregnancy disclosures: Understanding and overcoming the challenges of expectant motherhood at work. *Human Resource Management Review, 19,* 314–323.

King, E. B., Hebl, M. R., George, J. M., & Matusik, S. F. (2010). Understanding tokenism: Negative consequences of perceived gender discrimination in male-dominated organizations. *Journal of Management, 36,* 537–554.

King, E. B., Botsford, W., Hebl, M. R., Kazama, S., Dawson, J. F., & Perkins, A. (2012). Benevolent sexism at work: Gender differences in the distribution of challenging work experiences. *Journal of Management, 38,* 1835–1866.

Koch, S. C. (2005). Evaluative affect display toward male and female leaders of task-oriented groups. *Small Group Research, 36,* 678–703.

Linehan, M., & Scullion, H. (2008). The development of female global managers: The role of mentoring and networking. *Journal of Business Ethics, 83,* 29–40.

Lyness, K. A., & Heilman, M. E. (2006). When fit is fundamental: Performance evaluations and promotions of upper-level female and male managers. *Journal of Applied Psychology, 91,* 777–785.

Lyness, K. S., & Judiesch, M. K. (1999). Are women more likely to be hired or promoted into management positions? *Journal of Vocational Behavior, 54,* 158–173.

Morrison, A. M., White, R. P., & Van Velsor, E. (1987). *Breaking the glass ceiling: Can women reach the top of America's largest corporations.* Reading, MA: Addison-Wesley.

Powell, G. N., Butterfield, D. A., & Parent, J. D. (2002). Gender and managerial stereotypes: Have the times changed? *Journal of Management, 28,* 177–193.

Prime, J. L., Carter, N. M., & Welbourne, T. M. (2009). Women "take care," men "take charge": Managers' stereotypic perceptions of women and men leaders. *The Psychologist-Manager Journal, 12,* 25–49.

Ragins, B. R., Cornwell, J. M., & Miller, J. S. (2003). Heterosexism in the workplace: Do race and gender matter? *Group & Organization Management, 28,* 45–74.

Ridgeway, C. L., & Correll, S. J. (2004). Motherhood as a status characteristic. *Journal of Social Issues, 60,* 638–700.

Rudman, L. A. (1998). Self-promotion as a risk factor for women: The costs and benefits of counterstereotypical impression management. *Journal of Personality and Social Psychology, 74,* 629–645.

Rudman, L. A., & Fairchild, K. (2004). Reactions to counterstereotypic behavior: The role of backlash in cultural stereotype maintenance. *Journal of Personality and Social Psychology, 87,* 157–176.

Rudman, L. A., & Glick, P. (2001). Prescriptive gender stereotypes and backlash toward agentic women. *Journal of Social Issues, 57,* 743–762.

Ryan, M. K., & Haslam, S. A. (2005). The glass cliff: Evidence that women are over-represented in precarious leadership positions. *British Journal of Management, 16,* 81–90.

Schein, V. E. (1973). The relationship between sex role stereotypes and requisite management characteristics. *Journal of Applied Psychology, 57,* 95–100.

Schein, V. E. (1975). Relationships between sex role stereotypes and requisite management characteristics among female managers. *Journal of Applied Psychology, 60,* 340–344.

Schein, V. E. (2001). A global look at psychological barriers to women's progress in management. *Journal of Social Issues, 57,* 675–688.

Schneider, M., & Bos, A. (2013). Measuring stereotypes of female politicians. *Political Psychology, 35,* 245–256.

Seagram, S., & Daniluk, J. C. (2002). "It goes with the territory": The meaning and experience of maternal guilt for mothers of pre-adolescent children. *Women & Therapy, 25,* 61–88.

Seibert, S. E., Kraimer, M. L., & Liden, R. C. (2001). A social capital theory of career success. *Academy of Management Journal, 44,* 219–237.

Speitzer, G. M., McCall, M. W., & Mahoney, J. D. (1997). Early identification of international executive potential. *Journal of Applied Psychology, 82,* 6–29.

Stockdale, M. S., & Bhattacharya, G. (2009). Sexual harassment and the glass ceiling. In M. Barreto, M. K. Ryan, & M. T. Schmitt (Eds.), *The glass ceiling in the 21st century: Understanding barriers to gender inequality* (pp. 171–199). Washington, DC: APA Books.

Swim, J., Borgida, E., Maruyama, G., & Myers, D. G. (1989). McKay, Joan versus McKay, John—Do gender stereotypes bias evaluations? *Psychological Bulletin, 105,* 409–429.

Van Velsor, E., McCauley, C. D., & Moxley, R. S. (1998). Introduction: Our view of leadership development. *Handbook of leadership development* (pp. 1–28). San Francisco: Jossey-Bass Publishers.

Williams, J., Manvell, J., & Bornstein, S. (2006). "Opt out" or pushed out?: How the press covers work/family conflict—The untold story of why women leave the workplace. The Center for Worklife Law.

Yoder, J. D. (1991). Rethinking tokenism: Looking beyond the numbers. *Gender& Society, 5,* 178–192.

Congresswoman Debbie Wasserman Schultz

Congresswoman Wasserman Schultz represents Florida's 23rd Congressional District, encompassing parts of Broward and Miami-Dade counties.

Congresswoman Wasserman Schultz has been a strong advocate for women's health. Following her diagnosis with breast cancer in 2009, she introduced the Education and Awareness Requires Learning Young Act, which is legislation that directs the Centers for Disease Control and Prevention to implement a national education campaign on breast cancer to young women, especially women of certain national origins and races. Her bill became law in 2010 as part of the Affordable Health Care Act. According to Wasserman Schultz:

> Breast cancer is not just a disease that strikes at women. It strikes at the very heart of who we are as women: how others perceive us, how we perceive ourselves, how we live, work and raise our families—or whether we do these things at all.

Congresswoman Wasserman Schultz became a member of the Congressional Caucus for Women's Issues, a bipartisan members' organization which is devoted to women's health, and economic, legal, and educational concerns. She also is responsible for presidents since 2006 to proclaim Jewish American Heritage Month annually.

Source: http://wassermanschultz.house.gov/.

Chapter 9

Empowering Women Leaders to Rise above Microaggressions*

Kevin L. Nadal, Vanessa Meterko, Vivian M. Vargas, and Michelle Wideman

As several chapters in this volume have addressed, discrimination still exists in the United States, including the U.S. Congress, but instead may take more subtle forms (Nadal, 2008; Sue & Capodilupo, 2008). These subtle forms of discrimination can occur based on one's race, ethnicity, gender, sexual orientation, or other social identity; in recent years, such instances have been labeled as *microaggressions*.

Microaggressions are "brief and commonplace daily verbal, behavioral, or environmental indignities, whether intentional or unintentional, that communicate hostile, derogatory, or negative slights and insults toward members of oppressed groups" (Nadal, 2008, p. 23). Microaggressions occur on a daily basis and are so subtle that even the victims themselves may not know if the incident was directed at them because of their race, gender, sexual orientation, or religion or if it occurred because of some other reason. As a result, unlike the blatant racism prior to, and during, the civil rights movement, microaggressions become difficult to

*Portions of this chapter were previously published in M. Paludi & B Coates (Eds.). (2011). *Women as transformational leaders, vol. 2: Organizational obstacles and solutions* (pp. 207–231). Santa Barbara, CA: Praeger.

recognize and address Regardless of the intention of the enactor of the microaggression, these commonplace incidents of microaggressions can have a cumulative and detrimental effect on the mental health of members of nonprivileged groups.

The brief, commonplace, and subtle nature of microaggressions poses unique challenges for perpetrators and recipients alike. In contrast to overt forms of discrimination (e.g., racial slurs, sexual harassment, hate crimes), enactors of microaggressions may not recognize their behaviors and recipients may be confused and invalidated by the ambiguity of a microaggression. For example, when a white woman tells a black woman, "you're so articulate," the white person may genuinely believe that she is complimenting the person of color. However, she may not realize that her statement might actually be implying her bias that all black women are uneducated and inarticulate. On the contrary, because this statement may not be overtly racist or malicious in intention, the black woman might question whether or not she is being discriminated against. She may feel hurt while also questioning whether or not she is being "too sensitive." If she chooses to confront the individual, the white woman may rationalize or provide an explanation for the microaggression (e.g., "I was honestly just complimenting you"), which may in turn invalidate the recipient's experience of racism.

One of the biggest challenges of microaggressions is that a clash of worldviews may hinder one's ability to recognize such events. An incident that is perceived as hurtful by one individual in one context may not be perceived as harmful by another individual in another context. Moreover, an interaction that is perceived as a microaggression by an individual of the dominant identity group (e.g., whites, men, upper class, heterosexual individuals) may not be perceived as such by those of marginalized groups (e.g., people of color, women, lower class, or lesbian, gay, bisexual, or transgender). While the complexity of microaggressions makes it an elusive concept, recognizing their existence is the first step in stopping continued negative messages to various marginalized groups.

This chapter will describe the ways in which microaggressions affect the lives of women. Specifically, examples will focus on ways that microaggressions may influence women's leadership potential. The chapter will address microaggressions affecting women leaders in general and then will concentrate on the particular challenges that confront women of color, lesbian and bisexual women, and transgender women. Finally, the chapter will discuss the psychological impact of these subtle acts of discrimination, the coping mechanisms that women use, and implications and recommendations for addressing microaggressions in the workplace and in everyday life.

GENDER MICROAGGRESSIONS AND WOMEN

Women's Rights Campaigns have been making progress toward equality since major milestones in history, such as the Nineteenth Amendment and the Civil Rights Act in 1964 (Nadal, 2010; Swim & Cohen, 1997; Swim, Hyers, Cohen, & Ferguson, 2001). Despite steadfast efforts toward an egalitarian society, gender discrimination and sexism still exist today. Blatant forms of sexism are becoming increasingly less common and even looked down upon by society. However, subtle forms of sexism have become more commonplace and are harder to distinguish. Swim and Cohen (1997) define blatant and overt sexism as intentional, visible, and unambiguous, harmful, and unfair treatment of women. These forms of sexism are often easier to identify and are likely to fit the criteria for sexual harassment: unwelcome sexual advances, requests for sexual favors, and other verbal or physical conduct of a sexual nature. On the contrary, subtle or covert sexism usually goes unnoticed because it has been hidden by cultural and society norms (Swim & Cohen, 1997). Subtle sexism often does not fit the criteria for sexual harassment, even though subtle sexism creates hostile work environments and have negative consequences for women (Nadal, 2010). For example, a man who makes a stereotypical comment about women or who compliments a woman on her looks may not easily be defined as an unwelcome sexual advance or verbal conduct of a sexual nature. Thus, such behavior may not be reported or addressed and the behavior may continue.

Gender microaggressions are defined as "brief and commonplace daily verbal, behavioral, and environmental indignities that communicate hostile, derogatory, or negative sexist slights and insults toward women" (Nadal, 2010, p. 155). In a qualitative study, Capodilupo et al., (2010) found that female participants endorsed two main themes of gender microaggressions: *sexual objectification* and *assumption of traditional gender roles*. Sexual objectification at the workplace may be exemplified by a man who comments on a woman's outfit while staring at her body. While he may be intending to pay her a compliment, he is degrading her in the process. In addition, women are often assumed to maintain traditional gender roles. For example, when a career-driven woman is asked why she never got married or had kids, an indirect message is communicated that a woman's primary role in life is to raise children. While one may assume that asking such a question is innocuous or harmless, the woman who experiences this frequently may feel that others do not value her life choices or career.

In Capodilupo and colleagues' (2010) study, participants also reported other types of gender microaggressions: *second-class citizen, assumptions of inferiority, denial of reality of sexism, denial of individual sexism, use of sexist language, leaving gender at the door,* and *environmental invalidations*. An example of second-class citizenship may include a group of male employees who never invite a female coworker to join them at an event (e.g., sporting event) after work. Perhaps they assume that women would not be interested in sports, but perhaps they also exclude her because she is not viewed as important or worthy of an invitation. In addition, women are often assumed to be inferior to men (both physically and intellectually).

For example, when a woman's ideas are dismissed at a meeting or on the Senate floor or in the House of Representatives, while a man's are not, it is assumed that a man's opinions are more valuable than a woman's. Similarly, when women are assumed to need a man's help with passing legislation, a subtle message is communicated that all women need a man's help.

Denial of reality of sexism occurs when a man invalidates a woman's experiences with sexism by labeling her as "paranoid" or "oversensitive," while denial of individual sexism occurs when a man negates a woman who confronts him for perpetuating sexist acts. Sexist language occurs in both overt and covert forms; for example, jokes that belittle women politicians may be more intentional and explicit. However, when a man calls a female coworker "sweetie" or "honey" while he does not use the same language with male coworkers, he is unintentionally treating her in a condescending manner. Even marking the word "politicians" to inform the reader/listener that the politician is female is condescending. Women are often asked to "leave their genders at the door." This means that they are told (directly and indirectly) to not exhibit any feminine qualities (e.g., showing emotions) or complain about sexism. Finally, environmental microaggressions are instances where microaggressions are transmitted through systems, cultural norms, or the physical environment. For example, when a woman sees that there are very few women CEOs in the Fortune 500 companies or in politics, an indirect message is transmitted that women are inferior or do not make good leaders.

Gender microaggressions, whether intentional or unintentional, can have a lasting negative effect on women and their psychological well-being (Nadal, 2010). This negative effect can permeate every aspect of a woman's life, including her home life, her workplace, or her roles in society. Workplace discrimination and sexual harassment toward women may lead to reports of lower job satisfaction, and significant consequences for employee health like higher levels of anxiety and depression. Moreover, stereotypes and discrimination can affect women's ability to excel in their careers (Sipe, Johnson, & Fisher, 2009). Thus, eliminating gender microaggressions and other forms of discrimination can have beneficial effects on the workplace environment, including improved morale, organizational commitment, and retention (Sipe et al., 2009).

RACIAL MICROAGGRESSIONS AND WOMEN OF COLOR

Previous literature has found that people of color are often the victims of racial microaggressions. Racial microaggressions are defined as "brief and commonplace daily verbal, behavioral, or environmental indignities, whether intentional or unintentional, that communicate hostile, derogatory, or negative racial slights and insults to the target person or group" (Sue, Capodilupo, et al., 2007, p. 273). As with gender microaggressions, several categories of racial microaggressions have been identified: *alien in one's own land, ascription of intelligence, color blindness, criminality/assumption of criminal status, denial of individual racism, myth of meritocracy, pathologizing cultural values/communication styles, second-class citizen,* and *environmental microaggressions* (Sue, Capodilupo, et al., 2007). Many of these categories have been validated through research with African Americans (Sue, Nadal, et al., 2008), Latinos (Rivera, Forquer, & Rangel, 2010), and Asian Americans (Sue, Bucceri, Lin, Torino, & Nadal, 2007).

Alien in one's own land refers to instances where individuals are treated like foreigners, even though their family may have been in the United States for many generations; this can be exemplified by an employer telling an Asian American person that she "speaks good English" when she was born and raised in the United States and English is the only language she knows. Ascription of intelligence occurs when people assume others to have a certain intellectual capacity because of their race. For example, an employer who asks an Asian American employee to help fix a computer (who has indicated in no way that he is computer-savvy) may indicate the individual's biases or stereotypes about Asian Americans. This may be contrary to aforementioned examples of individuals assuming that African Americans are intellectually inferior or uneducated. Colorblindness may refer to instances when individuals make statements like "I don't see color" or "there is only one race—the human race." While these comments may be meant to be egalitarian sentiments, they indirectly invalidate the reality that the person of color is a racial and cultural being and that racism does exist in his or her life. An example may include a person of color who is followed around in a store, or a police officer pulling over a person of color for not doing anything wrong. While no one in these scenarios are using racist language or overtly discriminating the people of color in these cases, all of these experiences subtly communicate negative stereotypes about people of color.

The denial of individual racism occurs when an individual claims that he or she is racist, after someone confronts him or her on one's potentially racist behavior. The Myth of Meritocracy occurs when someone believes that anyone can succeed if he or she works hard enough. This belief suggests that if a person of color is not succeeding at work (e.g., not getting promoted, not getting elected to Congress), it must be due to laziness or a lack of effort on his or her part rather than to a systematic lack of social privilege. Pathologizing cultural values or communication styles occurs when individuals are expected to conform to white norms because their ways of doing things are unacceptable or inferior. For example, because assertiveness is an American value, it is expected that all individuals must utilize this communication style in the workplace; contrarily, while passivity may be viewed as a value in other cultures, it would be discouraged or viewed as substandard in many workplace settings. Finally, environmental microaggressions occur when cultural systems or the physical environment sends negative messages to people of color. For example,

seeing stereotypes of racial/ethnic minority groups on television or seeing a lack of people of color in leadership positions may send denigrating
messages to individuals of those groups.

Women of color may experience microaggressions that may occur due
to their gender, their race, or some combination of them all. For example,
Latina and Asian American women have often reported that they feel
exoticized because of both their race and gender (Rivera et al., 2010; Sue,
Bucceri, et al., 2007) African American women have reported experiencing
workplace microaggressions involving their hair (Sue, Nadal, et al., 2008).
Specifically, many African American women have been told (explicitly
and implicitly) that their hair was either "unprofessional" or "unique" and
sometimes are even asked if someone could touch their hair. All of these
types of microaggressions have negative implications. An African American woman who is told that her hairstyle is unprofessional is indirectly
being told that she needs to conform to white norms and have a hairstyle
similar to white women. Contrarily, an African American woman who is
told that her hair is "unique" or asked if someone could touch her hair is
implicitly being exoticized or treated like an object.

When women of color experience microaggressions, they may often
question if the incident is occurring because of their race, their gender,
or both. For example, when a male employer continually compliments an
Asian American woman on her looks, is he treating her like a sexual object
because of her race, her gender, or both? When an African American
woman is overlooked as a viable candidate for political office, is it because
of her race, her gender, or both? Again, it may be difficult to fully answer
these questions because the enactors may not recognize their behavior and
sometimes may even be well-intentioned. The man who continually calls
attention to the Asian American woman's looks may genuinely believe
that he is complimenting her, while the political party that overlooked the
African American woman as a candidate for office may genuinely believe
there were other factors as to why she wasn't the best candidate. Nonetheless, either of these situations may leave the woman of color to feel
confused, invalidated, frustrated, or saddened. As a result, these women
experience discrimination that is different than their white female counterparts who experience only sexism, as well as their men of color counterparts who experience only racism. Because of this, the stress of being
a "double minority" may have significant impacts on her self-esteem, her
mental health, and her performance.

Sexual Orientation Microaggressions and Lesbian and Bisexual Women

Lesbian, gay, and bisexual (LGB) individuals have been criminalized,
victimized, and marginalized throughout the history of the United States.
Records indicate that men were executed for the act of sodomy in colonial

America as early as 1624 (Herek, 1989). In contemporary times, hate crimes toward LGB people have continued to be on the rise; while the number of hate crimes based on race has been on the decline, hate crimes based on sexual orientation have increased over the past several years (Federal Bureau of Investigation, 2008). And while these numbers are still high, it is also important to recognize that many hate crimes based on sexual orientation are underreported, which means that the number of LGB hate crimes in the United States may even be higher (Herek, 2000). However, much like sexism and racism, discrimination toward LGB persons may also take on more subtle forms. Nadal, Rivera, and Corpus (2010) outline seven recurring types of microaggressions against LGB individuals: *use of heterosexist terminology* (e.g., people using the word "gay" to describe something negative), *endorsement of heteronormative culture/behaviors* (e.g., LGB individuals feeling pressured to appear heterosexual in order to be considered professional), *assumption of universal LGB experience* (e.g., others assuming that all LGB people fit into a neat stereotype or that one LGB person can speak for the entire community), *exoticization* (e.g., others glamorizing or objectifying lesbian and bisexual women as sex symbols or gay men as comedic relief), *discomfort/disapproval of LGB experience* (e.g., LGB people receiving disapproving stares from strangers when out in public with their partners), *denial of the reality of heterosexism* (e.g., a person denying that he or she treats LGB people any differently than he or she treats heterosexual people), and finally *assumption of sexual pathology/abnormality* (e.g., instances when LGB individuals are cast as overly sexual or sexually deviant).

There are many ways that lesbian and bisexual women experience these microaggressions two-fold because of the intersections of their identities. Lesbian and bisexual women have reported experiencing a variety of these types of microaggressions in the workplace, even at jobs that they describe as "gay friendly" (Giuffre, Dellinger, & Williams, 2008). These experiences have the potential to lead lesbian and bisexual women to have ambivalent or negative feelings about themselves, coworkers, their work environment, or some combination of them all. In some instances, encountering and addressing these issues directly has also been shown to facilitate learning about different groups of people in the workplace (Giuffre et al., 2008).

An example of a sexual orientation microaggression would be an opponent asking a bisexual woman candidate for political office personal questions about her dating life, her sex life, or her pregnancy (if applicable). While these questions may be well-meaning or may arise out of curiosity, and while some bisexual women may not mind "teaching" their heterosexual colleagues about bisexuality, others may feel singled out because other women do not have to field such personal questions. The woman may also feel pressure to speak on behalf of all bisexuals or act as a role model to disprove negative stereotypes about lesbians and bisexuals (Giuffre et al., 2008).

Another example of a sexual orientation microaggression involves the stereotype that LGB people embody characteristics of the opposite gender (e.g., gay men are considered feminine and lesbian women are considered masculine). This stereotype encourages a unique type of discrimination in any profession. For instance, a lesbian woman who worked at a "gay-friendly" but male-dominated company reported feeling uncomfortable when the men in the office made sexually crude comments about other women in her presence. She felt that because she was attracted to women, the men treated her as "one of the boys" and expected her to participate in the sexist objectification of other women, or at least to be less offended than a heterosexual woman might be (Giuffre et al., 2008).

While more employees and employers are open about their sexual orientations than in years past, there is still variability in the degree of openness at work ranging from explicit openness to lying in order to be perceived as heterosexual (Croteau, 1996). This continued hesitance to disclose sexual orientation at work and fear of discrimination may stem from the overt and covert discrimination that out lesbian and bisexual women still experience. In addition to being subject to the already well-documented gender-based discrimination in the workplace (e.g., lower pay for equal work, the proverbial "glass ceiling" and the lack of accommodation of motherhood at work), lesbian and bisexual women face unique types of discrimination in the workplace. From being the only woman in the office subjected to repeated probing questions about her personal life to being inappropriately treated as one of the boys, bisexual and lesbian women continue to face sexual orientation microaggressions in the workplace.

Transgender Microaggressions and Women of Transgender Experience

The word "transgender" is considered an "umbrella term" and is used to describe people who do not conform to traditional gender roles, including transgenderists, drag queens, cross-dressers, and transsexuals (Kenagy, 2002). People of transgender experience can identify as male-to-female or female-to-male. The former is a person who was assigned the male gender at birth but who identifies as female, and the latter is a person who was assigned the female gender at birth but who identifies as male (Kenagy, 2002). Individuals in the process of transitioning from one gender to another may identify as entirely female or entirely male, both female and male, or neither (Koken, Bimbi, & Parsons, 2009). Because American society sees sex and gender roles as "inherently immutable" it is difficult for some to accept others who do not fall into a simple male or female category (Kidd and Witten, 2007/2008). As such, *transwomen* or women of transgender experience are frequently socially marginalized and persistently stigmatized because of the way they live their lives. Some have argued that the inclusion of gender identity disorder in the *Diagnostic and Statistical Manual of Mental Disorders, Fourth Edition,* has only added to the discrimination and condemnation faced by this group on a daily basis (Koken et al., 2009).

As *gender nonconformists,* transwomen are often the victims of hate crimes and especially targeted because they are generally seen as men who are acting effeminate (Koken et al., 2009; Wilchins, 2008). Transwomen often provoke disgust and hate in those who wish to see "their kind" annihilated; this prejudice and hatred often results in especially brutal hate crimes (Kidd & Witten, 2007/2008). It is often believed that there is an underlying desire in these perpetrators "to eradicate the transgender-identified individual in order to alleviate his/her disgust and to avenge the sense of betrayal that precipitated the attack" (Kidd & Witten, 2007/2008, p. 34). Due to this overwhelming violence and palpable discrimination, many in the transgender community prefer to remain silent; thus, transgender people are slowly and collectively becoming an invisible minority ignored by many in law enforcement (Kidd & Witten, 2007/2008; Wilchins, 2008).

As gender nonconformists, transwomen face an exorbitant number of challenges on a daily basis. For individuals in society who are not familiar with members of the transgender community, "oohs" and "ahs" are frequent reactions along with questions of "why" and "how" with unsatisfactory answers. For example, many individuals ask invasive and private questions to transgender individuals about their body parts or their sexual activities. Because of this, many transwomen are unable to live "normal" lives, often encountering everything from stares, snickers, and insults to outright hostility, rejection, and aggression. Transgender individuals also deal with everything from rejection by family to denial of employment to limited educational opportunities (Leichtentritt & Davidson Arad, 2004; Sausa, Keatley, & Operario, 2007). Because of the limited literature about the transgender community, most members of society need to be educated about this community, in order to provide safer and more welcoming environments for them.

There are several categories of microaggressions that are directed toward transgender individuals. These categories include *use of transphobic language* (e.g., calling individuals by incorrect pronouns or using transphobic slurs), *endorsement of gender-normative/binary culture/behaviors* (e.g., assuming that men and women should dress a certain way), *assumption of universal transgender experience* (e.g., assuming that all transgender persons desire hormone treatment or reassignment surgery), *exocitization* (e.g., staring at transgender in awe or scrutiny), *discomfort/disapproval of transgender experience* (e.g., peering at a transgender person with condemnation), *denial of reality of transphobia* (e.g., invalidating a transgender person's experiences of discrimination), *assumption of sexual pathology/*

abnormality (e.g., stereotyping transgender people to all HIV/AIDS or to be sex workers), *denial of individual transphobia* (e.g., denying one's own transphobic biases), *denial of personal body privacy* (e.g., asking a transgender person inappropriate questions about his or her body parts), and *systemic and environmental microaggressions* (e.g., transphobic microaggressions that occur in the media, government, policies, and other institutions).

There are many ways that transgender microaggressions may occur in the workplace—on both systemic and interpersonal levels. A common example of an environmental/systemic microaggression includes how buildings usually have both a women's restroom and a men's restroom, but not a unisex option. This forced choice may cause a transgender employee to feel unwelcome or abnormal because he or she does not define himself or herself in such dichotomous terms. Moreover, when transgender individuals are transitioning from one gender to another, they may not feel comfortable using one bathroom over the other, or may be chastised for using the restroom of the gender they identify with (e.g., a transgender woman may want to use the women's restroom, but security guards may not let her). Another environmental transgender microaggression may involve a transgender employee who might also feel like a second-class citizen when he or she notices that there are no transgender CEOs or leaders within his or her company. This conspicuous absence sends the message that transgender people are invisible, less powerful, or less valued than those who endorse gender normative behaviors and identify with their biological sex.

Transgender microaggressions can also transpire through interpersonal interactions. For example, some transgender individuals report that coworkers repeatedly call them by the incorrect pronoun despite the fact that they had openly clarified their preferred gender pronoun on several occasions. When coworkers reply with "I don't even know what to call you" or continue to call the transgender person by his or her biological name and not by his or her preferred name, they are sending the message that the person's transgender experience is not valid or important. Again, although this may be explained away as confusion or carelessness, repeated microaggressions like these send the message that the transgender employee is abnormal and not worth respecting.

WOMEN'S COPING WITH MICROAGGRESSIONS

Some researchers have suggested specific actions to combat these types of subtle discrimination and create more accepting and productive work environments (see Sue, 2010, for a review). When individuals are the victims or recipients of microaggressions, there are several thought processes that may occur. Some authors have identified a "Catch 22" of whether or not they should react (Sue, Capodilupo, et al., 2007). If they do choose to respond to the microaggression, there is a potential of endangering their physical or psychological safety. For example, if a drunken man makes sexist remarks toward a woman at a bar, she may simply choose to ignore the statements because she worries that if she starts an argument with him he may potentially become violent. Thus, she may choose to avoid controversy and ignore him altogether in order to protect herself.

Psychological safety may be a more salient factor for addressing microaggressions in workplace settings. For instance, when a woman hears a sexist remark made by a coworker in the workplace, she has a difficult task of determining whether to respond. This is more pronounced during a political debate; thousands of individuals are watching and listening to the candidates. How the woman responds will be noted by individuals. Women realize that saying something about the microaggression may lead to tension between her and her opponent and will be interpreted by bystanders negatively. Moreover, she may want to avoid confronting him because she does not want to be seen as "oversensitive" and does not want any hard feelings to affect her reputation or opportunities within her campaign. Thus, she may feel it would be easier for her to not respond at all. Some may view this however as being unempowered.

However, for individuals who do not respond to microaggressions when they transpire, there are a myriad of physical and psychological consequences that may occur. For example, in the earlier illustration of the intoxicated man who makes a sexist remark at the bar, a woman may regret not saying anything to the man. While at the time, she may have been worried about her safety, on leaving the situation, she may feel disempowered for not being able to voice her opinion. She may also feel regret and worry that he will continue to make sexist remarks to other women, making her feel guilty that she should have said something to teach him a lesson. Thinking about what she "should have" or "could have" said may lead the woman to perseverate about the situation, which may then impact her self-esteem and may even negatively impact other aspects of her life.

There are emotional, behavioral, and cognitive reactions that women may experience in response to microaggressions. Women may experience various emotions that remain internalized (e.g., guilt, humiliation, and discomfort), as well as those that have been externalized and communicated to others (e.g., anger and fear). Women may utilize different behavioral techniques in response to microaggressions. Some women may remain passive and choose not to confront the enactor of the microaggression, while others attempt to protect themselves by actively engaging in behaviors that would make them less susceptible. For example, many women report that they walk in large groups in order to avoid being catcalled or bothered by men. Finally, women report many ways that they react cognitively to microaggressions: some become more resilient, others learn to accept microaggressions as a norm in society, and others have actively resisted microaggressions.

Finally, women of intersectional identities may cope with microaggressions in other ways. For example, Sue, Capodilupo, and Holder (2008) discuss how African Americans may deal with microaggressions. In a study with mostly female participants, many individuals report that they need a *sanity check,* in which they contact a friend or family member to confirm if their feelings and perceptions of a microaggression are valid. Moreover, this sanity check allows for these individuals to process their feelings in a safe and healing environment where they can feel validated and where they can be genuine without appearing to be an "angry minority." It is likely that women and other marginalized groups may also utilize this sanity check, in order to validate their perceptions and reactions to potential microaggressions and to verify that their reactions to microaggressions are legitimate.

RECOMMENDATIONS FOR WOMEN'S LEADERSHIP

In order to prevent microaggressions toward women (and other marginalized groups) and to promote women leaders in society, there are many changes that can be recommended. Although sexual harassment laws and policies are established and enforced in most states, microaggressions must also be discussed in workplace settings because sexual harassment laws and policies do not protect against subtle forms of discrimination. For example, because many microaggressions are so subtle and seemingly innocuous, it would be difficult for individuals to contend these instances in court. As a result, many workplace microaggressions are underreported because women and other marginalized persons do not feel that reporting such instances will lead to positive outcomes. Specifically, workplaces can implement many programs and policies to prevent or minimize microaggressions altogether. Some examples include:

(1) Integrating microaggressions into human resources diversity training programs. By discussing that subtle forms of discrimination is harmful in the same way that sexual harassment and overt discrimination is, the company is communicating that it is intolerant of discrimination and that it promotes culturally competent work environments.

(2) Incorporating microaggressions into sexual harassment policies and procedures. In the same ways that employees are informed about sexual harassment policies upon hiring, they should also be educated about microaggressions and subtle forms of discrimination. Again, this will serve as a way of promoting multiculturalism and social justice within the company.

(3) Creating safe environments where individuals can feel comfortable in discussing issues of race, gender, sexual orientation, and culture in the workplace. By being able to discuss cultural influences on communication styles, power dynamics, and other factors, institutions allow opportunities for individuals to address microaggressions as they occur. In doing so, individuals may feel more "safe" which would then lead to more productive working environments.

For families, there are many ways that individuals can address microaggressions in order to promote women's leadership and growth. However, one difficulty with addressing microaggressions in family systems is the complexity of family dynamics, gender roles, and culture. Each family is different because of its individual structures (e.g., whether it is a single-parent home, a two-parent home, or a home with guardians), gender roles (e.g., how much a family abides by traditional gender roles in behaviors, household chores, career choices), and culture (e.g., how one's ethnic and cultural values impact how one communicates, behaves, and perceives the other). Despite these unique factors, there are several ways that families of all kinds can promote women's leadership and minimize or prevent microaggressions:

(1) Teaching one's children about culture from an early age and encourage all children to succeed regardless of their gender, race, age, or social class. Doing so will allow children to develop a healthy self-esteem, which will hopefully lead to self-confidence, a good work ethic, and capacity for leadership.
(2) Helping children to understand the obstacles that may hinder their success, due to their gender, race, age, social class, or other identities. Some individuals may believe that social justice issues should not be taught to children because they fear that it will confuse them or taint their innocence. However, teaching them in small ways about social justice at early ages can help them to be prepared to deal with discrimination when they face it as adults. Sometimes, adults have difficulty discussing issues of race, gender, and culture because they never learned the language to discuss it in their formative years. Teaching children how to do so in their early years will hopefully allow them the comfort in discussing such issues as adults.
(3) Being aware of one's biases about gender and gender role expectations. In maintaining such awareness, individuals can be cognizant of how these biases affect the ways they encourage (or discourage) their children from engaging in behaviors or activities, as well as making career choices and striving for success.

In terms of everyday life, there are many ways that microaggressions can be minimized or diminished altogether. School systems can teach students about social justice issues from an early age and even well into adolescence. Religious institutions must be aware of ways that they perpetuate rigid roles, particularly in hindering women's leadership; perhaps changes can be made to empower women in a way that may not completely disregard tradition. The media must be more responsible regarding the sexist images that they portray about women, as well as the negative and stereotypical images they also portray of various racial/ethnic groups, LGBT people, and other sociocultural groups. Positive images and role models of women, including women of color, LGB women, and transgender women, will help to dispel stereotypes and negative assumptions about these groups. Government policies should reflect women's rights and encourage women to become leaders in all sectors; thus, perhaps this will foster more women's leadership and result in more women as elected officials.

REFERENCES

Capodilupo, C. M., Nadal, K. L., Corman, L., Hamit, S., Lyons, O., & Weinberg, A. (2010). The manifestation of gender microaggressions. In D. W. Sue (Ed.), *Microaggressions and marginality: Manifestation, dynamics, and impact.* New York, NY: Wiley & Sons.

Croteau, J. M. (1996). Research on the work experiences of lesbian, gay, and bisexual people: An integrative review of methodology and findings. *Journal of Vocational Behavior, 48,* 195–209.

Federal Bureau of Investigation (FBI). (2008). Hate crime statistics, 2007. Washington, DC: Author. Retrieved May 31, 2010, from https://www.fbi.gov/stats-services/crimestats/.

Giuffre, P., Dellinger, K., & Williams, C. L. (2008). "No retribution for being gay?" Inequality in gay-friendly workplaces. *Sociological Spectrum, 28,* 254–277.

Herek, G. M. (1989). Hate crimes against lesbians and gay men: Issues for research and policy. *American Psychologist, 44*(7), 948–955.

Herek, G. M. (2000). The psychology of sexual prejudice. *Current Directions in Psychological Science, 9,* 19–22.

Kenagy, G. (2002). HIV among transgendered people. *AIDS Care, 14,* 127–134.

Kidd, J. D., & Witten, T. M. (2007/2008). Transgender and trans sexual identities: The next strange fruit-hate crimes. Violence and genocide against the global trans-communities. *Journal of Hate Studies, 6*(1), 31–63.

Koken, J. A., Bimbi, D. S., & Parsons, J. T. (2009). Experiences of familial acceptance-rejection among transwomen of color. *Journal of Family Psychology, 23*(6), 853–860.

Leichtentritt, R. D., & Davidson Arad, B. (2004). Adolescent and young adult male-to-female transsexuals: Pathways to prostitution. *British Journal of Social Work, 34*(3), 349–374.

Nadal, K. L. (2008). Preventing racial, ethnic, gender, sexual minority, disability, and religious microaggressions: Recommendations for promoting positive mental health. *Prevention in Counseling Psychology: Theory, Research, Practice and Training, 2*(1), 22–27.

Nadal, K. L. (2010). Gender microaggressions and women: Implications for mental health. In M. A. Paludi (Ed.), *Feminism and women's rights worldwide, Volume 2: Mental and physical health* (pp. 155–175). Westport, CT: Praeger.

Nadal, K. L., Rivera, D. P., & Corpus, M. J. H. (2010). Sexual orientation and transgender microaggressions in everyday life: Experiences of lesbians, gays, bisexuals, and transgender individuals. In D. W. Sue (Ed.), *Microaggressions and marginality: Manifestation, dynamics, and impact* (pp. 217–240). New York, NY: Wiley & Sons.

Rivera, D. P., Forquer, E. E., & Rangel, R. (2010). Microaggressions and the life experience of Latina/o Americans. In D. W. Sue (Ed.), *Microaggressions and marginalized groups in society: Race, gender, sexual orientation, class and religious manifestations* (pp. 59–83). New York, NY: Wiley & Sons.

Sausa, L. A., Keatley, J., & Operario, D. (2007). Perceived risks and benefits of sex work among transgender women of color in San Francisco. *Archives of Sexual Behavior, 36*, 768–777.

Sipe, S., Johnson, D. C., & Fisher, D. K. (2009). University students' perceptions of gender discrimination in the workplace: Reality versus fiction. *Journal of Education for Business, 84*(6), 339–349.

Sue, D. W. (2010). *Microaggressions in everyday life: Race, gender, and sexual orientation.* New York, NY: Wiley & Sons.

Sue, D. W., Bucceri, J. M., Lin, A. I., Nadal, K. L., & Torino, G. C. (2007). Racial microaggressions and the Asian American experience. *Cultural Diversity and Ethnic Minority Psychology, 13*(1), 72–81.

Sue, D. W., & Capodilupo, C. M. (2008). Racial, gender, and sexual orientation microaggressions: Implications for counseling and psychotherapy. In D. W. Sue & D. Sue (Authors). *Counseling the culturally diverse,* 5th ed. New York, NY: John Wiley & Sons.

Sue, D. W., Capodilupo, C. M., & Holder, A. M. B. (2008). Racial microaggressions in the life experience of Black Americans. *Professional Psychology: Research and Practice, 39*(3), 329–336.

Sue, D. W., Capodilupo, C. M., Torino, G. C., Bucceri, J. M., Holder, A. M., Nadal, K. L., & Esquilin, M. E. (2007). Racial microaggressions in everyday life: Implications for counseling. *The American Psychologist, 62*(4), 271–286.

Sue, D. W., Nadal, K. L., Capodilupo, C. M., Lin, A. I., Rivera, D. P., & Torino, G. (2008). Racial microaggressions against Black Americans: Implications for counseling. *Journal of Counseling and Development, 86*(3), 330–338.

Swim, J. K., & Cohen, L. L. (1997). Overt, covert, and subtle sexism: A comparison between the attitudes toward women and modern sexism scales. *Psychology of Women Quarterly, 21*(1), 103–118.

Swim, J. K., Hyers, L. L., Cohen, L. L., & Ferguson, M. J. (2001). Everyday sexism: Evidence for its incidence, nature, and psychological impact from three daily diary studies. *Journal of Social Issues, 57*(1), 31–53.

Wilchins, R. (2008). An invisible war. *Advocate, 1005,* 33.

Senator Dianne Feinstein

Women have begun to see that if I go through that doorway, I take everybody through it.

Senator Feinstein has been an advocate for legislation on women's health, violence against women, and abducted children. She has raised more than $65 million for breast cancer research. In addition, Senator Feinstein has created nationwide AMBER alert communications network to assist law enforcement in locating children who have been abducted. She also has been key to providing survivors of violent crime a core set of procedural rights under federal law to ensure they have standing to assert their rights before a court.

Senator Feinstein also is a major supporter of hate crimes legislation. According to Senator Feinstein,

The criteria for serving one's country should be competence, courage and willingness to serve. When we deny people the chance to serve because of their sexual orientation, we deprive them of their rights of citizenship, and we deprive our armed forces the service of willing and capable Americans.

Source: http://www.feinstein.senate.gov/public/.

Chapter 10

Social Psychological Perspectives on Discrimination against Women Leaders*

Nicole L. Cundiff and Margaret S. Stockdale

GENDER DISCRIMINATION AGAINST FEMALE MANAGERS AND LEADERS

Prejudice and discrimination exist and are reinforced within organizational systems, which require effort and resources to change their culturally embedded processes that keep them grounded in the status quo. Discrimination against women in or for leadership positions in politics, business, or education can be manifested in terms of access or treatment. Disproportionately selecting men for leadership positions in politics (see Introduction, this volume) or for other career paths that could lead to leadership qualifies as access discrimination. Judging the performance of female leaders (or women in occupations with a leadership career path) to be inferior to men's; regarding such women as being less likable; shutting these women out of important developmental, mentoring, and networking opportunities; and creating a hostile or chilly work/campaign

*Portions of this chapter were previously published in M. Paludi & B. Coates (Eds.). (2011). *Women as transformational leaders, vol. 1: Cultural and organizational stereotypes, prejudice and discrimination* (pp. 177–199). Santa Barbara, CA: Praeger.

environment are examples of treatment discrimination. Ample evidence has amassed from experimental social-psychology-based laboratory studies, as well as field research, to document these forms of discrimination in a variety of samples (Blass, Brouer, Perrewe, & Ferris, 2007; Cuddy, Fiske, & Glick, 2004; Garcia-Retamero & López-Zafra, 2006; Green, 2009).

For instance, Garcia-Retamero and López-Zafra (2006) found that promotion perceptions for women were highest in feminized industries (i.e., clothing manufacturing), but in masculine (i.e., auto manufacturing) and gender-neutral industries (i.e., marketing), men were perceived as more promotable. Further, promotion perceptions of men in feminized industries were similar to the women in these industries. Therefore, women, though not disadvantaged, did not enjoy an advantage over men even in feminized industries. Men, on the other hand, were advantaged in both masculine and gender-neutral industries.

Through the popular press and personal experiences, working women are familiar with the concept of the glass ceiling—the point at which women's career advancement becomes stifled. However, obstacles in women's careers do not necessarily occur directly before reaching the upper echelons of organizations. Women encounter discrimination from early childhood and throughout their lives, which interferes and dissuades them from entering into the professions they want, including politics. For instance, women and girls are faced with disproportionate displays of heroes, historical figures, and role models of the opposing sex throughout their educational and professional advancement (Betz, 2005). This sends a message that women are not as important as men, potentially affecting young women's self-efficacy and self-esteem (Bandura, 2001; Lent, Brown, & Hackett, 1994). Exposing girls and women to female leaders in a variety of disciplines, including politics, can assist with their self-efficacy (see Introduction, this volume).

Other barriers that women face in their ascension to leader positions include lack of social support and mentors, sexual harassment and sexism, and maintaining multiple roles (family and work) (Betz, 2005; Eagly & Carli, 2007).

Eagly and Carli (2007) developed the metaphor of a labyrinth to illustrate the experiences and barriers facing women who aspire to leadership positions. They reported that women face a situation that can best be described as moving through a labyrinth when it comes to their careers, and that women have to learn to negotiate through this labyrinth in order to obtain top leadership positions, as opposed to straighter paths typically established for men. The theoretical labyrinth is full of dead ends and obstacles, yet it is perceivably surmountable where "paths to the top exist, and some women find them" (Eagly & Carli, 2007, p. 6). Reading the brief biographies of women in the U.S. Congress that are featured in this volume provides ample evidence of the labyrinth women politicians have faced and continue to face in their careers.

Women, who eventually progress through the glass ceiling or maneuver the labyrinth and achieve a leadership position, have many social expectations to maintain. First, some women may be in positions where they are tokens with restricted power and expectations to go along with customized ways of doing work (Eagly & Carli, 2007). Second, they may take on or display leader-appropriate behaviors and characteristics, therefore going against expectations that women display more communal behaviors (Eagly & Karau, 2002). In the introduction to this volume, Paludi describes this occurrence with some of the early women candidates for the U.S. presidency; they were evaluated more negatively when they adopted "masculine" political actions. When incongruities exist between displayed roles and expectations, evaluations of female leaders may be hindered. Heilman (2001) suggested that prescriptive stereotyping of women in organizational settings (expecting women to display stereotypical characteristics and admonishing those who do not) could limit their access into upper-echelon positions.

Networking or making connections with influential members of an organization or occupation is important in order to have a successful career. Female leaders encounter issues in networking due to culturally engrained practices within organizations, such as intentionally and unintentionally not being included in formal and informal communication channels. The appendices to this volume provide opportunities for women networking in politics.

Women also tend to encounter tokenism when they are promoted into leadership roles, in which they are not given as much authority or are not viewed as valuable as their male counterparts (Lyness & Thompson, 1997). Therefore, female leaders are less likely than male leaders to be included in their organization's social networks.

Finding suitable mentors can also be a problem for women because women in organizational leadership positions are scarce. Mentors, however, are necessary in order to create networks of relationships that will be sustained once the mentor leaves the organization, as well as to create links to informal social networks (Thomas, 2001). For instance, Blass et al. (2007) argued that mentoring helps to increase political skills necessary to succeed. Unfortunately when examining the amount of organizational politics mentees gained from their mentoring, they found that political understanding and networking occurred for men but not for women. In other words, women did not benefit from mentoring in terms of building influential social networks as did men. Therefore, finding suitable mentors for female leaders can be difficult and may potentially result in unsuccessful networking opportunities.

Gender role beliefs and stereotypes are other important factors that have strong impacts on discrimination and can wreak havoc on women's leadership trajectories at various career stages. For instance, stereotypes can impact women at the beginning of their career, while they are applying for a leadership position, during the interview process, or when interacting with followers.

SOCIAL PSYCHOLOGICAL FORCES SHAPING GENDER DISPARITIES IN LEADERSHIP

Women may be less likely than men to obtain leadership positions because of conflicts with other roles, self-doubts about their fitness for such roles, or others' beliefs that they are not appropriate for such roles. Well-entrenched patriarchic social structures that stress women's reproductive and care-giving capacities over economic and achievement-centered aspirations shape women's expectations about their own place in society as well as others' beliefs about appropriate roles for women. Although attitudes toward women and gender roles have become more progressive and egalitarian over the past several decades, as described later, these deeply rooted social systems still manifest insidious effects on the ability for women to obtain and succeed in leadership positions.

GENDER ROLE SOCIALIZATION

Differences in the social and economic roles that women and men hold in society is a major source of sex differences in social behavior, including one's own and others' expectations about family and career roles (Eagly, 1987, 1997). "The expectancies associated with gender roles act as normative pressures that foster behaviors consistent with these sex-typical work roles" (Eagly, 1997, p. 1381). For example, the gender role for women arises from the compassionate and nurturing activities that are performed as part of a family role and in many female-dominated occupations, such as teacher, nurse, and social worker. To the extent that expectations about gender roles become internalized, endorsement of gender roles may become part of individuals' self-concepts. But internalization is not necessary to produce gender differences. People can behave in gender-expected manners through self-fulfilling prophecies also known as behavioral confirmation (Zanna & Pack, 1975): "People communicate gender-stereotypic expectations in social interactions and can directly induce the targets of these expectations to engage in behavior that confirms these expectations" (Eagly, 1997, p. 1381).

Gender role beliefs have evolved, and both women and men espouse more egalitarian attitudes toward gender roles than in the past. Nonetheless, differences in such beliefs still exist, and those who endorse traditional gender role beliefs tend to follow career patterns that reinforce traditional disparities. For instance, Judge and Livingston (2008) examined the role of gender role attitudes in explaining the gender pay gap using data from the National Longitudinal Survey of Youth, which has been repeatedly administered to a national probability sample who were between the ages of 14 and 22 when first surveyed in 1979. The researchers found that over time possessing traditional attitudes toward gender roles (e.g., that a woman's place is in the home, not the office or shop) was associated with men pursuing high-paying male-dominated occupations and women pursuing low-paying female-dominated occupations.

The influences of gender inequity affect women beyond the office, since women have historically been responsible for the majority of domestic work and continue in this role. According to Catalyst (2009), 68% of women in their 20s and 30s cited a commitment to personal and family responsibilities as a barrier to women's advancement. In addition, Galinsky, Aumann, and Bond (2008) in a national probability sample found that 41% of workers believe that men should make the money and that women should take care of the home and family; only 67% of male workers believe that a working woman could be a good mother, whereas 80% of working women believe that working women are good mothers; men and women spend almost similar amounts of time with children on week days, although the roles they are playing during this interaction are not reported (3 hours for men and 3.8 hours for women); 67% of working women claim that they take the most responsibility in child care; and 70% of working women report doing most of the cooking in the household. Although, Galinsky et al. claim that attitudes toward women in the workforce and home are changing, it can be inferred that there is still a major gap between male and female domestic work. Further, it is encouraging to see increases in the amount of time men spend with their offspring. However, other areas of domestic work are inequitable and restrict the amount of time women can spend on their careers, potentially creating family–work conflict (Paludi, 2014).

To assess the impact of family–work conflict, Hoobler, Wayne, and Lemmon (2009) asked male and female workers about the amount of family–work conflict they were experiencing. Interestingly, even though women report being more responsible for the family than men, they reported less family–work conflict than men. However, perceptions of potential family–work conflict may still have an impact on women's careers. For instance, Hoobler et al. (2009) examined superiors' perceptions of female workers family–work conflict. They determined that women are expected to be the caregivers of a household by their bosses, which was found to interfere with perceptions of performance, person-job fit, and nominations for promotions. More specifically:

Women were rated lower on job and organizational fit and performance . . . [by] their managers' perceptions of their family–work conflict. In keeping with research on stereotypical attributes ascribed to women, it seems that women are less likely than men to be perceived as good "fits" and high performers because they are viewed as responsible for family, which may be seen as incompatible with holding leadership/managerial positions. It may be that managers feel that higher levels of family-work conflict make women less focused on their jobs and careers; consequently, managers presume that they are less committed. (Hoobler et al., 2009, p. 951)

Therefore, as women attempt to navigate their careers, home-life expectations may still interfere with their success.

Based on this research, it can be concluded that gender role socialization strongly shapes women's and men's role behavior and occupational decisions in politics as well as other professions. It also shapes expectations and beliefs about women and men in the workforce. In the next section, we discuss the role of stereotyping and bias and their basis for discrimination against female leaders.

STEREOTYPES

One of the most prevalent problems women in politics and other professions encounter is stereotypes. A stereotype is an automatic cognitive categorization of particular traits in connection with group membership, and they can lead to negative beliefs and reactions (Devine, 1989). For example, labeling women as warm and caring is a stereotype stemming from traditional socio-gender roles (Eagly & Karau, 2002). Further, negative emotion directed toward women is considered prejudice, whereas the actual treatment of a woman differently than a man based on their gender is discrimination.

Stereotyping can be both descriptive and prescriptive. Descriptive stereotyping is the process of attributing traits or characteristics to members of social categories, whereas prescriptive stereotyping describes attitudes toward individuals who enact characteristics believed to be appropriate for their social category, and by contrast, attitudes toward members who enact characteristics counter to those expected for their category—a process sometimes referred to as proscriptive stereotyping (Rudman & Glick, 2001).

Descriptive stereotyping often means that women are simply not perceived as leaders. For instance, in a study of male and female African American leaders, Peters, Kinsey, and Malloy (2004) found students were less likely to differentiate between female targets on leadership attributes than they were among male targets. That is, participants accurately perceived differences among male targets in whether they possessed leadership characteristics, but they uniformly perceived female targets as not possessing leadership characteristics. Therefore, women were less likely to emerge as leaders within workgroups (Peters et al., 2004). This research has direct implications for women candidates for public office, including why they receive fewer votes than men.

Perceivers tend to implicitly label women as non-leaders, whereas they differentiate men on leadership status and abilities. In another study, conducted by Fiske, Xu, Cuddy, and Glick (1999), lower-status people individuated (i.e., perceived individual differences and characteristics among a group of people) higher-status people, but high-status people did not individuate those of lower status. To put it another way, stereotypes are less likely applied to evaluations of higher-status individuals than to evaluations of lower-status individuals. Therefore, working women may be implicitly stereotyped and thus less likely to be categorized as leaders because of the widely held belief that the female gender role does not accord the same economic and social status as the male gender role.

Prescriptive stereotypes are estimations for how women in organizations *should* behave. Prescriptive stereotyping has the potential to affect evaluations of female leaders, depending on the alignment between prescripted leadership roles and salient demographic roles. For instance, women are commonly believed to express communal characteristics (i.e., being nurturing and calm) based on stereotypical prescriptions for appropriate female behaviors, whereas prescriptions for men are to express agentic qualities (i.e., being dominant and independent; Eagly & Karau, 2002).

Because many aspects of leadership subsume agentic qualities, aspiring female leaders are caught in a double bind. As women, they may not be perceived as having the requisite characteristics needed for leadership, but if they demonstrate their leadership capacity by enacting agentic traits, they are summarily disliked (Eagly & Karau, 2002). For example, self-promotion, which is commonly expected among leaders to verify their qualifications, is viewed much more negatively when enacted by women than by men (Moss-Racusin & Rudman, 2010). Similarly, female candidates who negotiate (an agentic behavior) are perceived more negatively than negotiating male candidates (Bowles, Babcock, & Lai, 2007).

Researchers have shown that regardless of parental status, individuals suspected to be low in warmth but high in competence are likely to evoke cooperation from most individuals as it is in their best interest to do so (Fiske, Cuddy, Glick, & Xu, 2002). However, historically such individuals tend to be treated in an active-hostile manner, such as being targets of physical aggression or sexual harassment (Berdahl, 2007). In contrast, groups perceived to be high in warmth and low in competence (i.e., working mothers) may receive help from fellow workers but be patronized in other ways. For instance, they may suffer from passive stereotyping, such as being labeled incompetent. Therefore, women are particularly susceptible to different forms of prejudice throughout their careers: they are perceived as warm and likable when they assume traditional female roles (motherhood) but are viewed as incompetent for other roles; when they prove their competence in nontraditional roles (e.g., leadership in politics), they are perceived as cold and unlikeable.

How women are perceived is going to influence whether they are selected for a leadership position and how they are sized up once in those positions. Inherently, people have different qualities or characteristics. Nonetheless, the same characteristic presented by a man or woman can be interpreted differently, thus affecting evaluations of the target individual (Eagly & Carli, 2007). This creates two-fold issues for female leaders. If women conform to traditional female stereotypes, they are not perceived to have characteristics of a competent leader. If they steer away from traditional stereotypes and enact agentic traits, then they are perceived to be competent, but unlikable.

WOMEN'S LEADERSHIP ADVANTAGE

Despite prescriptive and descriptive stereotyping that impedes the perception and evaluation of women as leaders, women may have a slight advantage with regard to the contemporarily popular notion of transformation leadership. Transformational leadership occurs when leaders are able to motivate followers toward organizational goals and increase followers' sense of group identity over self (Seltzer & Bass, 1990). Transformational leadership includes a variety of substyles, such as individualized consideration, intellectual stimulation, and inspirational motivation (also known as charisma), and it is perceived to be a highly effective leadership style (Avolio, Bass, & Jung, 1999). For instance, transformational leaders should be successful at obtaining the motivation and commitment from followers due to more personalized interactions, stemming from the individualized consideration subdimension.

Eagly and Johannesen-Schmidt (2001) found women to be slightly more transformational than men, whereas men more often than women took on a laissez-faire or unengaged leadership style. In addition, Eagly and Johnson (1990) conducted a meta-analysis examining leadership styles between women and men. They found that women have a more interpersonal style of leadership and men more task-oriented. In addition, Nye and Forsyth (1991) found that female leaders with the highest leadership effectiveness ratings were the ones who demonstrated more role-congruent socio-emotional or gender role–appropriate leadership orientations. However, for the most part, gender differences in leadership style have been small, and Eagly and Johnson's work shows that both women and men tend to exhibit effective leadership styles.

In more recent studies, perceptions of female leaders seem to be changing. For example, Powell, Butterfield, and Parent (2002) empirically examined stereotypical managerial characteristics, finding that "feminized leadership" was more accepted than what had been found in past studies. However, managerial characteristics were still more masculine than feminine. In addition, Eagly and Carli (2003) reviewed the literature and reported that female leadership styles are more effective in today's organizations, and male and female managers rated successful female managers as having similar characteristics as successful middle managers (Duehr & Bono, 2006). More specifically, Duehr and Bono (2006) looked at how different categories of people are associated with various leadership characteristics, such as agentic, communal, task-oriented, relationship-oriented, and transformational leadership. Male and female managers as well as female students were as likely to associate women with successful middle-management characteristics as they were men. Only male business students held that men but not women were similar to traits ascribed to successful managers. In general, they found both male and female managers are now being rated similarly on leadership characteristics by most groups of people.

Many studies have examined personality characteristics and leadership styles of male and female leaders. Based on these findings, we can conclude that there are only relatively small differences between men and women on these dimensions. Logically, no differences should be evident between women and men in selection into executive positions. However, objective measures depicting the raw numbers of men and women in top positions present a different story, most likely stemming from discriminatory practices toward women based on stereotypical perceptual bias.

FOLLOWERS' PERCEPTIONS OF LEADERS

Once a woman becomes a leader, barriers shift from those associated with access into leadership positions to those associated with gaining the trust of followers (a form of treatment discrimination). Vroom and Jago (2007) suggested that leadership is a two-way process: the leader influencing followers' behaviors and followers influencing the leader's behavior. According to role congruity theory, the juxtaposition of prototypically female roles with leadership roles creates perceptions of role incongruity, and thus, women are not perceived to be appropriate for leadership. For instance, Heilman, Block, Martell, and Simon (1989) found that men are perceived as leaders, but women, though viewed as similar to managers, were not categorized as leaders. Consequently, negative and automatic evaluations have the potential to influence female leaders' effectiveness in motivating and inspiring their followers.

If followers do not perceive deserving women as leaders, then female leaders are not likely to be viewed as charismatic (a subdimension of transformational leadership style), given that a characteristic of charisma is to stand out in the crowd or easily grasp the attention of the group. In addition, women may have a harder time achieving followers' loyalty if differentiation from one another is not present (Collinson, 2006).

As more women gain access to leadership positions, followers' perceptions and reactions to these new leaders are highly important. In accordance, Lord and Maher defined leadership as "the process of being *perceived* by others as a leader" (emphasis added; 1993, p. 11). Therefore, the way that employees perceptually categorize a manager or executive is critical to whether he or she is perceived as having leadership characteristics. Theoretically this perceptual process is influenced by schemas that followers hold for what constitutes a successful leader.

A schema represents knowledge and assumptions about abstract categories that is in an organized form. Leadership schemas are made up of prototypes and "they are stored in memory and are activated when followers interact with a person in a leadership position" (Epitropaki & Martin, 2004, p. 293). Understanding schemas in leadership perceptions is crucial, as much information processing occurs in leadership judgment and reaction. The perception of leadership takes on a top-down process, which is guided by the perceivers' schemas of appropriate leadership behavior and prototypical leadership characteristics (Lord & Emrich, 2001). Top-down processing is abstract processing based on information that has been stored in memory, whereas bottom-up processing is based on experiential data (Lord & Maher, 1993). For instance, assumptions and stereotypes about women are based on top-down processing. Lord and Emrich (2001) proposed that followers' schemas regarding leadership mediate leadership perceptions, such that followers' past experiences and general knowledge about leadership affect future perceptions of leaders.

Followers engage in both bottom-up and top-down processing in forming perceptions of leaders. A leader's outward characteristics, such as gender, along with contextual information from the organization (bottom-up processing) are used in conjunction with a follower's ideal representations of what constitutes a good leader (top-down processing) in order to categorize that person as a leader. Extending this thought, Hogg and Terry (2000) stated, "An intragroup prototypicality gradient exists—some people are or are perceived to be more prototypical than others" (p. 126). Therefore, some group members better match the expected prototype and are more likely to emerge as a leader (Hogg, 2001). Leadership prototypes have the potential to benefit prototypical homogeneous group members and could act against members of minority groups, such as women, leaving room for majority group members to emerge as leaders (i.e., men). However as we may be seeing in the current workforce, prototypical traits have the potential to shift over time and contexts (Hofstede, 1999; Hogg, 2001; Lord, Brown, & Freiberg, 1999).

Initial bias against women may dissipate quickly after followers get to know the female leader better; however, if there is enough information beforehand, then the bias may be moderated (Hogue & Lord, 2007). In other words, if there is enough information given to followers about a female leader before entering into a new position, then reduction in bias toward the leader can be expected (Landy, 2008). Some researchers, however, contend that additional information is not enough to create acceptance of female leaders. For instance, Heilman and Eagly (2008) stated that "the conditions that deter stereotyping are often absent in work settings. . . . Thus, stereotype-based perceptions of lack of fit are likely to take hold despite the availability of additional information" (p. 397).

Leadership prototypes may also change with environmental fluctuation in social expectations (Hogg, 2001; Hogue & Lord, 2007; Lord et al., 1999; Lord, Brown, Harvey, & Hall, 2001), relating to potentially shifting social/leadership roles when it comes to women (Eagly & Carli, 2007). For instance, features of the social environment, such as organizational hierarchies, exemplars, and social networks, serve as input that shapes perceivers' connections between social categories, such as male with leader. As the social environment shifts, the connections between characteristics that represent a prototypical leader fluctuate. However, the adjustments occur slowly through a feedback process as the perceiver matches his or her prototypical representations with leaders' behaviors. Thus, although there are more women in leadership positions, it is going to take some time before followers' perceptions of female leaders at executive levels change.

SPECIAL ISSUES FOR MINORITY FEMALE LEADERS

While representation of women in management is low, representation of minority women in leadership positions is even lower, demonstrating the importance of understanding additional career barriers for people categorized into multiple nonprivileged groups (Hite, 2004). The theory of compounding oppression allocates that there are different categories of prejudice that can adversely affect people who have multiple disadvantaged social identities, such as being a woman and an ethnic minority. For instance, although both white women and women of color are gaining access into organizations, the "glass ceiling" tends to be more prevalent for ethnic minority women than for white women (Eagly & Carli, 2007), which shows evidence that discrimination can have compounding effects on individuals depending on their unique characteristics. In accordance, Stanley (2009) reported that "in predominantly White organizations, power dynamics may cause disempowering experiences for African American women that can occur in the form of challenging, resisting, resenting, undermining, or even ignoring a person's authority" (p. 552). Further, when it comes to wages, women fair remarkably low in comparison to men and women of color have even lower wages, with Hispanic women receiving the lowest rate (Eagly & Carli, 2007).

The leadership labyrinth, consisting of career-path obstacles and dead ends, could be extended to nonmajority female groups to help explain the arduous path that they must take in order to obtain leadership positions within organizations. Eagly and Carli (2007) may be correct in their assertion that women no longer necessarily experience the "glass ceiling," and this career ceiling may be deteriorating for minority groups in the United States as well. The struggles that minority women experience and have to maneuver through tend to be even more strenuous than for white women due to additional stereotyping related to multiple visible identities.

As previously discussed, leaders need to be accepted by their followers in order to be effective; however, many female minorities may have a harder time being accepted as a leader. Stereotyping based on minority status presents additional barriers for such women as they attempt to navigate and shape their careers. If minority women have a harder time influencing followers' behaviors, then they would unfairly have to spend extra effort in order to gain the trust and loyalty of their followers (House, Javidan, & Dorfman, 2001). Political organizations need to be aware of the influences that multiple identities, such as gender and ethnicity, may have on their leaders, and extra steps need to be taken in order to ensure that the leaders will be supported during their crucial first weeks in office.

RECOMMENDATIONS

Many obstacles, some of them strenuous, seem to hinder women's advancement into leadership positions, and unfortunately the barriers to success do not stop once they get there. For instance, female leaders, once they start, have a harder time than their male counterparts at retaining tenure (Eagly & Carli, 2007). Many popular press publications on women in leadership instruct aspiring females to change their behaviors in a multitude of fashions. However, asking women to once again change in order to fit some prescribed standard is not only unfair but reinforces the standard instead of advocating for social change. If women are going to be perceived as equals to men, then social processes within organizations and society are going to have to change. Employees and employers alike are going to have to challenge themselves to understand personal biases and automatic perceptual processes, as recognition is the first step to stopping stereotypical effects.

Organizations should strive to create change within their culture, emphasizing on the inclusivity of female leaders. One possible cultural change that could help shift perceptions of female leaders is by directing organizational cultures to encompass values similar to feminine gender roles. For instance, Cundiff and Stockdale (2010) found that female leaders are perceived as more effective when they are embedded within collectivistic organizational cultures. Collectivistic cultures embrace team processes and group work, and reward team-based instead of individual efforts (Hofstede & Hofstede, 2005). These types of activities tend to be more congruent with traditional female gender roles, such as being nurturing and community oriented.

Organizations can also assist their female leaders by providing leadership development interventions that have been found to be equally successful for men and women. Leadership developmental programs, for instance, defined as "the development of the participant's knowledge, skills, ability, motivation, and/or perceived self-concept so as to enable him or her to exercise positive leadership influence" (Avolio, Mhatre, Norman, & Lester, 2009, p. 331), has had encouraging results for male and female aspiring leaders. Therefore, creating an equal opportunity-based leadership development program may help to decrease the differences found between male and female leaders.

REFERENCES

Avolio, B. J., Bass, B. M., & Jung, D. I. (1999). Re-examining the components of transformational and transactional leadership using the multifactor leadership questionnaire. *Journal of Occupational & Organizational Psychology, 72,* 441–462.

Avolio, B. J., Mhatre, K., Norman, S. M., & Lester, P. (2009). The moderating effect of gender of leadership intervention impact: An exploratory review. *Journal of Leadership & Organizational Studies, 15,* 325–341.

Bandura, A. (2001). Social cognitive theory: An agentic perspective. *Annual Review of Psychology, 52,* 1–26.

Berdahl, J. L. (2007). Harassment based on sex: Protecting social status in the context of gender hierarchy. *Academy of Management Review, 32,* 641–658.

Betz, N. E. (2005). Women's career development. In S. D. Brown & Robert W. Lent (Eds.), *Career development and counseling: Putting theory and research to work* (pp. 253–277). Hoboken, NJ: John Wiley & Sons, Inc.

Blass, F. R., Brouer, R. L., Perrewe, P. L., & Ferris, G. R. (2007). Politics understanding and networking ability as a function of mentoring: The roles of gender and race. *Journal of Leadership & Organizational Studies, 14,* 93–105.

Bowles, H. R., Babcock, L., & Lai, L. (2007). Social incentives for gender differences in the propensity to initiate negotiations: Sometimes it does hurt to ask. *Organizational Behavior and Human Decision Processes, 103,* 84–103.

Collinson, D. (2006). Rethinking followership: A post-structuralist analysis of follower identities. *The Leadership Quarterly, 17,* 179–189.

Cuddy, A. J. C., Fiske, S. T., & Glick, P. (2004). When professionals become mothers, warmth doesn't cut the ice. *Journal of Social Issues, 60,* 701–718.

Cundiff, N. L., & Stockdale, M. (2010, August). *Past cares in research show results today: Perceptions of female executive's effectiveness.* Roundtable discussion for Academy of Management, Montreal, Canada.

Devine, P. G. (1989). Stereotypes and prejudice: Their automatic and controlled components. *Journal of Personality and Social Psychology, 56,* 5–18.

Duehr, E. E., & Bono, J. E. (2006). Men, women, and managers: Are stereotypes finally changing? *Personnel Psychology, 59,* 815–846.

Eagly, A. H. (1987). *Sex differences in social behavior: A social-role interpretation.* Hillsdale, NJ: Lawrence Erlbaum Associates.

Eagly, A. H. (1997). Sex differences in social behavior: Comparing social role theory and evolutionary psychology. *American Psychologist, 52,* 1380–1383.

Eagly, A. H., & Carli, L. L. (2003). The female leadership advantage: An evaluation of the evidence. *Leadership Quarterly, 14,* 807–834.

Eagly, A. H., & Carli, L. L. (2007). *Through the labyrinth: The truth about how women become leaders.* Boston, MA: Harvard Business School Press.

Eagly, A. H., & Johannesen-Schmidt, M. C. (2001). The leadership styles of women and men. *Journal of Social Issues, 57,* 781–797.

Eagly, A. H., & Johnson, B. T. (1990). Gender and leadership style: A meta-analysis. *Psychological Bulletin, 108,* 233–256.

Eagly, A. H., & Karau, S. J. (2002). Role congruity theory of prejudice toward female leaders. *Psychological Review, 109,* 573–598.

Epitropaki, O., & Martin, R. (2004). Implicit leadership theories in applied settings: Factor structure, generalizability, and stability over time. *Journal of Applied Psychology, 89,* 293–310.

Fiske, S. T., Cuddy, A. J. C., Glick, P., & Xu, J. (2002). A model of (often mixed) stereotype content: Competence and warmth respectively follow from perceived status and competition. *Journal of Personality and Social Psychology, 82,* 878–902.

Fiske, S. T., Xu, J., Cuddy, A. J. C., & Glick, P. (1999). (Dis)respecting versus (dis)liking: Status and interdependence predict ambivalent stereotypes of competence and warmth. *Journal of Social Issues, 55,* 473–489.

Fortune. (2010). *Women CEOs.* Retrieved on May 26, 2010, from http://money.cnn.com/magazines/fortune/fortune500/2010/womenceos/.

Galinsky, E., Aumann, K., & Bond, J. T. (2008). Times are changing: Gender and generation at work and at home. Families and Work Institute, National Study of the Changing Workforce. Retrieved from www.familiesandwork.org.

Garcia-Retamero, R., & López-Zafra, E. (2006). Prejudice against women in male-congenial environments: Perceptions of gender role congruity in leadership. *Sex Roles, 55,* 51–61.

Green, F. (2009). Sex discrimination in job-related training. *British Journal of Industrial Relations, 29,* 295–304.

Heilman, M. (2001). Description and prescription: How gender stereotypes prevent women's ascent up the organizational ladder. *Journal of Social Issues, 57,* 657–674.

Heilman, M. E., Block, C. J., Martell, R. F., & Simon, M. C. (1989). Has anything changed? Current characterizations of men, women, and managers. *Journal of Applied Psychology, 74,* 935–942.

Heilman, M. E., & Eagly, A. H. (2008). Commentaries: Gender stereotypes are alive, well, and busy producing workplace discrimination. *Industrial and Organizational Psychology, 1,* 393–398.

Hite, L. M. (2004). Black and white women managers: Access to opportunity. *Human Resource Development Quarterly, 15,* 131–146.

Hofstede, G. (1999). Problems remain, but theories will change: The universal and the specific in 21st-century global management. *Organizational Dynamics, 28,* 34–44.

Hofstede, G., & Hofstede, G. J. (2005). *Cultures and organizations: Software of the mind,* 2nd ed. New York, NY: McGraw-Hill.

Hogg, M. A. (2001). A social identity theory of leadership. *Personality and Social Psychology Review, 5,* 184–200.

Hogg, M. A., & Terry, D. J. (2000). Social identity and self-categorization processes in organizational contexts. *Academy of Management Review, 25,* 121–140.

Hogue, M., & Lord, R. G. (2007). A multilevel, complexity theory approach to understanding gender bias in leadership. *Leadership Quarterly, 18,* 370–390.

Hoobler, J. M., Wayne, S. J., & Lemmon, G. (2009). Bosses' perceptions of family-work conflict and women's promotability: Glass ceiling effects. *Academy of Management Journal, 52,* 939–957.

House, R., Javidan, M., & Dorfman, P. (2001). Project GLOBE: An introduction. *Applied Psychology: An International Review, 50,* 489–505.

Judge, T. A., & Livingston, B. A. (2008). Is the gap more than gender? A longitudinal analysis of gender, gender role orientation, and earnings. *Journal of Applied Psychology, 93,* 994–1012.

Landy, F. J. (2008). Stereotypes, bias, and personnel decisions: Strange and stranger. *Industrial and Organizational Psychology: Perspectives on Science and Practice, 1,* 379–392.

Lent, R. W., Brown, S. D., & Hackett, G. (1994). Monograph: Toward a unifying social cognitive theory of career and academic interest, choice, and performance. *Journal of Vocational Behavior, 45,* 79–122.

Lord, R. G., Brown, D. J., & Freiberg, S. J. (1999). Understanding the dynamics of leadership: The role of follower self-concepts in the leader/follower relationship. *Organizational Behavior and Human Decision Processes, 78,* 167–203.

Lord, R. G., Brown, D. J., Harvey, J. L., & Hall, R. J. (2001). Contextual constraints on prototype generation and their multilevel consequences for leadership perceptions. *Leadership Quarterly, 12,* 311–338.

Lord, R. G., & Emrich, C. G. (2001). Thinking outside the box by looking inside the box: Extending the cognitive revolution in leadership research. *Leadership Quarterly, 11,* 551–579.

Lord, R. G., & Maher, K. J. (1993). *Leadership and information processing: Linking perceptions and performance.* New York, NY: Routledge.

Lyness, K. S., & Thompson, D. E. (1997). Above the glass ceiling? A comparison of matched samples of female and male executives. *Journal of Applied Psychology, 82,* 359–375.

Moss-Racusin, C. A., & Rudman, L. A. (2010). Disruptions in women's self-promotion: The backlash avoidance model. *Psychology of Women Quarterly, 34,* 186–202.

Nye, J. L., & Forsyth, D. R. (1991). The effects of prototype-based biases on leadership appraisals. *Small Group Research, 22,* 360–379.

Paludi, M. (Ed.). (2014). *Women, work and families.* Santa Barbara, CA: Praeger.

Peters, S., Kinsey, P., & Malloy, T. E. (2004). Gender and leadership perceptions among African Americans. *Basic and Applied Social Psychology, 26,* 93–101.

Powell, G. N., Butterfield, D. A., & Parent, J. D. (2002). Gender and managerial stereotypes: Have the times changed? *Journal of Management, 28,* 177–193.

Rudman, L. A., & Glick, P. (2001). Prescriptive gender stereotypes and backlash toward agentic women. *Journal of Social Issues, 57,* 743–762.

Seltzer, J., & Bass, B. M. (1990). Transformational leadership: Beyond initiation and consideration. *Journal of Management, 16,* 693–703.

Stanley, C. A. (2009). Giving voice from the perspectives of African American women leaders. *Advances in Developing Human Resources, 11,* 551–561.

Thomas, D. A. (2001, April). The truth about mentoring minorities: Race matters. *Harvard Business Review,* 99–107.

Vroom, V. H., & Jago, A. G. (2007). The role of the situation in leadership. *American Psychologist, 62,* 17–24.

Zanna, M. P., & Pack, S. J. (1975). On the self fulfilling nature of apparent sex differences in behavior. *Journal of Experimental Social Psychology, 11,* 583–591.

Congresswoman Nancy Pelosi

Congresswoman Pelosi has represented California's 12th district in the House of Representatives. This district includes most of San Francisco, Bayview, Chinatown, the Mission, North Beach, Presidio, and the Sunset. Pelosi is the first woman to head a major political party. From 2007 to 2011, Pelosi became the first woman to serve as Speaker of the House. In 2010, Pelosi led Congress in passing child nutrition legislation and food safety legislation and repealing the "Don't Ask, Don't Tell" policy which had prohibited lesbians and gays from serving openly in all branches of the military.

Source: http://pelosi.house.gov/.

Chapter 11

Men's Perceptions of Women Leaders[*]

Patti J. Berg, William Schweinle, and Betty Hulse

In 2008, Hillary Rodham Clinton nearly secured the Democratic Party nomination for president of the United States. Clinton won more than 18 million votes (including Michigan, in which her major opponent had withdrawn his name) and 46.0% of total delegate votes (Real Clear Politics, 2010a). In fact, she won 48.1% of the popular primary vote (when Michigan is included), compared to the 47.4% achieved by eventual President Barack Obama, making the primary race one of the most competitive in history. As president, Barack Obama appointed Clinton U.S. secretary of state, a position held by women (Madeleine Albright, 1997–2001, and Condoleezza Rice, 2005–2009) in two of the three four-year terms preceding her own. Clinton had gained the confidence of the populous at large and had earned the respect of her opponent, who appointed her to the highest-ranked Cabinet position within the executive branch, the fourth-ranked individual in the presidential line of succession should the president be unable to serve (U.S. Department of State, 2012). The secretary of state is responsible for developing and implementing foreign policy and oversees 30,000 employees with a budget of approximately $35 billion (White House, 2012). At the same time and until 2011, Nancy Pelosi was the first woman to serve as

[*]Portions of this chapter were published in M. Paludi (Ed.). (2013). *Women and management, vol. 2: Signs of solutions* (pp. 203–214). Santa Barbara, CA: Praeger.

Speaker of the House (second in the presidential line of succession), making her the highest-ranking woman in America's political history.

What is responsible for the underrepresentation of women at senior levels of leadership and management? There are several possible factors that may inhibit the ascent of women into top leadership positions. Among these are societal perceptions of women leaders and the dominant leadership paradigm present in our culture. Perceptions of women by men are of particular interest since men currently hold the majority of such coveted positions and may act as powerbrokers in the promotion of women through managerial ranks. Furthermore, it is of interest to examine how the gender assignment of leadership attributes is perpetuated by members holding positions of authority. While the focus of this chapter is on men's perceptions of women leaders and managers, we are reminded that gender and leadership identity is a dynamic process highly influenced by cultural and societal changes. In the following pages we review and summarize findings related to men's perceptions of women in leadership positions.

SOCIAL ROLE THEORY

According to Social Role Theory, people form beliefs about the attributes or characteristics of a person based on the roles they typically see performed by representatives of that person's gender. These exposure-formed beliefs then become widely held expectations of behaviors for people of that gender (see chapters in this volume). The homemaker–provider division of labor between women and men led women to learn domestic skills and men to learn skills that would gain them paid employment (Eagly, Wood, & Diekman, 2000). The behaviors stereotypically associated with homemaker and provider have been characterized as communal versus agentic (Eagly et al., 2000). Communal attributes, for instance, nurturance, helpfulness, kindness, and interpersonal sensitivity, have traditionally been ascribed to women, whereas agentic attributes, like ambition, dominance, independence, and self-confidence, have traditionally been ascribed to men (Eagly & Karau, 2002). Gender roles and their associated expectations influence behavior through accepted descriptive and injunctive societal norms. Descriptive norms refer to what is usual and typical (what we *do* or who we are) and suggests a degree of uniformity within a particular group; for instance, women are compassionate and men are competitive. Injunctive norms (also referred to as prescriptive norms) refer to what is proper, expected, acceptable, and desired (what we *should do*) and holds with it a degree of approval or disapproval by its group members (Eagly et al., 2000). For instance, men should enjoy attending or watching sports, while women should be interested in shopping.

While it is important to explore social roles as barriers to women with leadership aspirations, we must be careful not to oversimplify its influence in the workplace. Whitehead (2001) reminds us that gender identity is "grounded only in the incessant flux of intersubjective occurrence, identifiable only through prior social and cultural discursive configurations" (p. 94).

ROLE CONGRUITY

Stereotypical gender-assigned roles may be placed upon positions in society just as they are to individuals. In doing so, a search begins, attempting to bring together an individual and a societal position that are well matched. Leadership roles have been defined as historically congruent with prescriptive stereotypes of men and incongruent with prescriptive stereotypes of women. Women are often perceived as violating their prescribed role when taking on leadership positions. For instance, historically, leadership and managerial positions have been assigned agentic qualities, such as courage, control over subordinates, assertiveness, competitiveness, and independent success with tasks. The search to find a match for such a position is likely to begin with an individual who shares such qualities—the expectation being that a man is more likely to possess them. The agentic personality has become accepted as desirable and necessary for success as a leader or manager (Eagly, 1987; Eagly & Karau, 2002). Social Role Theory suggests a defining process ensues, with workplace position defined by gender attributes and men and women further defined by their role in these gender-assigned positions in the workplace.

Not uncommonly, men choose leaders based on observed societal norms and largely associate leadership with being male. Jackson, Engstrom, and Emmers-Sommer (2007) asked male and female U.S. university students to identify the leader of a group based on seating arrangement and head-of-table cue. Both male and female students chose a leader with the same gender as their own most often, but male subjects did so with significantly greater frequency than female subjects: 93.5% of the time male subjects selected a male leader, and 63.5% of the time female subjects selected a female leader (Jackson et al., 2007). When questioned about the reasons for their leadership choices, a number of male subjects indicated that men are "usually," "most likely," "generally" leaders, with none claiming or referring to males as being superior to females in leadership abilities (Jackson et al., 2007). Similar findings by Duehr and Bono (2006) indicate that male university students still view men and managers as more similar than women and managers.

Longitudinal research findings in populations of U.S. college students show attitudes toward women's roles grow more egalitarian for both genders over four years of college but that men's views are less egalitarian compared to women at matriculation and again four years later (Bryant, 2003). In other words, men's views of women's roles are more traditional upon college entry and are less likely to change as compared to women's views over this period of time.

In a more recent study, Bosak and Sczesny (2011) asked German undergraduate male and female business students to make decisions on shortlisting or hiring an applicant for a position in management. The students were also asked to rate the certainty of their decisions. Applicants were fictional and varied according to gender and role description (described as a leader or non-leader). When students were provided with evidence of an applicant's qualifications as a leader (leader role description), male and female subjects shortlisted and hired the "applicants" based on qualifications and independently of gender (Bosak & Sczesny, 2011). Female subjects shortlisted and hired non-leader male and female applicants with the same degree of certainty, and male subjects shortlisted these applicants with the same amount of certainty. However, for applicants with non-leader role descriptions, male subjects selected male applicants with greater certainty than female applicants (Bosak & Sczesny, 2011). These findings indicate that, in the absence of evidence qualifying a male or female for a leadership position, men continue to show bias for hiring men into management or leadership-type positions (Bosak & Sczesny, 2011).

Prime, Carter, and Welbourne (2009) found that senior male managers perceived women leaders as possessing statistically stronger feminine leadership behaviors (supporting, rewarding, mentoring, team-building, inspiring, and networking) than men leaders. Women were in agreement, and the distinction was more pronounced for these respondents. Male respondents (senior male managers) were more likely to prescribe masculine leadership behaviors (problem solving, delegating, and influencing upward) to men leaders than they were to women leaders. The authors also found a change in the way male managers view successful managers. Male respondents reported women leaders were more effective at supporting others and rewarding subordinates. Such biases inevitably infiltrate employment decision making.

Acceptance of leadership paradigms that are largely masculine have resulted in a perceived incongruence between feminine gender and leadership roles (Eagly, 1978). Historically, women who wished to achieve and succeed in management positions encountered the stereotype that women do not possess these agentic characteristics, and, found lacking, women were denied promotion or management positions altogether. In fact, under a paradigm that esteems leadership qualities as those that are "masculine," one of two possibilities exists for a woman interested in ascension to leadership position: (1) women demonstrate attributes imposed on the current leadership paradigm and (2) the paradigm shifts to equate leadership attributes with those that are "feminine." Acceptance of women in leadership roles would necessitate a change in how a women's sphere of competence is viewed or a shift in the perceived preferential attributes of a good leader from masculine to feminine. Yet Due Billing and Alvesson (2000) warn that modifying perceptions of the ideal leader by assigning feminine gender attributes to successful leadership may not be the best approach toward launching women into leadership positions since this reassignment does nothing to alter underlying societal norms and reinforces traditional attitudes that define idealized leadership potential by gender role divisions.

PARADIGM SHIFTS IN ROLE CONGRUITY

Over the past 30 years, workplace environments have evolved; successful businesses operate in a global economy, information is available instantaneously, menial tasks are now automatized, and communication is held at a premium with new ways to communicate with others to build partnerships and launch ideas. The evolved workplace has brought with it a reformed perspective about ideal leadership skills, and a shift has emerged in male perceptions of women's suitability to hold management positions.

The GLOBE Research Project on Leadership Worldwide collected data from 17,300 managers in nearly 1,000 different organizations representing 62 societal cultures to explore leadership attributes with the goal of discovering universal practices and values (Grove, 2005). A set of six culturally endorsed leadership dimensions were determined to be universal, four which were perceived to promote good leadership (charismatic/value based, team oriented, participative, humane oriented) and two which were perceived to impede good leadership (self-protective, autonomous) (Grove, 2005). The characteristics, abilities, and skills associated with the leadership dimensions promoting good leadership included ability to inspire and motivate, emphasizing team-building, involving others in decisions, supportive, considerate, compassionate, and generous (Grove, 2005). Characteristics describing dimensions that inhibit good leadership included independent/individualized leadership, self-centered, status conscious, and face-saver (Grove, 2005). These results support a new appreciation for communal attributes and hold particular agentic qualities accountable for inhibiting good leadership.

Research using male and female nontraditional undergraduate and graduate U.S. business students provides further evidence of the shift from a masculine leadership paradigm to a leadership paradigm with a greater balance between female and male characteristics (Atwater, Brett, Waldman, DiMare, & Hayden, 2004). Subjects utilized a modified version of Yukl's taxonomy of managerial subroles and rated each subrole as feminine or masculine. Of the 19 managerial subroles, subjects rated 7 subroles as more feminine and 6 subroles as more masculine (Atwater et al., 2004).

Sczesny, Bosak, Neff, and Schyns (2004) in a study of male and female management students in Germany, India, and Australia indicated a shift in the leadership paradigm to include person-oriented traits, a traditionally communal/feminine characteristic, as being an important characteristic for a leader to possess. People-oriented skills were viewed as more important for leaders-in-general than task-oriented traits by Australian and Indian students; task-oriented traits were viewed as more important than person-oriented traits by German students (Sczesny et al., 2004). In addition, male and female students from all three countries viewed women executives as having person-oriented traits to a greater degree than executives-in-general (Sczesny et al., 2004). However, male subjects of all three countries and female German subjects demonstrated bias toward men as leaders by imaging mainly male executives when considering questions pertaining to leaders-in-general (Sczesny et al., 2004).

The Pew Research Center Social and Demographic Trends Survey (2008) asked adult respondents to indicate whether the characteristics presented were "more true of men or more true of women." They were then asked to rate how important these characteristics were for leadership. Traits tested were honesty, intelligence, hardworking, decisiveness, creative, compassionate, outgoing, and ambitious (Taylor et al., 2008). The characteristics rated most important for leadership were honesty, intelligence, hardworking, and decisive, with honesty rated the highest (Taylor et al., 2008). Respondents rated women higher than men in honesty, intelligence, being outgoing, creativity, and compassion; respondents rated women and men equally in respect to hardworking and ambitious, and respondents rated men higher than women in decisiveness (Taylor et al., 2008). The majority of men and women in this survey believed that both men and women make good leaders (69% of men and 68% of women); 21% of respondents favored men as leaders, and only 6% favored women as leaders (Taylor et al., 2008). Only 4% of men believed women make better leaders than men compared to 8% of women believing women make better leaders than men (Taylor et al., 2008).

A survey distributed by Eagly and Johannesen-Schmidt (2001) prompted subjects to indicate how often a manager engaged in transformational, translational, and laissez-faire leadership-style behaviors. Women were rated higher than men on several scales: the attributes version of idealized influence, inspirational motivation and individualized consideration and contingent rewards (Eagly and Johannesen-Schmidt, 2001). On perceived effectiveness measures women were also rated significantly higher than men (Eagly and Johannesen-Schmidt, 2001).

Duehr and Bono (2006) sampled male middle managers, asking them to describe "women" and "managers." They found a robust positive correlation (ICC = 0.63, $p < .001$) between descriptors. Such a match between attributes of women and those of managers constitutes a dramatic shift in the views of male middle managers from previous research results (Heilman, Block, Martell, & Simon, 1989; Schein, 1973, 1975). The authors also found a change in the way male managers view successful managers.

Perhaps surprisingly, the views of male middle managers resulted in a correlation between "men managers" and "managers" as .74, in contrast to Heilman et al. (1989) ICC = .86 and to their own comparison of "women managers" and "managers" with an ICC = .81. Examining mean scale ratings across study samples for trends, male managers viewed successful managers as more communal and less agentic compared to Heilman et al. (1989) means. This change suggests a shift in the leadership paradigm to include a greater balance between agentic and communal characteristics (Duehr and Bono, 2006).

Interestingly, Rudman and Glick (1999) found that the feminization of management and leadership styles may present a backlash effect for women with more agentic work styles. The authors found that agentic women were penalized for lack of communal traits (e.g., kindness, generosity, concern, helpfulness, and compassion, traditionally considered feminine qualities) and were viewed as possessing less social aptitude than men with similar agentic qualities. In addition, there was a broader range of acceptable cross-gender workplace behaviors for men than there were for women. The results suggest that a workplace paradigm shift toward more androgynous leadership roles may benefit aspiring women more than taking on agentic qualities to remain competitive within the workplace.

A meta-analysis performed by Koenig, Eagly, Mitchell, and Ristikari (2011) determined that though there is strong evidence suggesting leadership is still associated with masculine attributes, these qualities are becoming increasingly androgynous over time. The group concluded that today's leadership now incorporates more feminine qualities such as sensitivity, understanding, and warmth but not at the expense of masculine dominance and strength.

Impact of Experience on the Social Role Paradigm Shift

Research supports that men with exposure to working women and women managers held more positive attitudes toward women managers. Male managers with working wives and male managers with past positive experiences with female coworkers were much less likely to attribute poor performance to gender-related characteristics and were much less likely to react punitively to lower performance evaluations compared to male managers without similar experience (Eskilson & Wiley, 1996).

There is evidence that exposure to women leaders in the political realm similarly influences a change in voter attitudes (Beaman, Chattopadhyay, Duflo, Pande, & Topalova, 2009). In 1998 Indian policy established gender quotas for leadership positions in certain geographical areas and required a percentage of leadership positions be reserved for women. The 2008 Indian election results showed significant gains for women contesting unreserved positions, with 18.5% of women elected to councils where positions had been reserved in contrast to 11% women in councils in which positions had never been reserved (Beaman et al., 2009). Further, the electoral gain by women was not due to incumbent advantage, as evidenced by an observed incumbent disadvantage for both reserved and unreserved positions (Beaman et al., 2009). Beaman and colleagues asked villagers to evaluate the effectiveness of a hypothetical leader, with manipulation of gender as the only variant between participants. Men living in villages where female position reservations had never occurred perceived the leader as significantly more effective when the leader's gender was experimentally manipulated to be male. In villages where female position reservation had occurred, male participants judged women and men as equally effective (Beaman et al., 2009). These results indicate that exposure to women leaders positively affects men's view of women's leadership effectiveness.

Beaman and colleagues used additional measures to investigate villagers' implicit and explicit taste for female leaders. Male and female villagers exhibited a strong same-gender preference for leadership, even in villages where reservations had occurred and male villagers explicitly admitted a preference for male leaders. This research indicates that in India exposure to women leaders does not reduce men's preference for a male leader but that exposure may make it more likely that men will associate women with leadership and leadership effectiveness (Beaman et al., 2009).

Current research reveals a paradigm shift toward a more androgynous leadership identity and points to men's evolved perceptions of women as capable, effective, and qualified for leadership positions. Also working in favor of women interested in taking on leadership positions is the improved confidence men have in their leadership abilities as men gain more experience working with women in such positions. Women are now visible in more positions of authority and power, increasing employee encounter frequencies with female leaders and redefining the leader–subordinate relationship (Koenig et al., 2011). Yet, in spite of changing perceptions and attitudes, disparities in hiring and the systematic promotion of women into management or leadership positions are statistically evident, and the marginalization of women in senior leadership positions persists.

CHANGING GENDER ROLES

The evolving organization of work has brought with it changing home dynamics and redefined family contexts. A change in the division of labor in society has accompanied the entrance of women into the workforce. Increasing numbers of men share responsibility for the care of children and domestic chores, reshaping gender roles and, in doing so, redefining masculine attributes. As men and women begin to assume roles traditionally imposed on their counterparts, masculine and feminine roles begin to share attributes, and the extension of these newly defined social roles infiltrates the leadership paradigm.

PATRIARCHY

Beyond social roles, socially and culturally reinforced stratifications prop the interests of men within organizations. From this perspective, women who want to achieve must make themselves indispensable to the organizational structure, effectively breaking through the "glass ceiling" (Whitehead, 2001). Such success often requires women invest their efforts in a corporate culture that thrives on negotiation and aggressive competitiveness, occasionally at the expense of personal consideration for others. Whitehead (2001) argues that the prospects of movement within a hierarchical structure bring with it alluring seductive qualities of potency and control as well as the perceived authority to change an organization.

Women negotiating their way through the hierarchical patriarchal structure are faced with subtle barriers in their pursuits toward promotion. At each level, women are confronted with the role incongruity challenge—ascension through the hierarchy brings with it status increases, and a broader breach between social role and leadership congruity emerges for women. Men, however, enjoy a closer match as they ascend. A Koenig et al. (2011) meta-analysis found that men, who are often beneficiaries of promotion and hold ultimate decision-making authority, devalue leadership by women and that men in such positions believe women do not possess the qualities of leaders. Women battle access challenges emboldened by implicit biases about leadership attributes.

Prime et al. (2009) contends that men are in a powerful position to close workplace gender gaps. She argues that, in order to transform the current male-dominated stratification, men must understand that the status quo is not beneficial to either gender, develop an awareness of gender biases, and actively challenge such biases. According to Prime, men with more enlightened perspectives about gender bias viewed the exclusion of women from leadership positions as disadvantageous to corporate competitiveness. Prime's research found that men are reluctant to deviate from social gender norms primarily because of the social penalties imposed on men who do not assume the "breadwinner" role. Men who had been mentored by women were more likely to hold such enlightened viewpoints.

JOINING RESEARCH WITH THE ANECDOTAL

Returning to the near rise of Hillary Clinton to the most powerful office in the United States, political systems offer an insightful approach to looking at perceptions of population subgroups, in this case a Democratic subgroup, since a single vote can be viewed as an indicator of confidence. While it is not possible to determine what percentage of those votes received by Clinton were cast by men, it is unlikely that all of her support was provided by women, suggesting a subgroup of men and women agreed Clinton possessed the skills and attributes to serve in the highest-ranking executive office in the United States. Yet, during her bid, Clinton was especially vulnerable to comments by political pundits, the new media, and talk-radio hosts referring to her as "emotional," often equated negatively with women and not a quality associated with the office of president, and "shrill," an unflattering description for a woman. Clinton's press image was all at once too feminine while at the same time not feminine enough.

What the research about men's perceptions of women with aspirations to hold high-ranking leadership positions in business or politics communicates is that social norms are shifting as are leadership paradigms. It appears, however, that much of this shift is felt at foundation and middle-management levels. Executive positions within the patriarchal hierarchy continue, by and large, to promote men, perpetuating the perception that women are unsuited for such leadership positions. In spite of this exclusion, women are increasingly visible in positions of authority, and, it appears, confidence in women's leadership skills by men with experience working with women is improving as more women work side by side with their male counterparts. Another important aspect of women candidates' visibility is Presidential Gender Watch 2016, a project of the Center for American Women and Politics that seeks to offer to the public an understanding of how gender influences candidate strategy, voter engagement, media coverage, and electoral outcomes for the U.S. presidency.

YouGov (2015; reported by the Center for Women in Government, 2015) noted that 67% of Americans stated that the United States is ready now for a woman president. Responses to Gender Watch 2016 regarding Hillary Clinton's announcement to seek the presidency in 2016 include:

> Hillary Clinton finally figured out how to talk about being a woman in presidential politics.

In a speech given in June 2015, Hillary Clinton quipped:

> I may not be the youngest candidate in this race, but will be the youngest woman president in the history of the United States. (quoted in Traister, 2015, p. 1)

REFERENCES

Atwater, L. E., Brett, J. F., Waldman, D., DiMare, L., & Hayden, M. (2004). Men's and women's perceptions of the gender typing of management subroles. *Sex Roles, 50,* 191–199.

Beaman, L., Chattopadhyay, R., Duflo, E., Pande, R., & Topalova, P. (2009). Powerful women: Does exposure reduce bias?. *Quarterly Journal of Economics, 124,* 1497–1540.

Bosak, J., & Sczesny, S. (2011). Gender bias in leader selection? Evidence from a hiring simulation study. *Sex Roles, 65,* 234–242. doi:10.1007/s11199-011-0012-7.

Bryant, A. N. (2003). Changes in attitudes toward women's roles: Predicting gender-role traditionalism among college students. *Sex Roles, 48,* 131–142.

Catalyst. (2009). *Engaging men in gender initiatives: What change agents need to know.* Retrieved on January 11, 2012, from http://www.catalyst.org/file/283/mdc-web.pdf.

Center for Women in Government. (2015). *Election watch.* Retrieved on June 16, 2015, from www.cawp.rutgers.edu.

Due Billing, Y., & Alvesson, M. (2000). Questioning the notion of feminine leadership: A critical perspective on the gender labeling of leadership. *Gender, Work &Organization, 7,* 144–157.

Duehr, E. E., & Bono, J. E. (2006). Men, women and managers: Are stereotypes finally changing?. *Personnel Psychology, 59,* 815–846.

Eagly, A. H. (1987). *Sex differences in social behavior: A social-role interpretation.* Hillsdale, NJ: Erlbaum.

Eagly, A. H., & Johannesen-Schmidt, M. C. (2001). The leadership styles of women and men. *Journal of Social Issues, 57,* 781.

Eagly, A. H., & Karau, S. J. (2002). Role congruity theory of prejudice toward female leaders. *Psychological Review, 109,* 573.

Eagly, A. H., Wood, W., & Diekman, A. B. (2000). Social role theory of sex differences and similarities: A current appraisal. In T. Eckes & H. M. Trautner (Eds.), *The developmental social psychology of gender* (pp. 123–174). Mahwah, NJ: Erlbaum.

Eskilson, A., & Wiley, M. (1996). The best teacher: Mediating effects of experience with employed women on men managers' responses to subordinates' mistakes. *Sex Roles, 34,* 237–252.

Grove, C. N. (2005). *Introduction to the GLOBE research project on leadership worldwide.* Retrieved on December 28, 2011, from *http://www.grovewell.com/pub-GLOBE-intro.html.*

Heilman, M. E., Block, C. J., Martell, R. F., & Simon, M. C. (1989). Has anything changed? Current characterizations of men, women, and managers. *Journal of Applied Psychology, 74,* 935.

Jackson, D., Engstrom, E., & Emmers-Sommer, T. (2007). Think leader, think male and female: Sex vs. seating arrangement as leadership cues. *Sex Roles, 57,* 713–723.

Koenig, A. M., Mitchell, A. A., Eagly, A. H., & Ristikari, T. (2011). Are leader stereotypes masculine? A meta-analysis of three research paradigms. *Psychological Bulletin, 137,* 616–642.

Pew Research Center. (2008). *A paradox in public attitudes. Men or women: Who's the better leader?.* Retrieved on January 15, 2012, from http://pewsocialtrends.org/files/2010/10/gender-leadership.pdf.

Prime, J. L., Carter, N. M., & Welbourne, T. M. (2009). Women "take care," men "take charge": Managers' stereotypic perceptions of women and men leaders. *Psychologist-Manager Journal, 12,* 25–49. doi:10.1080/10887150802371799.

Rudman, L. A., & Glick, P. (1999). Feminized management and backlash toward agentic women: The hidden costs to women of a kinder, gentler image of middle managers. *Journal of Personality and Social Psychology, 77,* 1004–1010. doi:10.1037/0022-3514.77.5.1004.

Schein, V. (1973). The relationship between sex role stereotypes and requisite management characteristics. *Journal of Applied Psychology, 57,* 95–100.

Schein, V. (1975). Relationships between sex role stereotypes and requisite management characteristics among female managers. *Journal of Applied Psychology, 60,* 340–344.

Sczesny, S., Bosak, J., Neff, D., & Schyns, B. (2004). Gender stereotypes and the attribution of leadership traits: A cross-cultural comparison. *Sex Roles, 51,* 631–645.

Traister, R. (2015). *Meet the new, old Hillary.* Retrieved on June 16, 2015, from www.newrepublic.com/article//122035/meet-new-old-hillary-clinton.

U.S. Department of State. (2012). *Diplomacy in action.* Retrieved on January 20, 2012, from http://www.state.gov/secretary.

Whitehead, S. (2001). Woman as manager: A seductive ontology. *Gender, Work & Organization, 8,* 84.

White House. (2012). *The executive branch.* Retrieved on January 28, 2012, from https://www.whitehouse.gov/1600/executive-branch.

Congresswoman Elise Stefanik

Congresswoman Stefanik represents the 21st district of New York. She is a member of the Armed Services Committee and the Committee on Education and the Workforce. Congresswoman Stefanik is the youngest woman to be elected to the U.S. Congress. In a recent interview (Gray, 2015), Stefanik noted: "The young girls in upstate New York—I hope they look to me as an example of what they can achieve" (p. 74).

Sources: https://stefanik.house.gov/; Gray, J. (2015). Road to Congress. *Capital Region Living,* May.

Chapter 12

"The Personal Is Political": From Personal Experiences with Sex Discrimination to Ensuring Equity for Girls and Women: Patsy Takemoto Mink

Michele A. Paludi

PATSY TAKEMOTO MINK (1927–2002)

Carol Hanisch (1970) has been attributed as saying "the personal is political," in which the relationships between our personal experiences and the larger political and social structures are noted. The phrase is used to empower women to be politically active about issues impacting them and their families as well as to ensure lawmakers are addressing women and women's lives rather than enacting laws that ignore women's realities.

In thinking about "the personal is political" when selecting a woman politician about which to write for the book, the choice was clear: Patsy Takemoto Mink. Why? Without her dedication to ensuring equity for women in education, Title IX of the 1972 Education Amendments would not have become reality. I have served as a Title IX Coordinator, trained Title IX Coordinators, and taught about Title IX in my courses in gender, women's studies, and educational psychology. And because of Congresswoman Mink's campaign to promote educational equity for women,

I experienced a different career after I graduated high school (in 1972) than I might have if not for her legislation. This is a brief biography of Patsy Takemoto Mink. But it is more than that; it is also a tribute and a thank you to Congresswoman Mink.

> We have to build things that we want to see accomplished, in life and in our country, based on our own personal experiences . . . to make sure that others do not have to suffer the same discrimination. (Patsy Takemoto Mink)

Congresswoman Mink is the first Asian American woman and woman of color to serve in Congress. She became the first Democratic woman to deliver a State of the Union response in 1970. In addition, President Carter appointed Patsy Mink as assistant secretary of state for Oceans and International Environmental and Scientific Affairs.

Congresswoman Mink served 12 terms in Congress, representing Hawaii's first and second congressional districts (Davidson, 1994). In her educational and work career she experienced discrimination. She once discussed the burden of stereotypes about Asian Americans: "And so as we carry around this baggage of being quiet, self-demeaning, self-effacing and acquiescent, it's extremely difficult for those who are impatient with that kind of stereotype to really make a stand on public issues without being labelled a radical or misfit" (reported in Cruz & Yamamoto, 2002, p. 588).

The University of Chicago law school would only accept her under its "foreign student quota," despite the fact she was born and raised in Hawaii (Cruz & Yamamoto, 2002). Following her graduation from law school she was denied employment at a law firm because she was a married woman. As a result of this experience, she decided to begin her own law practice. Despite the fact Congresswoman Mink had been born and raised in Hawaii, her husband had not, and consequently, this made her a "nonresident" of Hawaii. She argued her right to take the bar exam in Hawaii. She won this argument, took, and passed the bar exam and became the first Japanese American woman to be an attorney in Hawaiian history (Chan, 2012).

Congresswoman Mink's decision to pursue a career in law was a consequence of her being denied admission to medical school because of her sex. She had applied to 20 medical schools in 1948; none accepted women. Her choice of a career in law was based in part on her commitment to force medical schools to admit women. Simpson described Congresswoman Mink in the following way: "when one door closed she pushed another one open" (cited in Chan, 2012, p. 2).

In addition to experiencing sex discrimination, Congresswoman Mink was a target of race discrimination. For example, when attending the

University of Nebraska, she learned of the campus's racial segregation policy whereby students of color had to live in residence halls separate from white students. Congresswoman Mink organized a coalition that included administrators, staff, students, parents, alumni, and corporations who lobbied to end this segregation policy (Leavitt, 1985).

Dedicated to ensuring equity for women in education so her experiences with sex discrimination would not be experienced by other women, she collaborated with Congresswoman Edith Green and together they authored the Title IX Amendment of the 1972 Education Amendments. This legislation stated:

> No person in the United States shall, on the basis of sex, be excluded from participation in, be denied the benefits of, or be subjected to discrimination under any education program of activity receiving Federal financial assistance.

Title IX was the first comprehensive law to prohibit sex discrimination against students, faculty, and employees of educational institutions; it defines and ensures equality in education. Prior to it being signed into law by President Nixon in June 1972:

1. Girls and women were prohibited from taking certain courses, e.g., criminal justice and boys and men were banned from taking courses in home economics.
2. Women experienced quotas, e.g., most medical and law schools limited the number of women to 15 or fewer per school.
3. Women had to have higher standardized test scores and better grades than male applicants for college acceptance.
4. Women could not receive athletic scholarships.
5. Women professors were banned from faculty clubs; they were encouraged to join faculty wives' organizations instead.
6. Campuses had separate entrances depending on the sex of the student (Paludi, 2008).

The amendment to Title IX in 1987 expanded the definition of program or activity to include all the operations of an educational institution, governmental entity, or private employer that receives federal funds. Title IX prohibits sex discrimination in all college/university student services and academic programs, including, but not limited to, admissions, financial aid, academic advising, housing, athletics, recreational services, college residential life programs, health services, counseling and psychological services, registrar's office, classroom assignments, grading, and discipline.

In addition, Title IX prohibits discrimination because of sex in employment and recruitment consideration or selection, whether full-time or part-time, under any education program or activity operated by an institution receiving or benefiting from federal financial assistance ("recipient"). Also covered is sexual harassment and sexual violence. Furthermore, Title IX prohibits discrimination on the basis of pregnancy and parental status in educational programs and activities. According to the Title IX regulations, pregnancy discrimination is prohibited in admissions, hiring, coursework accommodations and completion, pregnancy leave policies, workplace protection, and health insurance coverage in educational programs and activities. Title IX specifically prohibits discrimination against a student based on pregnancy, childbirth, false pregnancy, termination of pregnancy, or recovery from any of these conditions. Title IX regulation also prohibits a school from applying any rule related to a student's parental, family, or marital status that treats students differently based on their sex.

According to Congresswoman Mink:

Because there were only eight women at the time who were Members of Congress. . . . I had a special burden to bear to speak for [all women], because they didn't have people who could express their concerns for them adequately. So, I always felt that we were serving a dual role in Congress, representing our own districts and, at the same time, having to voice the concerns of the total population of women in the country. (quoted in Gootman, 2002)

In 1976, Congresswoman Mink learned that she had taken part in an experiment during her pregnancy in 1951. The University of Chicago had prescribed "vitamins" to research participants; in reality they were pills containing the drug diethylstilbestrol (DES). Researchers had determined that DES caused cancer in women and fetuses. She learned that 1,000 women and their children were affected. She brought a class action law suit against the university and also the Eli Lilly Company. The settlement of this suit guaranteed all women and their children to receive free lifetime diagnostic testing and treatment if needed (Cruz & Yamamoto, 2002).

In 1974, Congresswoman Mink introduced the Women's Education Equity Act, which provided $30 million a year in educational funds for programs to promote gender equity in K-12, increase educational opportunities for women, and excise gender stereotypes from school curricula and textbooks.

Since 1972, Title IX has broadened to include sexual harassment and sexual misconduct: stalking, domestic violence, dating violence, and sexual assault, including rape. Despite its passage, issues of gender equity in education have still been present. For example, in 1975, Congress debated whether physical education classes should be separate for girls and boys.

Some members argued that separation does not mean equal. One vote was required to stop the change; Congresswoman Mink gave the deciding vote. According to Congresswoman Mink:

> "We all need to be reminded that since Title IX was put in place by a legislative body, it can be taken away by a legislative body."

> Title IX has been in front of Congress many more times (over 25) than most other pieces of legislation. Many schools are not in compliance with Title IX.

(Murphy, 2013)

In 2002 Congress renamed the Title IX Amendment of the Higher Education Act to the "Patsy T. Mink Equal Opportunity in Education Act."

Cruz and Yamamoto (2002) noted that Congresswoman Mink lived the values about which she fought:

> Patsy did more than speak about these causes—her life's work was a testament to what she believed in and spoke so vehemently about in public. Patsy's dedication to social justice was extraordinary. For even when the tide of public opinion was against her, she held steadfast to her beliefs and to her mission. (p. 569)

REFERENCES

Chan, K. (2012). The mother of Title IX: Patsy Mink. Retrieved on May 21, 2015, from http://www.womenssportsfoundation.org/home/she-network/education/patsy-mink.

Cruz, T., & Yamamoto, E. (2002). A tribute to Patsy Takemoto Mink. *Asian-Pacific Law & Policy Journal, 4*(2) (Summer 2003), 569–597.

Davidson, S. (1994). *Jeannette Rankin and Patsy Takemoto Mink: A heart in politics.* Seattle, WA: Seal Press.

Gootman, E. (2002). *Patsy Mink, veteran Hawaii congresswoman dies at 74.* Retrieved on May 23, 2015, from http://www.nytimes.com/2002/09/30/us/patsy-mink-veteran-hawaii-congresswoman-dies-at-74.html.

Hanisch, C. (1970). The personal is political. In B. Crow (Ed.), *Radical feminism: A documentary reader* (p. 113). New York: New York University Press.

Leavitt, J. (1985). *American women managers and administrators: A selective biographical dictionary of twentieth century leaders in business, education and government.* Westport, CT: Greenwood Press.

Murphy, W. (2013, August). *Violence against women on campus: How TITLE IX finally won its rightful seat at the Civil Rights table.* Presentation at the International Coalition against Sexual Harassment, New York, NY.

Paludi, M. (Ed.). (2008). *Understanding and preventing campus violence.* Westport, CT: Praeger.

Senator Barbara Mikulski

Senator Mikulski is the longest-serving woman in the Congress. She first won a seat on the Baltimore City Council in 1971. She won her bid for Congress in 1976. Senator Mikulski represented the third district in Maryland. She won election to the Senate in 1986 and won reelection four additional times. Senator Mikulski is credited as the first Democratic woman senator elected in her own right. Senator Mikulski is the dean of women, a role of mentor to newly elected women senators. This responsibility includes building coalitions among the women legislators.

Among her action areas in the Senate, Senator Mikulski has advocated for women to be included in clinical trials and medical research at the National Institutes of Health. Senator Mikulski also wrote the law that requires federal standards for mammograms. She has been committed to helping uninsured women get mammograms as well as treatment for cervical and breast cancer.

Source: http://www.mikulski.senate.gov/about-barbara/biography.

Chapter 13

"It's a Small Wonder Why There Aren't More Women. . .": Carol Moseley Braun, the First African American Woman in the Senate

Michele A. Paludi

And frankly, being a woman I think gives me a slightly different take on a lot of the issues and on a lot of the solutions to the
problems we face.

—Carol Moseley Braun

I owe my commitment to helping women candidates get elected to the
U.S. Congress to many women, including Carol Moseley Braun. In the
fall of 1991, I was riveted to the television as were most Americans, to
the Senate Judiciary Confirmation Hearings of Clarence Thomas. During the hearings, senators heard testimony from Professor Anita Hill,
who stated that while the director of the Equal Employment Opportunity Commission, Clarence Thomas subjected her to sexual harassment.
Dr. Hill claimed that Thomas asked her to date him and when she rebuffed
his advances, he sexually harassed her with inappropriate discussions of
sexual acts and pornographic films. Dr. Hill passed a polygraph test; the
results indicated she was telling the truth. Judge Thomas declined the test.

Dr. Hill's testimony was challenged as well as dismissed by the all-male Senate Judiciary Committee.

Eleanor Holmes Norton once noted that Dr. Hill's treatment by this Senate Committee contributed to the large number of women elected to Congress in 1992. According to Holmes Norton, "Women clearly went to the polls with the notion in mind that you had to have more women in Congress." Furthermore, the Senate Committee's treatment of Dr. Hill fostered the impetus for women to seek political office so as to effect change in the U.S. Congress. One of those women is Carol Moseley Braun. According to Senator Braun, "The Senate absolutely needed a healthy dose of democracy . . . it wasn't enough to have millionaire white males over the age of 50 representing all the people in the country" (U.S. House of Representatives, 2015).

Senator Braun entered the race for the Senate, representing Illinois, in opposition to Alan Dixon's support of Clarence Thomas as well as the need for the Senate to be more diverse. At the same time, I was providing media coverage of the Hill/Thomas hearings since I had been conducting research and publishing books on sexual harassment for five years previous to the hearings. Moseley Braun won the primary against two opponents, Alfred Hofeld and Dixon. In the general election she won against Richard Williamson (Perry, 1996). One of her campaign slogans was "we don't need another arrogant rich guy in the Senate." She became the first African American woman senator in the history of United States after winning 53% of the vote and subsequently served three terms representing Illinois (Rosen & Zerbonia, 2004).

Senator Moseley Braun's fist campaign was in 1992, a year labeled as "The Year of the Woman" in U.S. politics. This label was used to note the election of a number of women senators, including Senator Moseley Braun. Four women won Senate seats that year. Four. It was still only four. Senator Barbara Mikulski noted however that this label was not empowering: "Calling 1992 the Year of the Woman makes it sound like the Year of the Caribou or the Year of the Asparagus. We're not a fad, a fancy or a year."

President George H. W. Bush once was asked if the Republican Party would nominate a woman for president. Making reference to the slogan "Year of the Woman," President Bush stated: "This is supposed to be the year of the women in the Senate. Let's see how they do. I hope a lot of them lose" (Woolley & Peters, 1992).

Senator Moseley Braun was seen as a national symbol of equality and change in the Congress. In response to her being labeled as a "symbol" Senator Moseley Braun stated: "My job is emphatically not to be a celebrity or a full time symbol. Symbols will not create jobs and economic growth. They do not do the hard work of solving the health care crisis. They will not save the children of our cities from drugs and guns and murder" (Current Biography, 1992).

Senator Moseley Braun served on the Finance Committee of the Senate when Senator Daschle gave up his seat to her. She also served on the Senate Judiciary Committee, a committee that formerly was all male and initially prompted her to seek office. Furthermore, Senator Moseley Braun served on other committees, including Senate Banking, Housing, Small Business, and Urban Affairs Committee. Senator Moseley Braun convinced the Senate Judiciary Committee in 1993 to not renew the design patent for the United Daughters of the Confederacy since it contained the Confederate flag. She told the Senate that the flag "has no place in our modern times, place in this body, place in our society" (Dewar, 1993).

Her commitment to gender and race concerns was also evident in legislation she created to assist women who are widowed and divorced, noting: "Pension laws were never written for women . . . no wonder the vast majority of the elderly poor are women" (Dewar, 1993). Revisiting the issue of workplace sexual harassment that initially prompted her to seek office, Senator Moseley Braun joined other women senators in 1995 to request public hearings on sexual misconduct charges against Senator Packwood. The Senate rejected this request. Eventually the charges of sexual harassment, sexual abuse, and assault of women led to Senator Packwood's resignation from the Senate under threat of expulsion.

Senator Moseley Braun is quoted as saying: "I cannot escape the fact that I come to the Senate as a symbol of hope and change . . . nor would I want to, because my presence in and of itself will change the U.S. Senate" (Current Biography, 1994). After losing her reelection bid in 1998 Senator Moseley Braun was appointed ambassador to New Zealand by President Clinton. She served as ambassador throughout the Clinton administration.

In 2014 Senator Moseley Braun was interviewed about her career in the Senate. In this interview she stated: "To this day, I still question why it's hemlines, husbands and hair . . . women get marginalized in the political process by so many sets of negative preconceptions and prejudices that sometimes it can be very difficult. . . . Nobody cares if a male senator's pants are flooding" (Tam, 2014, p. 1). She further argued: "It's a small wonder why there aren't more women, women of color and women of color from not very privileged backgrounds getting involved" (Tam, 2014, p. 1).

REFERENCES

Current Biography. (1994). New York: Wilson.

Dewar, H. (1993, July 23). Senate bows to Braun on symbol of Confederacy. Washington Post, A1.

Perry, M. (1996). Carol E. Moseley Braun. In J. Smith (Ed.), Notable black American women (pp. 482–484). Detroit, MI: Gale Research.

Rosen, I., & Zerbonia, R. (2004). Carol Moseley Braun. In A. Henderson (Ed.), Contemporary black biography: Profiles from the international black community (Vol. 42, pp. 13–17). Farmington Hills, MI: Thomas Gale.

Tam, R. (2014). *Carol Moseley Braun: "Small wonder" there is not more diversity in Congress*. Retrieved on June 6, 2015, from http://www.washingtonpost.com/ blogs/she-the-people/wp2014/02/26/carol-moseley-braun.

U.S. House of Representatives. (2015). *Carol Moseley Braun*. Retrieved on June 6, 2015, from http://history.house.gov/People/Detail?id=18611.

Woolley, J., & Peters, G. (1992). Presidential debate at the University of Richmond. *The American Presidency Project*. Santa Barbara, CA: University of California.

Appendix A: Organizations Dealing with Women, Leadership, and Politics

Advancing Women in Leadership
www.advancingwomen.com/awl/awl.html

African American Women's Leadership
http://www.ncnw.org/centers/height.htm

Asian-Pacific American Women's Leadership Institute
http://www.apawli.org/

Athena Foundation
http://www.athenafoundation.org/

Black Career Women
https://bcwnetwork.com/

Black Women's Leadership Council
http://www.bwlc.com/

Business and Professional Women's Foundation
http://www.bpwpa.org/

Caribbean Institute for Women and Leadership
http://www.ciwil.org/

Catalyst
http://www.catalyst.org/

Center for Creative Leadership
http://www.ccl.org

Center for Leadership and Change Management
http://wlp.wharton.upenn.edu/leadership-center/

Center for Women's Business Research
http://womensbusinessresearch.org/

Center for Women's Global Leadership
http://www.cwgl.rutgers.edu

Center for Women's Intercultural Leadership
http://www.centerforwomeninleadership.org/#/

Center for Women's Leadership, Babson College
http://www.babson.edu/Academics/centers/cwel/Pages/home.aspx

Centre de Leadership Feminin
adfm@casanet.net.ma

Chattanooga Women's Leadership Institute
http://www.cwli.org/index.php

Council of Women World Leaders
http://www.unfoundation.org/features/cwwl.html

Courageous Leadership Consortium
http://www.courageousleadership.org/Leadership-Resources.cfm

Harpswell Foundation Leadership Centers for Women
http://harpswellfoundation.org/center/

Institute for Women's Leadership
http://www.womensleadership.com

Leadership America
http://leadership-women.org/programs/leadership-america

Leadership California
http://www.leadershipca.org

Leadership Illinois
http://leadershipillinois.org

Leadership Texas
http://leadership-women.org/programs/leadership-texas

National African American Women's Leadership Institute, Inc.
http:// www.naawli.org

National Association for Female Executives
http://nafe.com/?service=vpage/1474

National Hispana Leadership Institute
http://www.nhli.org

National Organization for Women
http://www.now.org/

National Women Business Owners Corporation
http://nwboc.org

Orange County Women's Leadership Fund
http://www.womensleadershipocny.org

Organization of Women Leaders
http://owls.wordpress.com/

Rutgers University Center for Women and Politics
http://www.cawp.rutgers.edu/

Seattle Women's Commission
http://www.seattle.gov/womenscommission/resources.htm

Soroptimist International
http://www.soroptimistinternational.org/

South Asian Women's Leadership Forum
http://www.southasianwomen.org/

Susan B. Anthony Center for
Women's Leadership
http://www.rochester.edu/SBA/

United States Women's
Chamber of Commerce
http://www.uswcc.org/

Virginia Women's Institute for
Leadership
http://www.mbc.edu/vwil/

The White House Project: Vote,
Run, Lead
http://www.voterunlead.org/

Women Executive Leadership
http://www.
womenexecutiveleadership.com/

Women in Leadership
Foundation
http://www.womeninleader
ship.ca/

Women in Leadership Retreat
http://executive.berkeley.edu/
programs/women-leadership/

Women Leaders Online
http://www.wlo.org

Women of Color Leadership
Institute
http://leadingwomenofcolor.org/
about-us/

Women Presidents Organization
http://www.wprog.com/index.htm

Women's Executive Network
http://www.wxnetwork.com

Women's Institute for
Leadership Development for
Human Rights
http://www.nonprofitfacts.com/
CA/Womens-Institute-For-
Leadership-Development-Fo
r-Human-Rights.html

Women's Leadership Circles
https://www.marlboro.edu/
admissions/professional/wlc

Women's Leadership Exchange
http://www.
womensleadershipexchange.com/

Women's Leadership Forum
http://www.exed.hbs.edu/
programs/wlf/

Women's Leadership Institute
http://www.mills.edu/WLI/wli
.home.html

Women's Leadership Network
http://wlnnews.com/

Women's Leadership Program
http://www.ccl.org/leadership/
programs/WLPOverview.aspx

WomenWatch
http://www.un.org/womenwatch

Worldwide Guide to Women in
Leadership
http://www
.guide2womenleaders.com

Zonta International
http://www.zonta.org/

Appendix B: National Resources: Campaign Trainings for Women

EMERGE AMERICA

Political leadership training for Democratic women that is offered throughout the United States. Goals include identifying, educating, and inspiring Democratic women to seek local and state political offices.
contact@emergeamerica.org

EMILY'S LIST CAMPAIGN TRAININGS

Training for Democratic pro-choice women elected at state and federal levels.
Attention is paid to empowering women to protect and defend their seats when new district lines are drawn.

EMILY'S LIST POLITICAL OPPORTUNITY PROGRAM TRAINING

Training offered to state and local women candidates who are Democrats and pro-choice.
mstephenson@emilyslist.org

EXCELLENCE IN PUBLIC SERVICE SERIES

Encourages mentoring of Republican women leaders to seek more involvement in government and politics.
ctdudley@aol.com

NEXT STEP

Political training to women aged 23–27 who have a passion for politics.
info@runningstartonline.org

NFRW CAMPAIGN MANAGEMENT SCHOOL

The National Federation of Republican Women sponsors training to teach candidates fund-raising, campaign plans, volunteer organizing, and communications with voters.
political@nfrw.org

PATH TO POLITICS

Seminar to give women aged 21–45 information to seek elected office.
info@runningstartonline.org

POLITICAL INSTITUTE FOR WOMEN

Training for women seeking elected office. Training includes policy issues.
Kimberly@politicalinstituteforwomen.org

PROJECT GOPINK

Goals are to recruit, train, mentor, and network women in public service.
Empowering Republican women to seek local, state, and federal offices.

READY TO RUN

Training for women who are seeking elected office or are newly appointed.
sinzzdak@rci.rutgers.edu

VOICES OF CONSERVATIVE WOMEN

Organization encourages more women to be involved in public policy. It also trains women for elected office.
info@voicesofconservativewomen.org

WOMEN WORTH WATCHING

Offers assistance to women who are building competitive campaigns.
info@wcfonline.org

WOMEN'S CAMPAIGN SCHOOL AT YALE UNIVERSITY

Training program for women seeking elected office or moving to higher
elective offices.
info@wcsyale.org

About the Editor and Contributors

MICHELE A. PALUDI, PhD, is the series editor for Women's Psychology and for Women and Careers in Management for Praeger. She is the author/editor of 35 college textbooks, and more than 160 scholarly articles and conference presentations on sexual harassment, campus violence, psychology of women, gender, and discrimination. Her book *Ivory Power: Sexual Harassment on Campus* (SUNY Press, 1990) received the 1992 Myers Center Award for Outstanding Book on Human Rights in the United States. Dr. Paludi served as chair of the U.S. Department of Education's Subpanel on the Prevention of Violence, Sexual Harassment, and Alcohol and Other Drug Problems in Higher Education. She was one of six scholars in the United States to be selected for this subpanel. She also was a consultant to and a member of former New York State Governor Mario Cuomo's Task Force on Sexual Harassment. Dr. Paludi serves as an expert witness for court proceedings and administrative hearings on sexual harassment. She has had extensive experience in conducting training programs and investigations of sexual harassment and other Equal Employment Opportunity issues for businesses and educational institutions. In addition, Dr. Paludi has held faculty positions at Franklin & Marshall College, Kent State University, Hunter College, Union College, and Union Graduate College, where she directs the human resource management certificate program. She is on the faculty in the School of Management at Union Graduate College. She is also the program director for psychology at Excelsior College.

MELISSA ALEXANDER is a physician assistant in Sioux Falls, South Dakota. She earned a bachelor of science degree at the University of Nebraska Lincoln and a master's of science at the University of South

Dakota. She taught physician assistant medicine at her alma mater before returning to full-time practice. Her medical practice expertise is in cardiology, interventional radiology, and family practice where she now provides medical care to underserved populations.

SUSAN A. BASOW is Charles A. Dana Professor of Psychology at Lafayette College. A licensed clinical psychologist, Prof. Basow focuses her teaching and writing on gender issues. She is the author of the textbook *Gender: Stereotypes and Roles,* as well as chapters on gender socialization, gender and education, body image, gender identity development, and gendered communication. She has conducted numerous research studies on gender issues in students' evaluations of female and male faculty as well as on other topics, such as women's body objectification and gendered perceptions of relational aggression. A fellow of the American Psychological Association in three divisions (Society for the Psychology of Women; Society for the Psychological Study of Lesbian, Gay, and Bisexual Issues; Society for the Psychological Study of Social Issues), Professor Basow currently is on the executive committee of Div. 35, the Society for the Psychology of Women.

PATTI J. BERG serves as assistant professor in the University of South Dakota School of Health Sciences. She has been recognized by the American Physical Therapy Association as a neurologic clinical specialist, and her interest areas include neurology, infant and child development, memory, and motivational attributes.

BREENA E. COATES is professor of global strategy in the Department of Management in the College of Business and Public Administration at California State University, San Bernardino (CSUSB). She received her PhD in organizational behavior and public policy from the University of Pittsburgh. She taught at San Diego State University and retired in 2007 as associate professor emeritus, when she was selected to teach high-level military personnel from the United States and other countries in the master of strategic studies program at the United States Army War College, Carlisle, Pennsylvania. Dr. Coates came to CSUSB in September 2009.

Her research interests include corporate and public policy impacts on strategic corporate social responsibility, and implications of constitutional, statutory, and case law on business. She currently teaches in the area of global strategy in the capstone class for MBA students at CSUSB. In her academic career she has served on over 30 theses and projects. Dr. Coates has 37 publications, including peer-reviewed journal articles, books, and book chapters, and 21 peer-reviewed conference publications. In the past 10 years, Dr. Coates has received 10 prestigious university awards for teaching, learning, research, and university service.

Dr. Coates was born and raised in India, and received her baccalaureate degree from Calcutta University, India.

NICOLE L. CUNDIFF, PhD, 2010, Southern Illinois University Carbondale, is the director of the Northern Leadership Center and assistant professor of management at the University of Alaska-Fairbanks. She specializes in gender in leadership and organizational diversity. Nicole has published in venues such as the *Journal of Leadership and Organizational Studies* and *Management Research Review.*

VERONICA L. GILRANE is currently pursuing her doctoral degree in industrial organizational psychology at George Mason University. Working closely with her advisor, Dr. Eden King, Ms. Gilrane conducts research in the area of workplace diversity and inclusion. In particular, a primary focus of her research explores the experiences and perceptions of women and minorities in leadership positions. Ms. Gilrane has presented her research at the annual conference for the Society for Industrial and Organizational Psychology. In addition to her scholastic endeavors, Ms. Gilrane has gained applied research experience relating to the retention of officers in the U.S. armed forces.

BETTY HULSE is a certified physician assistant and member of the faculty for the South Dakota Physician Assistant Studies Program. Her research includes clinical education of physician assistant students, laboratory medicine applications in physician assistant education, and provision of primary care to underserved populations. She practices at the Keystone Treatment Center in Canton, South Dakota.

EDEN B. KING joined the faculty of the Industrial Organizational Psychology program at George Mason University after earning her PhD from Rice University in 2006. Dr. King is pursuing a program of research that seeks to guide the equitable and effective management of diverse organizations. Her research, which has appeared in outlets such as the *Journal of Applied Psychology, Human Resource Management, Perspectives of IO Psychology, and Group and Organization Management,* integrates organizational and social psychological theories in conceptualizing social stigma and the work–life interface. This research addresses three primary themes: (1) current manifestations of discrimination and barriers to work–life balance in organizations, (2) consequences of such challenges for its targets and their workplaces, and (3) individual and organizational strategies for reducing discrimination and increasing support for families. In addition to her academic positions, Dr. King has consulted on applied projects related to climate initiatives, selection systems, and diversity training programs, and has worked as a trial consultant. She is currently on the editorial board of the *Journal of Management* and the *Journal of Business and Psychology.*

LORI M. KUMLER is assistant professor of political science and international studies at University of Mount Union in Alliance, Ohio. She has been a feminist in her native Ohio and in several other states and countries in which she has lived over the years, including Rhode Island, Scotland, Oregon, Maryland, Brazil, and Michigan. She received an MAT from Tufts University, and an MS and a PhD from the University of Michigan. She recalls her formal feminist awareness starting in ninth grade when she completed a project for English class on women in advertising.

PAULA K. LUNDBERG-LOVE is professor of psychology at the University of Texas at Tyler (UTT) and Ben R. Fisch Endowed Professor in Humanitarian Affairs for 2001–2004. Her undergraduate degree was in chemistry, and she worked as a chemist at a pharmaceutical company for five years prior to earning her doctorate in physiological psychology with an emphasis in psychopharmacology. After a three-year postdoctoral fellowship in nutrition and behavior in the Department of Preventive Medicine at Washington University School of Medicine in St. Louis, she assumed her academic position at UTT where she teaches classes in psychopharmacology, behavioral neuroscience, physiological psychology, sexual victimization, and family violence. Subsequent to her academic appointment, Dr. Lundberg-Love pursued postgraduate training and is a licensed professional counselor. She is a member of Tyler Counseling and Assessment Center, where she provides therapeutic services for victims of sexual assault, child sexual abuse, and domestic violence. She has conducted a long-term research study on women who were victims of childhood incestuous abuse, constructed a therapeutic program for their recovery, and documented its effectiveness upon their recovery. She is the author of nearly 100 publications and presentations and is coeditor of *Violence and Sexual Abuse at Home: Current Issues in Spousal Battering and Child Maltreatment* as well as *Intimate Violence against Women: When Spouses, Partners, or Lovers Attack*. As a result of her training in psychopharmacology and child maltreatment, her expertise has been sought as a consultant on various death penalty appellate cases in the state of Texas.

JENNIFER L. MARTIN, PhD, is assistant professor of education at the University of Mount Union. Prior to working in higher education, Dr. Martin worked in public education for 17 years, 15 of those as the department chair of English at an urban alternative high school for students labeled at-risk for school failure in metropolitan Detroit. In addition, she taught graduate and undergraduate courses in research methods, multicultural education, educational leadership, and women and gender studies. Currently, she teaches graduate courses in curriculum and undergraduate courses in multicultural education, gender studies, and content area literacy. Dr. Martin is committed to incorporating diverse texts in all her courses and inspiring culturally responsive pedagogical practices in current and future educators. She is the editor of the two-volume series *Women as Leaders in Education: Succeeding despite Inequity, Discrimination, and Other Challenges* (Praeger, 2011), which examines the intersections of class, race, gender, and sexuality for current and aspiring leaders from a variety of perspectives. Dr. Martin's current book project is *Racial Battle Fatigue: Insights from the Front Lines of Social Justice Advocacy,* which contains personal stories of the repercussions of doing social justice work in the field and in the university. Activists and scholars share experiences of microaggressions, racial battle fatigue, and retaliation because of who they are, for whom they advocate, and what they study. Dr. Martin has numerous publications on bullying and harassment, educational equity, and issues of social justice. She is currently studying the development of culturally responsive leadership practices.

TRACY C. MCCAUSLAND is a second-year doctoral student in the Industrial Organizational Psychology program at George Mason University. She completed her BS from Davidson College in 2009. Her teaching responsibilities include undergraduate psychology research methods as well graduate advanced statistics and research methods. Her research interests consist of leadership, teamwork, training, and age diversity. In addition to her academic responsibilities and pursuits, Ms. McCausland also serves as the president of the Industrial Organizational Psychology Student Association at George Mason University.

LINDSEY M. MEEKS is assistant professor in the Department of Communication at the University of Oklahoma. Her research interests include gender, political communication, and media, with a focus on how these areas intersect within elections.

VANESSA METERKO earned her master's degree in forensic psychology from John Jay College of Criminal Justice in New York City. In addition to her education in psychology, she has a background in health care research and experience with crisis counseling. Her current research interests include wrongful convictions, bias crime, and subtle discrimination.

FELICIA L. MIRGHASSEMI has received a bachelor's of science in psychology and a master's degree in clinical neuropsychology from The University of Texas at Tyler. She is currently focusing on receiving her Licensed Professional Counselor Intern license to further develop her clinical skills. She is interested in providing therapeutic interventions to individuals facing psychological distress due to major life changes. Her research interests include understanding the development of empathy burnout in helping professions, as well as treatment and prevention methods. Her long-term goals are to contribute to policy changes that improve access to quality mental health for community members.

WHITNEY BOTSFORD MORGAN received her doctorate in Industrial and Organizational Psychology from George Mason University in 2009. She is currently assistant professor of management at the University of Houston–Downtown. Dr. Morgan teaches organizational behavior, principles of management, and leadership. The overarching goal of her program of research is to provide theoretical and empirical evidence guiding the advancement of women and mothers in the workplace. Her line of research touches a variety of content areas, including performance appraisal, developmental opportunities, extra-role behavior, and retention. She has published in *Human Resource Management Review, Journal of Occupational Health Psychology, Equal Opportunities International,* and *Sex Roles*; she is also a reviewer for *Equal Opportunities International, Human Relations,* and for the Academy of Management and Society for Industrial and Organizational Psychology annual conferences. Dr. Morgan has consulted on several applied projects related to selection, competency modeling, and leader development initiatives.

KEVIN L. NADAL, PhD, is associate professor of psychology and mental health counseling at John Jay College of Criminal Justice–City University of New York, who earned his doctorate in counseling psychology from Columbia University. He has published several works focusing on Filipino American, ethnic minority, and LGBTQ issues in the fields of psychology and education. He is a fellow of the Robert Wood Johnson Foundation and is the author of the books *Filipino American Psychology: A Handbook of Theory, Research, and Clinical Practice* and *Filipino American Psychology: A Collection of Personal Narratives.*

WILLIAM SCHWEINLE earned a PhD in quantitative and social psychology at the University of Texas at Arlington and received postdoctoral training in quantitative psychology at the University of Missouri, Columbia. He is currently associate professor of biostatistics and director of research development in the University of South Dakota School of Health Sciences where he teaches statistics and research methods. He also is the chair of the USD IRB and is the statistical editor for the *Journal of Physician Assistant Education.* Although his research activity is varied, his primary area of inquiry has been the psychology of men who abuse their partners and men who sexually harass women.

KATHERINE A. SCOTT has worked in numerous research and academic settings and is currently focusing on expanding her clinical testing and counseling skills. Her primary research interests lie in memory performance and cognitive dysfunction in relation to traumatic brain injury, mild cognitive impairment, Alzheimer's disease and other dementias, and the rates of deterioration associated with the aforementioned disorders. She is also interested in the neurophysiological underpinnings of post-traumatic stress disorder, and the consolidation and retrieval of memory related to traumatic experiences. Katherine Anne holds a bachelor's degree in psychology and a master's degree in clinical psychology with a specialization in neuropsychology.

MARGARET S. STOCKDALE, PhD, 1990, Kansas State University, is professor of psychology and program director of applied psychology at Southern Illinois University Carbondale. She is the author and editor of over 40 publications, including 5 books primarily in the field of employment justice and gender issues in the workplace. Peggy is a fellow of the American Psychological Association and associate editor of *Psychology of Women Quarterly*.

VIVIAN M. VARGAS received her master's in forensic psychology from John Jay College of Criminal Justice. Her career goals are to work with juveniles within the criminal justice system. She currently resides in New Jersey and continues to research microaggressions toward various minority groups.

MICHELLE WIDEMAN attained a masters in forensic mental health counseling from John Jay College of Criminal Justice–City University of New York. She currently lives in Virginia and has research interests in microaggressions toward special identity groups.

Index